Ready-to-Use

SELF-ESTEEM &
CONFLICT-SOLVING
ACTIVITIES

for Grades 4-8

Ready-to-Use
SELF-ESTEEM & CONFLICT-SOLVING ACTIVITIES
for Grades 4-8

BETH TEOLIS

Illustrated by Carol Giguere, Alex Li, and Beth Teolis

JOSSEY-BASS
A Wiley Imprint
www.josseybass.com

Published by Jossey-Bass
A Wiley Imprint
989 Market Street, San Francisco, CA 94103-1741   www.josseybass.com

Jossey-Bass books and products are available through most bookstores. To contact Jossey-Bass directly call our Customer Care Department within the U.S. at (800) 956-7739, outside the U.S. at (317) 572-3986 or fax (317) 572-4002.

Jossey-Bass also publishes its books in a variety of electronic formats. Some content that appears in print may not be available in electronic books.

Library of Congress Cataloging-in-Publication Data

Teolis, Beth.
     Ready-to-use self-esteem & conflict-solving activities for grades
4–8 / Beth Teolis.
       p.   cm.
     Includes bibliographical references.
     ISBN 0-13-045256-4
     1. School children—United States—Psychology—Handbooks,
manuals, etc.   2. Self-esteem in children—United States—Handbooks,
manuals, etc.   3. Conflict management—Study and teaching
(Elementary)—United States—Handbooks, manuals, etc.   4. Social
skills—Study and teaching (Elementary)—United States—
Handbooks, manuals, etc.   I. Title.
LB1117.T43   1995   95-33581
370.15'3—dc20

Printed in the United States of America
FIRST EDITION
PB Printing 10 9 8 7 6 5 4

DEDICATION

Many children receive some encouragement from at least one person who takes an interest in them. This book is dedicated to all the children who do *not* have such a person in their lives. It is my hope that the content within these pages will help to inspire educators to be those significant people who will make all the difference in a child's life!

ACKNOWLEDGMENTS

There is acknowledgment for only one name under "author" of this book, yet so many names should be included in that space along with my name. The completion of this book has been a unified effort among my wonderful family, friends, fellow educators, mentors, editors, and publisher. I thank each and every one of you!

Michael O'Keefe, Superintendent of Program Design for the Metro Separate School Board in Toronto, supported my workshops and pilot school program. He asked the Board to publish this book in its first rough form. I am so grateful for his unflinching support of all my ideas.

Rob Greenaway, President of the School Division of Prentice Hall Canada, read the book which was published by the Metro Separate School Board and felt there is a widespread need for it. Suggesting that I revise it, he devoted his efforts to making this vision a reality. His perseverance resulted in Winfield Huppuch, Education Editor of Prentice Hall, also encouraging me to revise my book for publication. Their enthusiasm spurred me on and I thank both of them for believing in and supporting the concept from the onset.

I was assisted all along by the editing expertise and helpful activities suggestions of my Education Editor, Susan Kolwicz. The final thorough review was accomplished by my Development Editor, Diane Turso. I am so grateful for their invaluable, patient assistance.

My wonderful husband, John Teolis, worked endless hours right beside me to produce this book. My children, Cortleigh and Johnny, gave me all the space and support I needed to complete my work. My parents, brother, and friends provided esteem for the esteemer and I thank them. I especially thank *Emily McAteer*, *Patsy Posak Rosart* and *Dorothy Polito Etherington* for encouraging me from the beginning to write this book.

The illustrators, Carole Giguere and Alex Li, who assisted me with a large part of the art work, succeeded in giving the book the fun, up-to-date 90's look I wanted for the children to enjoy!

Much of the content of the following pages is based on the teachings of Dr. Michele Borba, whose teaching has paved the way for all educators in the field of self-esteem. Her *Esteem Builders* and her seminars have educated me about the components of self-esteem and have given me invaluable inspiration.

Robert Reasoner, author of *Building Self-Esteem: A Comprehensive Program*, has provided a foundation for our studies of the components of self-esteem with his thorough analysis of self-theory. He also encouraged me to write this book. His research and activities ideas have assisted countless educators in many countries to build students' self-esteem.

My training with Jack Canfield in his Facilitating Self-Esteem Seminars empowered me to write for educators about ways we can help our students. He has made such a positive difference in the lives of so many people, including mine first and foremost.

My Skills for Life Pilot School liaisons in the Metro Separate School Board helped with many of the bulletin board and art and celebration ideas found in this book. They are: Evelisa Ricci, Sandra Loberto, Anna Monaco, Judy Vella, Barb Ruhr, Norah Shanque, Mary Elizabeth Stubbings, Mary Valtellini, Austin Dale, Kelly Brown, Rose Ientile, and Josie Huhn. My thanks also to Rosalyn Harris for sharing with me her own school's naturalization experiences.

FOREWORD

Recent studies indicate that almost one-third of our youth are failing to contribute to society due to drug and alcohol abuse, lack of school completion, teenage pregnancy, suicide, or crime and violence. These young people end up being a financial drain on society and its resources. Research indicates that lack of positive relationships with adults and low self-esteem are two major contributing factors to this problem.

This material, developed by Beth Teolis, offers teachers and other educators hope as well as practical solutions for addressing this problem. The program is based on research which has shown that activities such as these can foster more positive relationships with adults and build the elements of self-esteem so badly needed by so many students. The conflict solving section will prove to be especially helpful in reducing conflicts and behavior problems in school.

The section on self-esteem empowerment for the educator is particularly important for it recognizes that the self-esteem of the teacher can have a major impact on how students feel about themselves. Those who use the materials will be amazed at how easily these student activities can be integrated into the normal curriculum and the enthusiasm with which they are received by the students.

I would urge all schools concerned about how to prepare students for productive, contributing citizenship to consider implementing this program.

Robert W. Reasoner

Robert W. Reasoner, President of the International Council for Self-Esteem; author of *Building Self-Esteem in the Elementary School* and co-author of *Building Self-Esteem in Secondary Schools.*

ABOUT THE AUTHOR

Beth Teolis, B.S., M.Ed., Indiana State University, taught elementary grades for over 12 years in Indiana and in Toronto, Ontario. She noted repeatedly the correlation between children's levels of self-esteem and their academic and social progress. She now devotes her professional career to building students' self-esteem and conflict solving skills. She is an active keynote speaker at professional conferences and presents workshops to educators, parents, and students as well as to a broad range of business people.

Ms. Teolis has also written *Skills for Life Resource Guide*, published by Metro Separate School Board of Toronto in 1993, which is presently used by principals, vice principals, classroom and special education teachers, social workers, and guidance counselors in Ontario. She has initiated 27 Skills for Life Pilot Schools in the Metro Toronto Separate School Board.

Ms. Teolis is available for seminars, workshops, and consultive work through Life Skills Associates, 149 Coldstream Avenue, Toronto, Ontario M5N 1X7; phone 416-484-8113, e-mail jwt@blakes.ca, or fax 416-863-2653. More important, she would like to know how this book is helping you to help your students.

WHAT THIS BOOK WILL DO FOR YOU

"I saw reflected in my teacher's eyes somebody I could be."

— *A CHILD WITH HOPE*

When a teacher is willing to make an investment in building positive **self-esteem and conflict solving skills** in children, both academic and social progress will follow. These are **skills for life** children will carry with themselves long after they have left your classroom. These skills for life can be easily woven into your curriculum so that teaching them is *not* an additional time burden for you.

Improved student behavior may include: fewer victims of anorexia, of drug and alcohol abuse, less school truancy, and fewer school dropouts. Fewer children will need to affiliate with gangs. Gender inequity will cease to be a problem as equity is a natural outcome of learning skills for life. All of the above problems can be attributed, in large part, to a child's low self-image. Especially needy are at-risk children who do not feel a sense of physical and emotional safety in their homes. These children need to feel free of humiliation and physical harm when they walk through your doors. Many children have to learn that they *do* possess positive qualities and what these qualities are. How can we help these at-risk and other low self-esteem children? Together we will share the journey to implement ways in which we can make each child feel valuable, capable, and lovable.

What Makes *This* Classroom So Special?

I decided to discover why it was that in some classrooms I entered, the energy was so warm I could almost embrace it. Why did I walk into other classrooms to meet a negative spirit of indifference and unhappiness emanating from the students? I began to study the interaction between the classroom teacher and the students as well as the level of self-esteem displayed by the teacher. During my hundreds of workshops in the schools, I began to observe that teachers with the warm "family" classroom atmospheres possessed two common points: they *felt good about themselves* and *unconditionally cared for their students*. They found something positive in each child, and had clearly decided they were going to make a positive impact on the lives of their students. What makes certain classrooms special? Their successes can be attributed to teachers who have a *caring attitude* toward each of their students, which overflows to create a positive, warm climate. For some children, it will be their first and last opportunity to be touched by a person who will be significant as a positive motivator in their lives.

How Can You Build Positive Self-Esteem in Students?

You have about nine months in which to give your students what may be, for many, the gift of believing in themselves. They may not receive this gift—the building blocks of positive self-esteem—from anyone else. They may begin to listen, for the first time in many cases, to positive qualities they possess, once a feeling of security (the foundation of Maslow's hierarchy of needs) has been established in your classroom. Based upon Robert Reasoner's *Building Self-Esteem: A Comprehensive Program* (Palo Alto, CA: Consulting Psychologists Press, 1982), our journey toward making each child feel valuable, lovable and capable will instill the components of self-esteem in sequential order: **Security**, **Positive Identity**, **Friendship Building**, **Goal Setting**, and **Competence**.

To begin, all children need to learn in an environment in which they feel free from humiliation and physical harm. When children have experienced physical and/or emotional abuse in the home, before academic learning can take place, it is crucial to develop in them a sense of **security**.

The next component of self-esteem builds a sense of selfhood in the child. Because our goal is to instill positive feelings about themselves while accepting their limitations, we will call it the component of **positive identity**. They are then more capable of forming skills needed to build **friendships**. Qualities needed to attract and to keep friends are taught. This is an important skill for life they will use all their lives. **Goal setting** encourages children to dream and then plan to turn those dreams into goals they can achieve. Included in goal-setting are creative problem-solving skills that will provide essential building blocks for conflict solving. **Competence** encourages children to look outside themselves toward helping others. An "I can!" approach to obstacles, risks, and challenges is evident. This section teaches capable decision-making when faced with today's issues and inevitable peer pressure.

How Can You Enable Children to Solve Conflicts Peacefully?

Have you lamented not only the violent acts being committed in our schools and communities, but also the lack of empathy or repentance young offenders show for their victims of violence? We ask, "Isn't it too bad that *someone* couldn't have reached one of those young offenders before the violence occurred?" So many factors determine a child's path to violence; you may find it difficult to believe that, as the teacher of a child for one or two years, you *can* make a difference in the direction of the path a student is going to take. You may find yourself saying, "I can only do . . . *so much!*" You're right. You can do *so much!*

Once students have a foundation in the components of self-esteem, you can *then* begin to teach them how to deal with **conflict solving** within themselves and with others. They will be prepared to accept the BBQ Strategy for cooling off their anger before using the TLC Approach Steps to collaborative problem solving as well as active listening and mediation skills, all found in the Conflict Solving section of this book. A child will also begin to realize his or her individual global significance as a peace contributor. As a sense of peace develops within the child, he or she becomes capable of peaceful relationships with others.

What Legacy Can I Give to My Students?

You are the most important resource for your students. For that reason, a special teacher empowerment section, just for you, is included at the beginning of this book. Years from now, your students may not remember all the facts you taught them, but they *will* remember your essence— the empathy, honesty, and kindness you have within yourself that you modeled to them. Most of all, they'll recall how you encouraged them in some way, the respect you gave them, and how you made them feel about themselves.

Let's continue our journey toward making this "dream" for our children a reality in our classrooms.

Beth Teolis

> "No printed word nor spoken plea
> Can teach young minds what men should be.
> Not all the books on all the shelves
> But what the teachers are themselves."
> —ANONYMOUS

ABOUT THIS RESOURCE

Included in this resource are over 100 ready-to-use classroom activities to build **positive self-esteem** and **conflict solving skills** within your students. Here are exercises in *skills for life* that students will carry within themselves long after they leave your classroom. Suggested ideas for easily integrating them into your daily schedules are listed below. All activities have been previously classroom-enjoyed by students and teachers!

The five components of self-esteem build upon one another, with security forming the solid foundation for the others. The remaining components may overlap. For example, security and friendship-building skills often overlap. When you enable a child to feel safe and comfortable in your classroom and promote a feeling of warmth among your students, friendship skills often emerge. Goal setting and competence overlap when instilling an "I can!" attitude in children to make their dreams realities and to dare to take reasonable risks. Positive identity and competence are both components that point out students' strengths along with recognition and acceptance of their limitations, giving them a feeling of capability and confidence.

The section on conflict solving is effectively taught *once the child has this self-esteem foundation* formed. How can children be expected to deal with their anger toward others before their anger within has not been at least partially resolved? If children don't feel security and trust with their teachers in their classrooms, if they don't see *anything* positive about themselves, if the only affiliation they know is with the "wrong" group of kids or a gang, if they don't care about goals, if their attitude in life is "I *can't*, so why bother trying?" how can we expect them to control their outer-directed anger, to be able to cool down and plan a collaborative solution? Build the foundation for conflict solving by teaching the components of self-esteem and the conflict-solving skills will then more readily be learned.

You will find *concepts repeated* on different activity sheets for each component. The purpose of this repetition is not only to give you the choice of activities, but also to provide different activities to give students a refresher, after you move on to another component.

Activities Curriculum Integration

- **Drama:** Through role playing real-life situations students can relate to, they learn they are responsible for their feelings about themselves, what they can do about negative days, how to feel and express empathy for others, how to deal with peer pressure, and how to have fun with class bloopers!

- **Language Arts:** Poems, autobiographies, and multicultural booklets enable students to express their feelings about themselves through creative-writing activities. Literature links to related topics are provided.

- **Art:** Ideas for displays around the room, school hall collective art activities, bulletin board captions, and student art work are all integrated with the objective of forming positive identities and solving conflicts peacefully.

- **Music:** Suggestions are given for the use of music in the classroom on an ongoing basis. Specific songs linked to activities are provided as well as special Peace Activities Celebration, Self-Esteem Day, and Graduation selections.

Special Activities

- **School Ground Naturalization Plan:** Plotting ideas for starting a school ground naturalization project are given in detail.

- **Relaxation:** Exercises are given to teach visualization.

- **Games:** Various games enable students to put themselves in another's shoes. Critical thinking, values formation, and creative problem-solving skills are presented in game formats such as crossword puzzles, dominoes, scrambled letters, and the classroom game, "It Is! It Isn't!"

- **Special Celebrations:** Ideas for a classroom or schoolwide Peace Activities Celebration, Skills for Life Activities Day, and a Multicultural Celebration are all provided step-by-step for you to implement.

- **Skills for Life Workshop Outline:** Step-by-step suggestions for presenting your own workshop.

Special Features of This Resource

Educator Self-Esteem Empowerment • Behavior That's Driving You Up the Wall • Skills for Life Activities Day • Peace Activities Celebration • "I Dig My Roots" Multicultural Celebration • Grams • Inspirational Candle Quotes • Parents as Partners • Letters to Parents • How to Set Up Your Own Skills for Life School Program • How to Present a Skills for Life Workshop • Student Tests and Evaluations • Rationale, Goals and Intended Outcome Statements for Students • Anorexia Reading List for Kids • Relaxation Exercises • School Ground Naturalization Plans • Self-Esteem and Conflict-Solving Bibliographies • Just-for-fun activity sheet at end of each section • Skills for Life Resources for Parents

START YOUR OWN "SKILLS FOR LIFE" PILOT PROGRAM

Is there a "Skills for Life Program" in your area? If not, why not be the person to start one? Here are some simple steps, skeleton ideas to get you started; then you can fill in more ideas of your own as you get going. What is really needed to get any pilot program off the ground is your enthusiastic belief that kids will benefit by the program and you will have the impetus to get started! If you have the desire, the following suggestions will help you along. Not only will it be challenging and lots of fun, but most of all, it will be one of the most rewarding experiences you will have when you see the results of your efforts. And you will see those results in the eyes of your students, which will no longer be vacant, defiant, hostile or fearful; they will hold a new light. That light will come from hope.

- *How will you begin?* Form a **small team** along with any others in your school who are interested in building self-esteem and conflict solving in your children. Hold **group meetings** to share ideas as to activities that are working, bulletin board and hall display ideas, Peace Activities Celebration plans, a Self-Esteem Day Assembly, or School Grounds Naturalization, along with your own ideas. The ideas from these meetings are **shared with the faculty at faculty meetings**. You only need about five to ten minutes to report on your group meetings and suggestions for the faculty to use. Sign-up sheets could be presented at the faculty meetings to plan for participating teachers and dates for the assemblies. Any **faculty empowerment activities** could be done at this time such as initiating the activity "Guess Who?" "WOW" or another idea from the Teacher Empowerment section. Introduce an activity by saying, "This activity was used and made a hit with the kids . . ." Pages from this book along with other sources that have been used with a class could be displayed on the faculty table for others to see as examples they may also want to try with their classes. As with any good recipe, you taste it, like it and then want to know how to do it yourself!

- *How can you expand when you're ready?* If there are several schools in your area that would like to be included after you have begun your own pilot program, ask for a **liaison** from each school to meet together periodically to share ideas among yourselves. It is important that the same liaison(s) attend the meetings for the continuity needed for this program. Agree on a **convenient meeting site**, **date**, and **time**. Starting a "Pilot School Photo Scrapbook" is a great way to share what's going on in the different pilot schools. Each liaison takes photos of self-esteem and conflict-solving activities, assemblies, skits, and bulletin board and hall display ideas going on in each pilot school and takes them to the liaison meetings where they are assembled in the scrapbook.

- *Where will you get ideas for your pilot program?* Ideas from various resource guides are just a start to the creativity teachers show when they get going in this program— they take the ideas and run! Educators enjoy the creativity and the kids love it, thus everyone benefits!

- *How can you present a workshop?* Each liaison may provide a **workshop for the faculty**. It is not important to be an experienced presenter. If you have a sincere dedication to self-esteem and conflict-solving skill building in children and you feel it will benefit your students, that is all you need to get going. A **workshop presentation outline** (which you can creatively edit) follows to guide you along step by step.

Although it can be frustrating at times when you are discouraged by those who feel self-esteem and conflict solving skill-building activities are a waste of school time along with the fact that you won't see positive results immediately, you will feel fulfilled once you begin to see the benefits. You will see a more positive school climate, educators validating one another as well as their students, students validating each other with fewer put-downs, children being more positive with family members in the home (where they can continue the validation process), improved academic performance, fewer fights and less bullying, kids *wanting* to come to school, children feeling less need to affiliate with gangs, and gender equity—all as a result of the "Skills for Life" Program you helped to create!

SELF-ESTEEM
AND CONFLICT-SOLVING WORKSHOPS

Time: Approximately 2-1/2 to 3 hours for each workshop
Theme: I Can Only Do . . . So Much!

1. Self-Esteem Workshop

Materials Needed:

One enthusiastic presenter dedicated to giving a workshop that will empower teachers to empower their children; candle, matches, and soft music; candle forms provided in Section 1 (may be cut out and mounted on yellow bristol board); six candles made of yellow bristol board or construction paper with quotations of your choice (some quotations are found in Section 1) attached and numerals one to six written on each candle (distribute candle quotations at various seats before participants enter); props and cards with lines for the skits you plan to use; activity sheet "WOW" from Section 2; small gift, such as a purse mirror, wrapped in four or five layers of gift wrap; "One at a Time" starfish story found in Section 1; samples of students' work from this resource, such as, "What Makes Me Pop," "WOW," or "Just Blading By," and bulletin board and hall ideas you have made or collected from liaison meetings; "Pilot School Photo Scrapbook" to pass around during your break; and "My Goals" scrapbook (which you have made yourself to show your group).

Introduction:

To create a warm atmosphere as participants enter, have a candle lit, lights softened, and music playing, such as "Candle in the Wind" by Elton John, "The Dance" by Garth Brooks, "I Know" by Beautiful World, or relaxing classical music.

Begin by asking your group members if they can recall a teacher who encouraged them in some area that they still carry with them today—a love of reading, sports, music or a general belief in themselves they have never lost—someone who put a light in their eyes. Pass the candle form for everyone to sign the name of that teacher on the candle along with how he or she was encouraging to them. After all have signed the candle, display it in your faculty room, on a bulletin board, or in a corner designated for teacher empowerment. Explain to your group that the theme of your workshop will be "I Can Only Do . . . *So Much!*" Ask how they would feel if one day, a student of theirs were asked to sign a candle recalling a teacher who encouraged him or her in some way and that student chose them?

First Part of Workshop—Teacher Empowerment:

Explain that before we can model positive self-esteem and treat students with a positive attitude, we must first feel positive about ourselves. So, to begin, ask teachers to get comfortable because for the first part of the workshop you are going to do some self-esteem empowerment for the educators—a time just for them!

Validations—Giving and Receiving: In order for teachers to create a positive feeling in their schools among one another, they need to take time to validate each other. To illustrate validations, pass a small gift (a purse mirror or a notepad to write validations to others) wrapped in four or five layers. Begin the process by giving a specific, sincere compliment to someone you would like to validate. For example, pass the gift to a teacher, principal or vice principal you have noticed being patient and kind to a student, spending extra time to help a student or give support to a colleague when needed. Each recipient takes off one layer of paper before passing it on. The one who takes off the last layer keeps the gift. An important part of this exercise is not only to learn to give validations, but also how to receive and gracefully accept positive comments given to us without feeling we don't deserve them! (This is an exercise in which teachers are often very touched by recognition from their colleagues.)

To extend validations to one another, ask teachers to form teams of six, and then pass out "WOW" activity sheets. Ask them to first write their names at the tops of their sheets, then to pass them to the left for everyone on the team to write how that colleague WOWS them! As they write their validations, play the song "Hero" by Mariah Carey as background music. This is a powerful song they may want to add to their class selections so that students may seek to find the hero that lies within themselves. To further illustrate the importance of using this activity with their students, point out that validations from peers have a lasting impact on children and may be, for many, the *only positive comments about themselves they ever receive.*

Ongoing Candle Readings: Ask for the numbered candle readings (which you distributed before the workshop) to be read during your workshop at various intervals. Pause and ask for the number of the saying to be read, perhaps after each activity. They only take a moment to read, yet the quotations provide so much thought for reflection.

A Time Just for You—A Relaxation Exercise: Ask your participants to get comfortable for a relaxation exercise. Tell them that this will be a time just for them! You may prefer to choose your own description for this activity, calling it "imagination" or "visualization." Advise them, when doing this exercise with their classes, to be sensitive to some children who may feel reluctant to visualize, even though this exercise involves simply imagining climbing a mountain and looking for your inner strengths. Step-by-step instructions for leading your participants on this imaginative adventure are found in the activity "A Peaceful Journey" in Section 7. Dim the lights so that all can relax by your flickering candle. Choose relaxing background music to create a mellow mood. Speak in a soft voice and don't rush this activity. Pause to give participants time to reflect. Continue to play relaxing music and leave the lights dimmed as they begin their break. This ends the Teacher Empowerment portion of the workshop.

Break: Offer coffee, tea, juice, and simple refreshments. During the break, seek out two people to take the roles of "Granny" and "Wilbert" for one of the skits. Genders are best reversed for this skit, with a male playing "Granny" and a female in the role of "Wilbert." (Lines for this skit are in "A Geeky Play" in Section 6.) The large flowered hat for "Granny" and hat or goggles worn atop "Wilbert's" head along with a crazy tie or scarf really do make for a good laugh among colleagues!

Second Part of Workshop—Empower Your Students:

Play "Life Is a Highway" by Tom Cochrane or another lively song as participants reassemble.

The Tiffany Skit: Start off the second part of the workshop, which focuses on empowering students, with "The Tiffany Skit" found in Section 3. Ask for volunteers to play the various characters. Assure everyone that although the skit has a message and it's extremely valuable to do with their classes and for assemblies, it's also a favorite activity of this workshop, lots of fun, and nobody has more than two or three lines!

After the skit, reflect on the fact that many students do have one day after another hearing only negatives. Discuss ways of dealing with how to help students who face constant negativism: teaching them that nobody can make them feel low if they don't allow it; their feelings about themselves are what they believe they are and not what others tell them they are—or are not. At this point, announce you would like the group to welcome two visitors to your workshop, Granny and her grandson, Wilbert. (*Lead the group in applause for "Granny" and "Wilbert."*)

The Granny and Wilbert Skit: "Granny" hobbles in wearing her flowered hat and "Wilbert," in his geeky attire, follows. This is a humorous skit and also carries the message that you are responsible for how you feel about yourself; you are who *you* believe you are; not what someone else tells you who you are. Explain that children should be led to the awareness that they are in charge of their reactions to an event. Play the song "Life Is a Highway" by Tom Cochrane and point out to the teachers that they are the drivers, driving along their own highways of life. To further illustrate that we have within ourselves the power to make a positive experience out of a potentially negative experience, tell "The Coupon Story."

The Coupon Story: This is the true story of a young girl who had her first job at a large hardware store. A rude customer came to her cash register, demanding cash for his large collection of store coupons. She explained that the coupons were only redeemable in merchandise, not in cash. After several more demands for cash and more patient explanations from the girl, the angry man tore up the coupons, swore at the girl, and threw them in her face. Screaming loudly, he left the store, shouting and swearing. The young girl quietly picked up each coupon and said thoughtfully, "Later I'll tape all these coupons together. There should be enough to lay away a Walkman I've been wanting!" Customers who had witnessed the angry man's scene expected the young girl to be shaken, possibly crying, asking for a break; instead she *chose* how she would react to the situation. She chose to make a positive outcome out of a negative event.

The Five Components of Self-Esteem: *Security*, *Positive Identity*, *Friendship Building*, *Goal Setting*, and *Competence* are introduced and displayed visually on an overhead, chart or board for all to view as you speak about each component. It is important that you fully understand the rationale and goals behind teaching each of the components so that you can share it with your participants and are able to answer their questions. A full bibliography is available for you at the back of this book to give you references for your workshop information. Emphasize to teachers that only *after* the students have received a foundation in the components of self-esteem should conflict-solving skills be introduced.

2. Conflict-Solving Workshop

Materials Needed:

Masking tape to divide room; list of controversial topics; collection of magazine "gifts" or real items, with some that are fun trying to convince others to give up; cards containing conflict situations for mediation; props for role playing; and samples of students' work.

First Part of Workshop—Games to Introduce Conflict-Solving Concepts:

(All of the following activities are found in Section 7.) Have the room prepared for the game, "It Is! It Isn't!" to illustrate the point that conflict is inevitable in our lives and we need to have the ability to see the problem from the other's point of view; not only through our own eyes. Play the game, "I Want What You Have."

Introduce Conflict Styles: Discuss the five conflict styles. Give a problem-solving situation to groups of five or six. After several minutes of group problem solving, ask participants to evaluate the conflict style they used. Introduce the BBQ and TLC guidelines for collaborative problem solving.

Role Playing: Role playing is effective in reviewing aggressive vs. assertive approaches and active listening skills. Play "What's Wrong with This Picture?" to point out body language in active listening. Make up a role play situation pointing out the differences between "pushy" aggressive and assertive behavior.

Break: Offer coffee, tea, juice, and simple refreshments.

Second Part of Workshop—Active, Hands-on Conflict Solving

Play "I Know" by Beautiful World or "Forever Yesterday, for the Children" by Gladys Knight as participants reassemble. Check music suggested for Peace Celebrations.

Triggers 'n' Traps 'n' Tricks: With a partner or small group, introduce and discuss one of your anger Triggers 'n' Traps (what often "sets you off" and you get stuck in) 'n' Tricks (when the real issue is in the past, not the present issue.)

Plug in to Mediation: Give conflicts to triads for each to take a turn in the role of mediator.

Peace Activities: Pass out the teacher directions and activity sheets for planning a Peace Activities Celebration.

For Both Workshops: Samples Displayed:

Share some completed student activity pages of your choice, bulletin board and hall display samples, and art and language arts ideas. We all like to see what has worked well with classes as well as what the finished product looks like!

Closing for Either Workshop:

Read "One at a Time" (found in Section 1) to point out to teachers the power they have to make a positive difference to even one child who passes through their classroom doors. Ask them to sign the name of a child they want to help on the starfish included in Section 1. For a closing activity, listen together to "Children Will Listen" by Barbra Streisand or "Hero" by Mariah Carey. These songs embody all we are trying to accomplish with our children. Form a circle around your candle, hands clasped together as you reflect on the significant role you play in the lives of the children who pass through your doors. If one day someone asks one of them to sign a teacher's name on a candle, as we did during our opening activity, perhaps his or her eyes will light up remembering *you* as the teacher who made a difference in his or her life.

HOW TO PLAN A "SKILLS FOR LIFE" ACTIVITIES DAY

Does the idea of having a "Skills for Life" Activities Day (or you may prefer to call it "Self-Esteem Activities Day") at your school sound appealing? Yes, but a lot of work? Are you asking, "Who would be in charge? Not me!!" Let the following pages do your planning for you, step by step. Even a ready-to-hang sign-up sheet is provided! What you will need to do as the one in charge (that's *you* because you're still reading this!) is to enlist several willing participants. Talk with some of your colleagues about this fun and rewarding activities day and, with the support of some enthusiasts, ask the principal for time to discuss it at the next faculty meeting. All you have to supply is a desire to make these ideas a reality.

Once the faculty agrees to a "Skills for Life" Activities Day, decide together on either a full- or half-day program and whether the entire school or certain divisions will be participating. Next, **introduce the activities** from which teachers may choose (activity suggestions are provided on the following sheet). Tell them to feel free, if they prefer, to make up their own activities. Provide the **sign-up sheet** (also included here) to be hung in a convenient place with the **tried-and-true kids' activities sheets attached**. Participants are asked to indicate on the sign-up sheet the activity they will enjoy doing with their groups.

Twenty-minute sessions work well. The oldest students in your school can act as **monitors** and assist the younger children as they move from one class to another. They can also help teachers prepare for activities, assist them during the sessions and, afterwards, display the students' work in the halls or on bulletin boards. If the entire school is participating, the bell could ring after 20 minutes and again for the start of the next session. Allow **five minutes** for students **to rotate**. Kids should wear nametags so that all the teachers will be able to identify the students by their names.

An all-school **assembly or celebration** in the gym is an enjoyable culminating activity. "A Geeky Play," the Wilbert and Granny skit, is always enjoyed by students. For fun, a couple of teachers or the principal and/or vice principal could dress up as Granny and Wilbert—the kids would love it! Some favorite "Class Bloopers!" role plays could be performed. Teachers may want to add to this bloopers act also. The oldest class in your school may choose activities of their own to present—skits they have made up. Some of the most creative products, slogans and ads (if groups did the activity, "Create an Ad!") could be presented by their creators and posters done by all the groups displayed in the gym. The opening song might be a portion of "Celebration" by Kool and the Gang to provide a celebratory entrance as the children file in for the assembly. If classes have learned one or more songs, they can sing them to close the assembly.

Most important, enjoy your day!

SOME TRIED-AND-TRUE KIDS' ACTIVITIES FOR "SKILLS FOR LIFE" DAY

1. **What Makes Me Pop!** Write sizzling qualities inside the kernels and decorate, cut out, and display the boxes in hall with the caption "What Makes Us Pop." (See Section 3.)

2. **I CAN!** This activity is for primary students. Cut forms in the shapes of cans from brightly colored paper, with lines provided for students to print the things they *can* do. You could also provide booklets with an I CAN! cover to include stories and illustrations of themselves in successful situations.

3. **Music.** Teach an inspiring song to each class for a sing-along at an assembly. Some suggestions are: "Hero" by Mariah Carey, "The Greatest Love of All" by Whitney Houston, or "I Can" by Baldy.

4. **Detectives!** Give problems for students to solve creatively. Cut out magnifying glasses or detective hats from colored paper with creative problems (from this book or one of the puzzle books listed in the Bibliography) written on them. Pass one to each team for brainstorming solutions together. Copy suggested solutions onto cards that can be passed out near the end of the session; however, if the teams' answers work, they are right! Encourage all creative solutions. (See Section 5.)

5. **Create an Ad!** Here's a creative problem-solving opportunity for kids to come up with a new product, or to choose an existing product and create a slogan and ad to market it. Students make posters to advertise the product, or they could perform live ads for a TV ad. If a video is available, some ads could be taped. These ads may be done individually or in small teams. Emphasize creativity!

6. **Drama Corner.** Have students rehearse their skits and perhaps perform them at an assembly. "A Geeky Play" (Granny and Wilbert skit) could be included. Suggested props and attire need to be available. (See Section 6.)

7. **Class Bloopers!** Create role plays from humorous classroom incidents. These role plays could be written by the oldest students in your school and printed on cards for you to pass out to teams to perform. (See Section 2.)

8. **It's Video Time!** for older students and **Times of My Life** for primary students in which students turn life events into movie material. (See Section 2.)

9. **Plant a Positive Tree**—or **Tree of Special Kids**. Give leaves to students to write the positive things they are going to say to themselves, replacing negative self-talk. Hang all the leaves on a huge paper tree in the hall to create a School Positive Tree. Rose forms could be made and substituted for leaves and a huge rosebush could be hung, "Everything's Coming Up Roses!" (See Section 3.)

10. **Our Forest of Friends**. This is a fingerpainting activity for primary students. Trees are decorated and hung together to create a forest of friends. (See Section 4.)

MORE TRIED-AND-TRUE KIDS' ACTIVITIES . . .

11. **Any Way You Slice It, I'm Deluxe!** Make pizzas of yellow bristol board with "toppings" of positive qualities about the child. Toppings could also be used for hot dogs, hamburgers, or ice cream cones. (See Section 3.)

12. **WOW!** Teams of six write validations on each person's "Wow" sheet. Kids decorate their sheets and display them with the caption, "Here's How We WOW Each Other!"(See Section 2.)

13. **Stars.** Qualities of good friends or students' goals are written inside the stars. Paper cut into shapes of clouds could also be hung along with the stars. Set up a center with glitter pens or glue and sparkles for students to decorate and hang stars with the captions, "At _____ We Have Goals," "Our Stars Shine at _____," or "Our Dreams Can Come True!" (See Section 4.)

15. **(Name of School) Is Building a Solid Foundation.** Have bricks or grams ready to pass out to students, who write their ideas for building a better school or why they feel their school is special. Hang all bricks or grams in your front hall under the caption, "We Are Building a Firm Foundation" or, if grams are used, the name or initials of the school are formed with the grams. (See Sections 2 and 9.)

16. **Life Is a Highway and You're the Driver.** Play the song "Life Is a Highway" by Tom Cochrane. Invite students to sing (and drive) along. Explain the purpose of the activity is that they realize they are in charge of their own highways of life. The activity sheet asks students how they will handle detours and roadblocks on their own highways. (See Section 6.)

17. **We're a Hit with Our CD'S.** Have CD plastic covers available for students to trace on colorful bristol board with a song about themselves written inside the cover. Or a Character Description could be written. Silver foil "discs" (laminated, if possible) inside make for a realistic CD! (See Section 2.) *Activity for primary students*: Each child glues white circles or silver foil circles onto a black "record" with the child's name and something special written about the child. If displayed, the caption is "Our Top (number of students) Hits!" (See Section 2.)

18. **We Make (Name of School) a Barrel of Fun!** This is a display activity for primary students. Children decorate little brown bears with small white faces on which they can sprinkle glitter and glue. Their names are written on the bears. A bear in a barrel with the name of your school is in the center of the large hall or bulletin board display.

19. **At (Name of School) We Have Goals.** Students' top three goals are written on signposts and hung on a display with the saying: "Which of the two roads should I take?" Alice asked the rabbit. "It doesn't matter," said the rabbit. "Because without a goal, you're never going to get there!"

20. **My Loot Bag of Goodies.** This activity is for primary students. Draw and trace a party loot bag and several candies (suckers, gumdrops, taffy, etc.) onto paper. Children write out or dictate the qualities they feel are special about themselves to be written inside the candies. They then cut out the loot bags and the candies, and paste the candies inside the loot bags. Loot bags are then colored and decorated.

"SKILLS FOR LIFE" DAY SIGN-UP SHEET

Sign up below for one of our "Skills for Life" Day activities! If you have an activity of your own, please feel free to use it. If you're looking for an idea, check the attached list.

	Name:	Activity:
1.	_____	_____
2.	_____	_____
3.	_____	_____
4.	_____	_____
5.	_____	_____
6.	_____	_____
7.	_____	_____
8.	_____	_____
9.	_____	_____
10.	_____	_____
11.	_____	_____
12.	_____	_____
13.	_____	_____
14.	_____	_____
15.	_____	_____
16.	_____	_____
17.	_____	_____
18.	_____	_____
19.	_____	_____
20.	_____	_____

PARENTS AS PARTNERS

Enlist the parent(s) or guardians of the children you teach as your partners. Welcome them warmly into the school to talk with you as early in the school year as possible; let them know your academic and skills for life objectives. Enlist their help at home, too. Consistency is so important to the success of the child. This meeting is intended to be held in addition to your fall Open House or the evening when parents come *en masse* to hear about your program for the year. Taking the time to talk privately with each parent will break down any barriers that may have been present. Some parents, for many reasons, do not want to ask questions about the school program publicly. However, if they feel comfortable with you privately, they may ask you questions that will help them understand better what will be taking place in your classroom during the year. They will become your allies, and all of you working together will benefit the child so much more than having inconsistency in the home, breaking down much of what you are trying to accomplish with the child in school.

If a parent complains about your teaching *values* to his or her child, take the time to explain which values you will be teaching and carrying out in your classroom, and in most cases, once the question, "Which values will my child's teacher be teaching?" is answered, parents will usually find you all want to instill the same values in your children. These include nonviolent ways of dealing with anger and conflict, empathy for others if you hurt them, honesty, and alternatives to joining gangs which promote violence.

If parents express opposition to self-esteem and conflict-solving skills building, ask them, "What are your fears about this?" You may find that the self-esteem of the opposing parent(s) is sometimes low and he or she will resist any kind of work dealing with this topic, which is to him or her a painful process. Go over the program with parents so they will realize your aim is to enable the child to feel capable and positive about his or her abilities, which will lead to improved academic success and to improved behavior. A "Skills for Life Workshop for Parents" may begin with empowering their self-esteem and then proceed to explain to them the components of self-esteem and conflict-solving skills you will be teaching their children. Use the Skills for Life Workshop plans in this book which may be adapted for parents. If the mystique of this program is removed, you will most likely receive their full support. Their questions are, after all, justified as they were probably not taught skills for life during their own school years; it is an area many parents would like to have explained to them. Once it is outlined to them, most parents realize these are important skills from which they also would have benefited during their own elementary and junior high years!

Some may oppose, for religious reasons, any imagination exercises you will do. You may want to assure those parents that no religion is mentioned, the exercises are simply relaxing, a peaceful timeout for the child. If they still do not want their children to participate, assure them you will give their child another activity to do at that time.

If a child is misbehaving, find out from the parents what is taking place in other areas of the child's life that may be contributing to the misbehavior. Stress to them the importance of finding something positive in the child to point out. Ask them to try to overlook all the negatives for two or three weeks (unless it involves physical harm which, of course, cannot be ignored)—as difficult as it may be—and instead to focus on positive feedback for efforts that may have previously gone unnoticed. Explain that they will probably be put to the test, but to make every effort to avoid the old pattern of negative feedback, concentrating only on the positive. Assure parents you are making the same efforts at school and feel that after a few weeks of being patient with bids for negative attention, you may all begin to see some improvement.

Most of all, form a team that consists of yourself, the parent(s) or guardian(s), and the child. Your team goal is to instill in the child the desire to be the best he or she can be in every area, both academic and nonacademic. Send them invitations (provided in this book or you may prefer to have the children make their own) to your Skills for Life Activities Day, I Dig My Roots Multicultural Festival and your Peace Activities Day Celebrations. Arrange a time for them to come in to visit for an hour or so to informally view your everyday routine. Ask parents to come in to share their skills with your class. Encourage factory workers who could educate students about the topic "team productivity" and what contributes to team productivity in their work places. Many of the components of team management can be applied to children playing on sports teams, groups in the classroom, and other team activities. Learning to be a team player and a team leader is a skill for life they will use for many years in so many areas of their lives! Computer technologists could report on their vision of the role of the Information Highway in the year 2000 and beyond and how students should be preparing for those future jobs.

A parenting list of reference material is included in this book, available for you to offer a parent if he or she is interested in complementing your skills for life program at home.

Once the parents become your partners, together you can make all the difference to a discouraged, low self-esteem child. This collaborative approach assures that *everybody* wins!

CONTENTS

SECTION 7
Conflict Solving • 189

Rationale, Goals, and Intended Outcomes • 190

SECTION 8
Behavior That's Driving You Up the Wall • 263

SECTION 9
Ready-To-Use Handouts • 271

BIBLIOGRAPHY • 289

Ready-to-Use
SELF-ESTEEM &
CONFLICT-SOLVING
ACTIVITIES
for Grades 4-8

1
Teacher Empowerment

1–1. GIVE ME A LITTLE MORE R–E–S–P–E–C–T

YOU are the well that students draw from. What if YOU are in a DROUGHT STATE?

1. Rescript your self-talk. Turn negative thoughts into positive thoughts by picturing the way you would like it to be, then rewording the thought. **Example:** "I am only a teacher." (*negative self-talk*) "I have the ability to positively influence these thirty plus children for life." (*positive self-talk*)

2. Listen to empowering tapes on the way to work. Attend professional seminars and inservice training. Read educational journals. Welcome new knowledge.

3. Make sure you have MUSIC (many different kinds) in your room daily. Play music as students enter the room—classical, rock, country, etc. Notice how noise level will soften as students hear background music. Share some of their music favorites also!

4. Select a piece of clothing with two pockets. Put a quantity of paper chips in one pocket. Each time during the day that you say something negative to yourself, put a paper clip in the other pocket. At the end of the day, tally your negative comments. Use this activity to measure your response to a colleague, student, or loved one.

5. Be proactive. Be the one at your school to be *positive* in the staff room about other students, parents, and colleagues. Try to avoid being with consistently negative colleagues. Camaraderie is too often built around mutual negativity. It can be a partly sunny day or a partly cloudy day—it's up to you.

6. Ask yourself, "What have I done lately to lean toward the risk or to get out of my comfort zone?"

7. Model high self-esteem. Teachers who feel good about themselves are more successful at producing students with high self-esteem. They try to bring out the best in each student. They encourage students to set goals and reach their true potentials because they have done so themselves. Conversely, a teacher with a low self-esteem often displays a negative self-attitude when dealing with students. If you need to criticize a colleague, friend, relative or student in order to feel positive about yourself, you probably need to raise your own self-esteem.

1–2. MY SUCCESSES

Directions: Divide your life into three equal age periods (for example, birth –15, 16–30, 31–45) and list three successes for each period on the spaces provided below. In the last section list three successes you would like to have in the next five years.

First Third:

1. _____
2. _____
3. _____

Second Third:

1. _____
2. _____
3. _____

Third Third:

1. _____
2. _____
3. _____

Next Five Years:

1. _____
2. _____
3. _____

Success Symbol Activity:

Form pairs. If you could bring one symbol to show your partner one of the times in your life when you felt successful, what would you choose? Some life successes cannot be represented by an object. If that is your experience, share with your partner your fond memory of a successful event.

Jack Canfield, Self-Esteem Seminars
6035 Bristol Parkway, Culver City, CA 90230, 1-310-337-9222

Used with permission.

1–3. LET YOUR BEST POINTS SHINE!

We are born into this world as shining stars. If the lustre fades a bit, we need to renew its splendor. **Directions:** Write your name on the top of this sheet. Pass your star to those who will write one of your "bright points" *inside* the star points. Then, add in the center of the star what *you* think makes you shine so brightly!

1-4. GUESS WHICH COLLEAGUE IS THIS?

Pass this sheet to colleagues and place their guesses in the question mark.

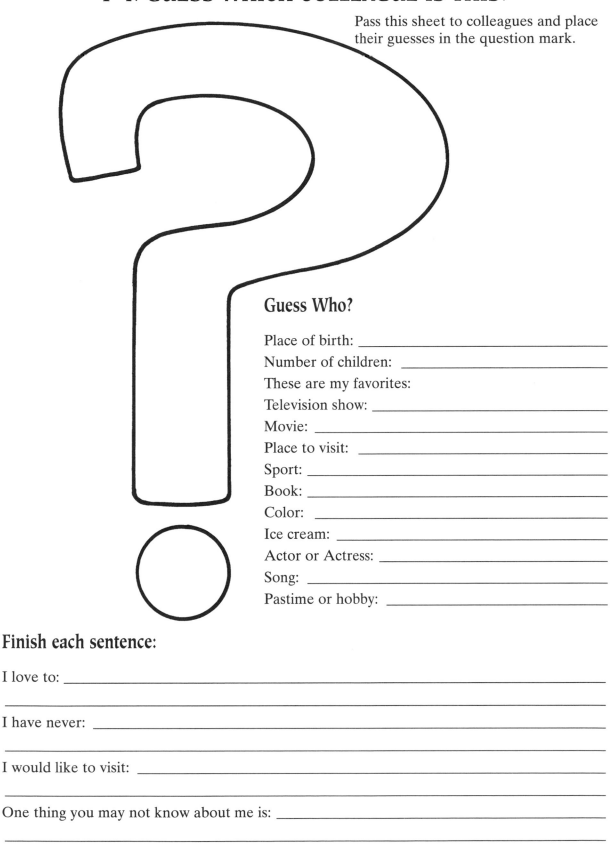

Guess Who?

Place of birth: _____

Number of children: _____

These are my favorites:

Television show: _____

Movie: _____

Place to visit: _____

Sport: _____

Book: _____

Color: _____

Ice cream: _____

Actor or Actress: _____

Song: _____

Pastime or hobby: _____

Finish each sentence:

I love to: _____

_____

I have never: _____

_____

I would like to visit: _____

_____

One thing you may not know about me is: _____

_____

1–5. CANDLE QUOTATIONS

Here are quotes you can cut out and attach to copies of the candle pattern.

"I cannot think of a single psychological problem—from anxiety to depression, to fear of intimacy or success to suicide and crimes of violence—that is not traceable to the problem of poor self-concept. Positive self-esteem is a cardinal requirement of a fulfilling life."

DR. NATHANIEL BRANDEN

"When one door closes, another opens."

HELEN KELLER

"Sure, it's vital to teach Johnny and Mary how to read and write and think and compute—but if they don't learn to love themselves and each other, the rest isn't worth anything. Self-esteem and the capacity for loving are the most basic skills each human being has the need and right to learn about."

JOSEPH M. BROOKS

"We all make mistakes. But to commit a wrong, to lower the dignity of a child and not be aware that the dignity has been impaired is much more serious than the child's skipping of words during oral reading."

C. MOUSTAKAS

"You need not worry about whether you will make a difference in your students' lives. This is a given. The question is whether you will make a positive or a negative difference."

TONY ARMENTA

"No one can make you feel inferior without your consent."

ELEANOR ROOSEVELT

1–5. CANDLE QUOTATIONS

Here are quotes you can cut out and attach to copies of the candle pattern.

"Once you see a child's self-image begin to improve, you will see significant gains in achievement areas, but even more importantly, you will see a child who is beginning to enjoy life more."

DR. WAYNE DYER

"You may be disappointed if you fail, but you are doomed if you don't try."

BEVERLY SILLS

"Self-esteem is learned. If it is learned, you can teach it."

DR. MICHELE BORBA

"Spread love everywhere you go; first of all in your own house. Give love to your children, to your wife or husband, to a next door neighbor. . . . Let no one ever come to you without leaving better and happier."

MOTHER TERESA

"Teaching self-esteem, after all, is simply a way to help students overcome their negative ideas about themselves and to discover their unique potentials. But the success of such education is absolutely dependent upon the educator knowing his or her own essential self-worth so he or she can communicate that feeling of self-worth to others."

JACK CANFIELD

"To create and build may take the devotion and energy of a life time. To destroy can be the thoughtless and inconsiderate act of a moment."

WINSTON CHURCHILL

7

1–6. ONE AT A TIME

A friend of ours was walking down a deserted Mexican beach at sunset. As he walked along, he began to see another man in the distance. As he grew nearer, he noticed that the local native kept leaning down, picking something up, and throwing it out into the water. Time and again he kept hurling things out into the ocean.

As our friend approached even closer, he noticed that the man was picking up starfish that had been washed up on the beach and, one at a time, he was throwing them back into the water.

Our friend was puzzled. He approached the man and said, "Good evening, friend. I was wondering what you are doing."

"I'm throwing these starfish back into the ocean. You see, it's low tide right now and all of these starfish have been washed up onto the shore. If I don't throw them back into the sea, they'll die up here from lack of oxygen."

"I understand," my friend replied, "but there must be thousands of starfish on this beach. You can't possibly get to all of them. There are simply too many. And don't you realize this is probably happening on hundreds of beaches all up and down this coast? Can't you see that you can't possibly make a difference?"

The local native smiled, bent down and picked up yet another starfish, and as he threw it back into the sea, he replied, "Made a difference to that one!"

JACK CANFIELD AND MARK V. HANSEN

Taken from *Chicken Soup for the Soul: 101 Stories to Open the Heart and Rekindle the Spirit* by Jack Canfield and Mark V. Hansen, 1993, Health Communications. Used with permission.

STARFISH ACTIVITY

Fill in the starfish names of at-risk, low self-esteem students, abuse victims, or any other discouraged child to whom you will make a difference. Place the starfish (or make a large starfish) in your faculty room and ask colleagues to sign their names of a child to whom they *will make a difference*!

2
Security

SECURITY

Rationale:

Security is the first component of self-esteem to be developed in students. It is the foundation upon which the other components of self-esteem should follow sequentially. Based upon Abraham Maslow's Hierarchy of Needs, security or safety is a need that must be met in order for a child to move forward socially and academically.

Goals:

- Set up cooperative groups in which each student feels secure in sharing with members.
- Create a feeling of physical and emotional safety in a caring, positive classroom.
- Alleviate in your students any fear of being shamed or embarrassed so that they feel trust.
- Set and enforce consistent, fair classroom rules and consequences. Let students have a role in setting some guidelines and displaying them in the classroom.
- Demonstrate unconditional caring by letting your students know they are cared for even if they earn a poor grade or misbehave.
- Treat each student as your favorite.
- Acknowledge all the special people in the students' lives who contribute to their feelings of security.

Intended Outcome Statements for Students:

- "My classroom is a safe place for me."
- "I understand what is expected of me in this classroom."
- "I know I will not be embarrassed if I 'mess up.' I am proud of my race and my language."
- "In return for the respect I receive in my classroom, I will respect the classroom rules."
- "My teacher may not always like my grades or my behavior, but she always cares for me!"
- "I have special people I care about and they care about me."
- "Our classroom rules are fair. I even helped make some of them!"
- "I am in a team in my class with our own name. It feels good to share and listen to each other."

2-1. DIRECTIONS FOR THE SECURITY QUIZ

This quiz may be used as a pre-test before the Security component is introduced in your classroom. After you feel your students have completed a sufficient number of security-building activities, the quiz may again be given and the results compared with the pre-test.

Below are the Security components you are assessing. If a student answer differs from the answer key below, it may be an indicator of weakness in that component and you will know specifically what his or her needs are.

Feelings of security to be instilled in students are:

- Emotional Safety—Freedom from humiliation, ridicule or put-downs.
- Physical Safety—Freedom from bodily harm.
- Racial Pride—Pride in one's culture, knowledge of roots.
- Rules and Consequences—Knowledge of consistent rules and consequences.
- Unconditional Caring—Secure feeling of being cared for regardless of mistakes made.

Answer Key:

1. NO; Emotional Safety
2. YES; All Components
3. NO; All Components
4. YES; Emotional Safety, Unconditional Caring
5. YES; Physical Safety
6. YES; Unconditional Caring
7. NO; Racial Pride, Emotional Safety
8. YES; Rules and Consequences
9. NO; Racial Pride, Emotional Safety
10. YES; Rules and Consequences, Emotional and Physical Safety

- -

Teacher Evaluation—Notes on Weak Areas:

Student: _____Date: _____

Observed behavior in the area of: _____

_____

My plan to help strengthen that area: _____

_____

_____

Name _____ Date _____

STUDENT SECURITY QUIZ

Directions: Circle YES or NO depending how you *usually* feel about the statement. Your answers will not be shared with the rest of the class.

YES	**NO**	1.	I am afraid kids will laugh at me if I read or answer aloud in class.
YES	**NO**	2.	No matter what is going on in my life, when I walk into my classroom I feel better.
YES	**NO**	3.	Often my stomach feels sick, my head aches or I feel like crying.
YES	**NO**	4.	I have someone I can feel comfortable telling my problems to in my classroom.
YES	**NO**	5.	I feel safe from physical harm when I am in my classroom.
YES	**NO**	6.	I trust my teacher will still like me if I make a mistake.
YES	**NO**	7.	I feel that kids in my classroom pick on me because of my race.
YES	**NO**	8.	In my classroom, I know the rules and the results for me if I do not follow the rules.
YES	**NO**	9.	I am embarrassed to speak in class because my English is poor.
YES	**NO**	10.	I think our classroom rules and the results if they are not followed are mostly fair.

Why I answered YES or NO on number(s): _____

_____

_____

_____

_____

_____

_____

Here are some of my ideas that I could do to help myself feel more secure:

_____

_____

_____

_____

_____

2-2. MY SCHOOL IS A WARM PLACE

The time spent in your classroom is probably close to the waking hours you and your students spend in your home. Why not make it a comfortable, warm "home away from home"? A feeling of security and safety is instilled in children as a result of seeing their classrooms as safe, warm havens in which they will not be physically or emotionally harmed.

Materials Needed:

- "My School Is a Warm Place" activity sheet
- White bristol board or chart paper cut into large puffs of smoke (*optional*)
- Black felt pens, pens or pencils
- Brick Dittos from activity 2–14, "What a Hoot" (*optional*)
- Paste, scissors

Directions:

1. Lead a class discussion by asking students, "What makes you look forward to coming to our school?" *Responses:* "My friends are here. I look forward to being with my friends." "I know what's expected of me at school." "I won't be hurt at my school—unless by accident." "My teacher cares about me."

2. Include any negative comments in the discussion; do not disregard them. Together with the class or privately with the student who expressed negativism (whichever approach you feel is appropriate), brainstorm some possible solutions to the factors involved in a student's not feeling good about his or her school.

3. Ask students what makes them feel warm when they walk into your classroom. *Responses:* "My friends are here." "My teacher will still care about me if I make a mistake." "I like our bright bulletin boards and seeing my work displayed." "I love our cozy old rug." "I like our routine."

4. Pass out activity sheets. Instruct students to put their thoughts about their feelings for their school and classroom into words inside the smoke puffs. Each different puff should contain a different "favorite" thought about what makes them feel warm about their school, why it is a special place to them.

Cooperative Art Activity/Bulletin Board Link:

Cooperative groups will each be given one large puff of smoke (made from white bristol board or lined chart paper cut in the shape of smoke puffs) or a brick. (See Activity "What a Hoot," for a brick ditto.) Each group discusses what makes it feel good about its classroom and/or school. One person from each group may copy the group comments onto the puffs or bricks and hang them next to a chimney or in the front hall to build a school foundation that could be built with the bricks with the caption OUR SCHOOL/CLASSROOM IS A WARM PLACE or WE'RE ALL PUFFED UP ABOUT OUR SCHOOL/CLASSROOM.

MY SCHOOL IS A WARM PLACE

What makes you feel warm
when you come to school?
Fill in the smoke puffs with
what you feel good about, what
makes it special. *Example:*
Do you feel safe? Why? Do
you have friends there? Who?
What makes you feel warm
when you walk into your classroom?

2–3. OUR CLASSROOM RULES

Students are given the opportunity to contribute to some of the classroom rules in this activity. A basis for building security in students is to create fair, consistent classroom guidelines and consequences. This contributes to structure in the child's life, which he or she may not receive at home, where rules may be inconsistent or threatening with little or no consequences congruent with the child's behavior. In this way, students will know what is expected of them and what will follow if they do not meet those expectations. Students are also reminded to give "Boosters" or compliments if they are pleased about fair, kind treatment by the teacher or classmates.

Materials Needed:

- "Our Classroom Rules" activity sheet
- Small box labeled "Mutual Respect Box" or "On My Mind Box"

Directions:

1. Discuss school and playground rules with students. Elicit from students the reasons for these guidelines. *Responses:* "For kids' safety." "To teach kids how to treat others and how to behave in the right way." "To let kids know what is expected of them."

2. Review your classroom rules with your students. Discuss each rule and listen to feedback from the students. Ask children if there are some rules they feel have been neglected, rules they feel should be added to the classroom list. *Response:* "We need rules to deal with kids who give put-downs, kids who disrupt the class a lot, annoying bullies."

3. Give students an opportunity to offer some suggestions for dealing fairly and effectively with concerns they have expressed. Workable ideas could be written on a chart or the board to become new classroom rules added to your present rules.

4. Students may copy their established classroom rules along with their newly formed rules onto the pennants on the activity sheets. If the class has come up with several workable suggestions for classroom rules, you may want to have only the new rules copied onto the pennants.

5. Announce that your classroom is going to have a new addition as an opportunity for students to voice their concerns and boosters (don't forget the teacher and/or students who have treated others fairly or helped children in time of need). A student committee could be responsible for covering a box entitled "Mutual Respect Box" (students respect the rules of the classroom and know their concerns will be respected) or "On My Mind Box."

6. Several copies of the "tear-off" at the bottom of the activity sheet should be available beside the box for use whenever a student feels the need to express a concern or a booster. Names signed on the sheets could be optional.

OUR CLASSROOM RULES

After discussing our classroom rules together, copy them down on your pennant. Sign your name agreeing to doing your best at all times to keep those rules.

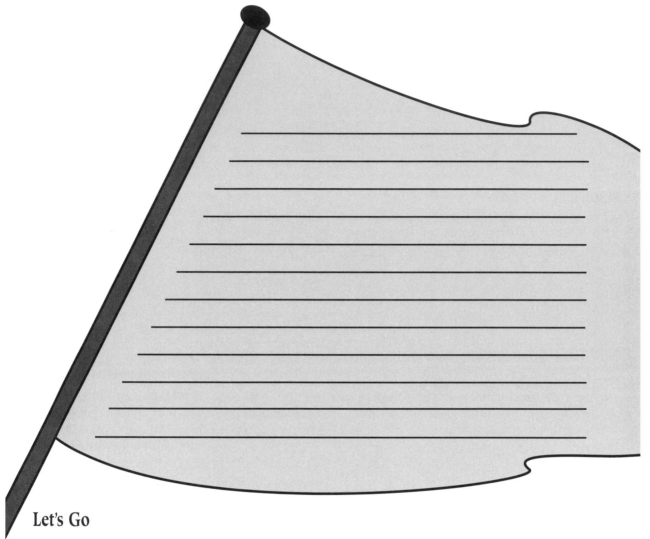

Let's Go

Your teacher will sign to agree to reading your concerns that may come up in the classroom "MUTUAL RESPECT BOX" or "ON MY MIND BOX."

Place the tear-off sheet in our "MUTUAL RESPECT BOX" when you have a question, suggestion or concern about a classroom rule. DON'T forget to add your BOOSTERS also.

Here is my suggestion, Booster, or concern about:

_____

_____

_____

Date: _____ Signed: _____

2–4. I'M JUST BLADING BY WITH SOME CD'S! (CLASS DECREES)

Why not hear from the students ideas they themselves find effective in dealing with class decrees—rules and consequences? A basic tenet of building security in students is creating fair, consistent classroom guidelines and consequences. This structure enables students to know what is expected of them and what will follow if they do not meet those expectations. Often children do not receive this structure at home, where they may receive threats of punishment that are never carried out or punishment incongruent with the misbehavior.

If students are given an opportunity to voice their ideas about some of the class rules and consequences, the result will be classroom guidelines to which everyone has contributed. The most responsible ways students suggest to handle safety, academic achievement, moral issues (all to be compliant with school rules) as well as suggestions to help students going through difficult times at home may be combined into a set of the students' own rules.

Materials Needed:

* "I'm Just Blading By with Some CD'S!" activity sheet
* Bristol board or construction paper, cellophane tape, markers (*optional*)

Directions:

1. Announce to your students you feel they are capable of taking responsibility for some of their own classroom rules. While making it clear to them that there are school and playground rules and standards of behavior that are already established, you would like to hear some of their ideas for rules and consequences.

2. Pass activity sheets to the students. Decide whether you want to read and discuss each classroom issue listed on the sheets as a whole-group or cooperative-group activity before asking students to write their individual classroom decrees (or CD's).

3. Write the term "decree" on a chart or the board and ask for meanings from students. *Responses:* "An official order, decision, rule, or guideline."

4. After discussion about each listed issue, ask students to fill in their activity sheets. Sheets may then be collected and—those you feel are the best ideas for your class decrees—may be compiled into one large CD (perhaps made by some volunteers) to be displayed prominently in the classroom.

Bulletin Board Link:

Students may also enjoy making their own CD's of bristol board or construction paper with their individual rules inside. CD's may be made by tracing a CD cover and taping another square that is one thumb less in width onto the top with the caption or title "OUR CD's." Aluminum foil cut into a round shape could contain class decrees or the students' own written **c**haracter **d**escriptions (CD's) of themselves in song form written on paper and glued onto the foil. They can choose their own titles, if writing their character descriptions. If possible, laminate.

Name _____ Date _____

I'M JUST BLADING BY WITH SOME CD'S!
(Class Decrees)

What guidelines would you suggest for your ideal classroom, remembering that you are responsible for both student and teacher safety, academic achievement, and moral issues arising in the classroom. Your teacher will compile the most responsible ideas into a large CD outline to be hung in the classroom. How would you help deal with these issues?

- student and teacher classroom safety

  _____

  _____

- a student's incomplete homework assignments

  _____

  _____

- a student's consistently poor test grades

  _____

  _____

- class clowns, bullies and loners (all of whom need help feeling better about themselves— how would you help them?)

  _____

  _____

- students caught stealing or cheating

  _____

  _____

- students who are victims of abuse (how would you help?)

  _____

  _____

- gangs who threaten violence

  _____

  _____

- other CD issues

  _____

  _____

2–5. MAKE A SCENE

The following activity presents the opportunity for students to create the ideal classroom! They may design their own classroom spaces. Having a comfortable as well as functional space makes your "home away from home" a welcoming haven of security for all who enter.

Materials Needed:

- "Make a Scene" activity sheet
- Colored pencils, crayons

Directions:

1. Announce to your class that the following activity is going to be an opportunity for them to create their ideal classrooms! Tell them this is an activity to encourage them to combine comfort and practicality (getting rid of all desks, for example, would make it difficult to write) in a creative use of classroom space, one in which both students and teacher can function well.
2. Pass out the activity sheets. Go over with students all the points for them to consider and advise them to sketch a draft of the redesigned room before they put their plans inside the curtain on the activity sheet.
3. Students may draw their own symbol keys for the furniture, computers, etc., or, if keys are not used, they may draw the actual objects inside the curtain on the activity sheet. Tell students to indicate inside the curtain where their designated areas are to go, such as computer area, library and reading area, etc. (Abbreviations for these areas could be used, e.g., CA and L&RA.)
4. Creative solutions to practical needs are to be encouraged in this activity. You may wish to create *your own* "ideal" classroom space!

Math Link:

You may want to make up a "pretend budget" of available funds for this classroom design and a "pretend price list" for each item to be included. Students will learn to keep their ideas within the budget by adding the cost of each new item they choose. Remind them of the practicality of using any present furniture, equipment, rugs, display boards, etc., in helping to keep costs down, unless you decide to have your students purchase all-new items for their classroom designs. Here are some possibilities from which to choose if you would like to make budget a factor in this activity:

1. Students will be asked to rearrange the classroom with what is in your classroom right now, with a budget for one new piece of equipment, one new piece of furniture, and one added "facelift" feature: choice of color for fresh paint, new display boards, floor coverings, or other ideas from the students to brighten the classroom.
2. Students will have a specific budget provided by you for their new designs. (Your "pretend" new costs of furniture, equipment, floor coverings, display boards, etc., could be written on the board or a chart or prepared on handouts.) Students could combine new purchases with what they plan to keep that is already in the classroom or, if your budget allows, make all new purchases.
3. Students may make up their own budgets for their new classroom designs. They would also research approximate prices for the items they plan to purchase for their new classrooms. They could choose between combining old and new objects (the most realistic) and purchasing all new furnishings, equipment, and objects for the classroom (the most fun!)

MAKE A SCENE

Here's your chance to "make a scene" about your classroom! Design a space you feel would be ideal for the needs of the teacher and students. Keep in mind the practical needs of students. For example, you cannot overlook the need for desks or tables on which to write (so beanbags or cushions for everyone would not be practical!). Place furniture, equipment, and special areas where you want them to go inside the curtain. Dream, but be practical so that your dream might really work!

Symbol Key: (Optional)

Include the following points in your classroom design renovation:

1. Teacher's space for desk and any equipment (telephone, copier, etc.) you feel he or she needs.
2. Desks, tables, writing surfaces, and chairs for students. Describe them.
3. Chalkboards, display boards, or other invention for class to view material.
4. What will your walls look like? Color? What will occupy the wall and *ceiling* spaces? Door?
5. Other equipment, floor covering, coat and backpack storage space, music area, library and reading area, computer area, other ideas.

2–6. I DIG MY ROOTS!

Appreciating where we come from, our family roots, enables us to celebrate ourselves. Opportunities in this activity to have students gather information about their ancestors' origins and customs encourage them to appreciate and respect one another's multicultural differences.

Materials Needed:

- "Dig It" activity sheet (bottom part of sheet duplicated 11 times for each student)
- Books displayed on countries and people of same origins as students
- Construction paper for title cover pages for students' booklets

Directions:

1. Tell students they are about to discover some information about their family roots or origins. An outcome of this activity will be a greater appreciation of their own cultural heritages as well as respect for diverse cultural differences within your class.

2. Write the following words on a chart or the board and discuss meanings:

   Genealogy—"Recorded history of one's ancestry or the study of family descent."

   Genealogist—"One who studies or traces genealogies or descents."

   Culture—"The ideas, customs, skills, arts, etc., of a given people in a given period."

   Ethnic—"A group distinguished by customs, language, common history, etc.; *ethnical*— a member of a minority or nationality group that is part of a larger community."

   Ancestor—"Any person from whom one is descended earlier in a family line than a grand-parent."

   Tradition—"Stories, beliefs, customs, etc., handed down from generation to generation."

   Race—"Any geographical, national, or tribal ethnic grouping; also known as *ethnic stock.*"

   Heritage—"Something handed down from one's ancestors or the past."

3. Tell students they are going to be amateur genealogists as you pass them the activity sheets. They are going to "dig up" facts about their family histories. They will make booklets consisting of 11 pages, each page containing a letter of "I Dig My Roots" with information for that page.

4. Go through instructions for each page and letter of "I Dig My Roots." Be sensitive to foster or adopted children who worry that they do not have information on their birth families' backgrounds. You could suggest they research their adoptive or foster family roots. Another alternative for a child with no access to birth information would be to help him or her choose a book from the display table that contains information about a country or ethnic group they find interesting. They could make a booklet about the country or the ethnic group and the customs of its people.

5. Instruct students to fill in the page number and letter for each page, along with information and sources of information needed for each page. If photos or objects are unavailable, pictures of the requirements may be drawn from information the student

2-6 I DIG MY ROOTS ACTIVITY (cont'd)

obtains from his or her oldest living relatives. Covers can be made of construction paper with student's name, title, and a picture of themselves. Completed booklets may be stapled together.

Class Multicultural Celebration:

If a class celebration is of interest to all, each child could have several choices in which to participate in a multicultural party: a sampling of family food, dolls, clothing, art objects, music, tribal utensils, holiday or religious celebration objects, or other ancestral reminders. If you wish to inform parents of this celebration, an announcement follows. Because it will be difficult for some working parents to attend day celebrations, you may want to hold an evening party or invite those who are able to attend a day event. Another idea would be to hold several different cluster celebrations of students with same backgrounds, e.g., Caribbean Celebration, Spanish Fiesta, Roman Revival, etc. Perhaps a different group could be celebrated every month.

 **MEMO**

To: PARENTS AND GUARDIANS
From: CLASSROOM CELEBRATION COMMITTEE
Subject: CLASSROOM MULTICULTURAL CELEBRATIONS!

We are having a CELEBRATION! We will "dig" our family roots to celebrate our class multiculturalism. We are very interested in your family traditions, your country of origin, music, clothing, and other aspects of your culture.

Will you please help your child make this a special celebration by sending something you think will give the children a token of your origins? You could send a food sampling the children could taste, a clothing sample, or a traditional family object for our display table.

If you are able to come to the classroom on this special day, we welcome you. Please let us know if you can attend.

Even if you can't attend or send along a sampling, please help your child complete his or her "I Dig My Roots" Celebration Booklet.

OUR CELEBRATION DATE: _____TIME: _____

NO. OF STUDENTS: _____

Thank you!

(Please return the form below with your child.)

- -

_____ I am unable to attend the celebration. However, I will send _____.

_____Yes, I will attend the celebration.

Comments:

Signed: _____

DIG IT!

Dig up some information about your family roots. **Genealogy** is the recorded history of your ancestry, where your forefathers came from and some of your traditional customs. It will help you celebrate your heritage. Enjoy learning about and celebrating multicultural differences within your class. Follow the letters in **I-D-I-G-M-Y-R-O-O-T-S** and the directions below for each of the 11 pages to form your Celebration Booklet. Interview relatives and collect and ask permission to bring to school any traditional family objects. Record in the pages of your booklet all the information you gather. Celebrate and be proud of who you are!

Page 1 — I: Information gathering. Ask parents about their birthplaces and child-hood memories.

Page 2 — D: Dad's parents, grandparents, great-grandparents. Ask about jobs, skills, interests.

Page 3 — I: Interview oldest relatives still living. Ask about their favorite child-hood memories.

Page 4 — G: Genealogy Tree. Fill tree's branches with relatives from both Mom's and Dad's sides.

Page 5 — M: Mom's parents, grandparents, great-grandparents. Ask about jobs, skills, interests.

Page 6 — Y: Young photos of relatives or stories from them about "the good old days!"

Page 7 — R: Recipes! Ask Mom and Dad for favorite recipes handed down in their families.

Page 8 — O: Origin of ancestors. Find out towns and countries they came from and the years.

Page 9 — O: Objects of interest. Draw pictures of old family utensils, dolls, coat-of-arms, etc.

Page 10 — T: Traditional customs of dress, gift giving, holiday celebra-tions, religious celebrations, parties, art, language, and others.

Page 11 — S: Summarize your gathered information. Tell why you are proud of your heritage.

- -

Letter for this page: _____

Information needed for this page: _____

_____

_____

Source of information: _____

2–7. TIMES OF MY LIFE WHEN I FELT LIKE A STAR

Recalling times when a child felt like he or she succeeded in some way with family and/or friends is the goal of this activity. Having positive experiences with family and friends enhances a feeling of security in the child.

Materials Needed:

- "Times of My Life When I Felt Like a Star" activity sheet
- Colored pencils, crayons, markers

Directions:

1. Ask students to recall some events in their lives when they felt like a "star." Hold a class discussion in which they share some of these times. Encourage children to remember family gatherings, times spent with friends, or other times when they felt pleased with themselves.

2. Ask students, "Is it important for others to give you praise in order for you to feel like a star?" *Response:* "Praise from others is nice, but not necessary if I feel good about what I've done."

3. Distribute activity sheets and instruct students to draw scenes of the times of their lives when they felt happy about something they have accomplished. Pictures of scenes should include people special to them. Tell students that each frame can be part of one "star" event for a movie or each frame could be a scene from several different happy events. Some children may choose to write in the frames about their events rather than to draw the events.

Art Activity:

Students may trace from stencil forms large yellow stars made of bristol board or construction paper. Inside each of the points of the star, they may choose to draw, write about, or include photos of "star" events in their lives.

Name _____

Date _____

TIMES OF MY LIFE WHEN I FELT LIKE A STAR

Make a movie in which you're the star! Fill in the frames with pictures or write about scenes of yourself with people who are special to you.

2–8. IT'S VIDEO TIME!

This activity provides the opportunity for students to write about themselves and star in their own videos! Role playing their scripts after they are completed or doing their scripts for an actual video recording (if a video recorder is available) will be an enjoyable part of this activity.

Materials Needed:

- "It's Video Time!" activity sheet
- Individual "props" for playing out video scripts

Directions:

1. Pass out activity sheets while announcing to students that they are going to have the opportunity to write the script and star in their own videos.

2. Direct the attention to some possible ideas for their scripts or words to be used in their videos. Six suggestions are offered at the top of the activity sheet. You may want to add some other possibilities on a chart or the board. Some children may choose to create their own ideas.

3. Students should write a draft of their scripts before filling in the video form on the activity sheet. If longer scripts are desired, additional pages may be added.

4. Ask the students for some titles of videos that have held appeal to them and made them want to see the video. Point out that the title is a capsule overview of what people are going to see and enables you to say, "That looks like a fun, interesting, educational, or thrilling video." Tell students to think of several possible titles before selecting the best one they feel will draw people to their videos! Ask, "Does that title invite you to view the video? Why? Why not?"

5. If not actually video recorded, students may role play their videos. They may want to choose classmates for various characters in their scripts.

IT'S VIDEO TIME!

It's your turn to write, direct, and star in your very own video! Some possibilities may include:

- A typical day in the life of . . .
- A crazy experience I had . . .
- My face was REALLY RED when . . .
- The Best of . . .
- Ways to avoid . . .
- My invention to improve _____ is _____ .

Use a real video if you have access to a school recorder or hand in your written script with the option of role playing. Select a slick title and cover for your BLOCKBUSTER!

DIRECTOR: _____

TITLE: _____

My Script

2–9. IT'S A RUNAWAY BESTSELLER!

Students are given the opportunity to write their own autobiographies for this activity. They may choose real events in their lives or they may choose to combine both real and imagined events to create a bestseller.

Materials Needed:

- "It's a Runaway Bestseller" activity sheet
- Current bestseller list from newspapers and title lists from bookstores (for title ideas)
- Autobiographies displayed of historical figures, athletes, astronauts, and other figures who hold interest to students
- Lined paper cut to the size of the runaway book cover

Directions:

1. Write "autobiography" on a chart or the board and ask students for the definition. *Response:* "The story someone writes of his or her own life."

2. Go over the titles on the bestseller and book lists with your class. Determine how many of the books are autobiographies. Study the titles together and decide which titles spark students' interest in reading the autobiography. Tell students to think of titles that encourage people to want to read the book when they write their own book titles.

3. Ask students what they hope to find out about a person when they read his or her autobiography. *Responses:* "To learn how they got to be so successful to have people interested enough in their lives to want to read a book about them." "To learn how they combine professional success and their personal lives, their hobbies, and their goals." Remind students to keep these points of interest in mind when they write their own autobiographies.

4. Pass out activity sheets and explain the "runaway book" activity sheet is to be the cover page. They should create an inviting title page. Pages completed for the autobiographies may be stapled together along with the cover.

5. Encourage the class to recall highlights of their lives and combine them with imaginative events to write their life stories. Explain that if not all the incidents in their books are real, the book is not a true "autobiography"; because fiction is included, it would be known as a "biographical novel."

Bulletin Board Link:

A large "Book Person" announces "Our Class Runaway Bestsellers" with class booklets of their own "bestsellers" on display.

IT'S A RUNAWAY BESTSELLER!

2–10. MAKE AWESOME WAVES TOGETHER!

This activity is a valuable tool in gathering information about students' interests. Answers on the activity sheets can be matched up for the purpose of forming circle groups for future class cooperative-group activities to consist of six students per group. Students will enjoy having commonalities among members of their groups and will feel more comfortable during groups activities when asked to form their circles.

Materials Needed:

- "Make Awesome Waves Together!" activity sheet
- Colored pencils, pens

Directions:

1. After passing out the activity sheets, ask the students if any of them would like to share their experiences on a waterslide. After these experiences are shared, ask the students if they enjoy being with others who like some of the same activities as they do. Lead a discussion about "good times" students with common interests have shared together.

2. Tell the students they are about to complete a pleasant activity—listing their "favorites" in the waterslide on the activity sheet. Ask them to complete the fill-ins next to the numerals on the waterslide with their answers that correspond to the numbered questions about "favorites."

3. Collecting and reading these activity sheets will provide you with insight into some personal interests of each of your students when having "chill-out" time with individual students as well as forming class cooperative groups. A couple of students could assist you in forming class groups of six, based upon several answers matching on one another's waterslides. In order to facilitate orderly future movement into their new groups, names could be given to each group, the group members listed under the group names, and this group information displayed in the classroom in easy view of the class. Forming groups by common interests is one way of providing security for students, especially helpful to low self-esteem students.

4. After matching up common interests among students and putting them into groups of six students per group, pass the sheets back to the students and call out the names of students to form new groups. In their new groups, they can discuss and decide upon their group names.

Music Link:

"Slip Slidin' Away" by Paul Simon.

Art Activity:

Ask a group of students to draw a long, winding waterslide for a bulletin board or to place above the boards in the classroom. The names of the newly formed groups could be carried along by one member from each group zooming down the slide with the group names placed visibly on their watermats.

Name _____ Date _____

MAKE AWESOME WAVES TOGETHER!

Write *what you enjoy doing the most* in the *even* numbers 2, 4, 6, 8, 10, 12.
Write your *school subjects in order of favorites* in the *odd* numbers 1, 3, 5, 7, 9, 11, 13.

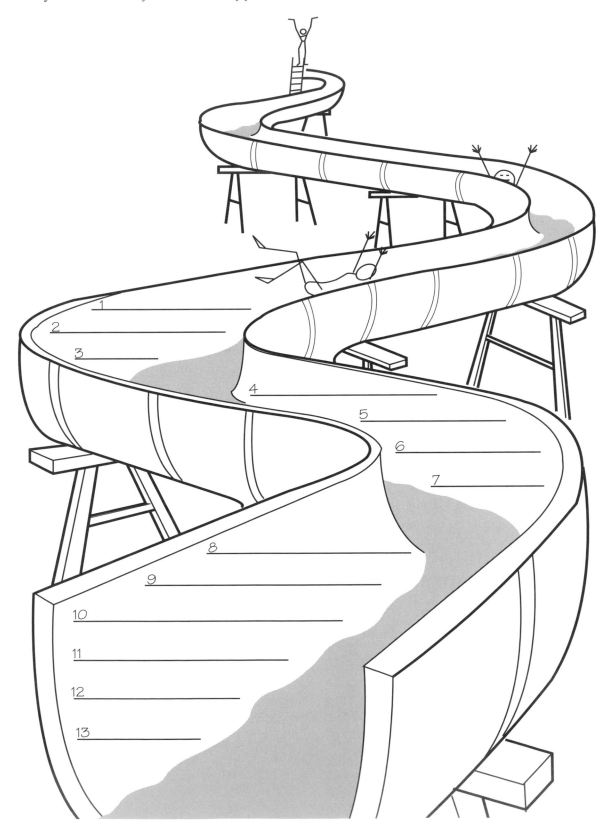

2–11. SOLID GOLD CLASS BLOOPERS!!

Sharing humorous situations and having a good time together enhances the security component in the classroom. Students and teachers will have fun recalling some *class bloopers* they can role play.

Materials Needed:

- "Solid Gold Class Bloopers" activity sheet
- Props for role plays (*optional*)

Directions:

1. Explain the meaning of "Solid Gold" to students. A song that is a bestseller reaches a point of selling enough copies to become a solid gold recording. We are going to call our bloopers "Solid Gold Bloopers." Ask for class meanings of the term "bloopers." *Response:* "Funny incidents when something that was not meant to go wrong, goes wrong!" Ask for some examples of bloopers they have had or seen.

2. Hold a class discussion about the distinction between a "put-down" and a "blooper." *Responses:* "Put-downs make a person feel laughed *at*, not laughed *along with*." "Bloopers make people laugh if they share the humor and don't feel they are being made fun of or embarrassed."

3. Explain to students that the bloopers they choose to role play should be incidents in which all the people involved agree that the event was in good fun. Ask for and enjoy together some bloopers they have experienced or seen.

4. Pass out the activity sheet and ask a student to orally read the directions along with the array of possibilities for student role-plays. An option for bloopers requested by students not listed is a possible choice in the last selection, "I thought of another great BLOOPER," which you may wish to confirm with the student before rehearsal begins. They may choose to role play individually or with a partner(s).

5. After what you feel is an adequate period of preparation, students may perform their blooper role-plays.

6. Enjoy this activity! (You may wish to join the act should you ever recall *yourself* in a blooper situation!)

Art Link:

Display the heading CLASS BLOOPERS! with either student drawings of blooper incidents with accompanying explanations *or* photos taken of blooper role-plays hung with scenario explanations below.

Name _____ Date _____

Solid Gold CLASS *BLOOPERS!*

The ability to look on the funny, humorous side of situations is a life skill that may sometimes help you during difficult times. Below are some situations from which you can choose to role play. They should be fun incidents that have occurred inside the classroom or in your school during the time you have attended your school. Remember, making fun of or mocking another at the expense of hurting his or her feelings is not acceptable subject matter.

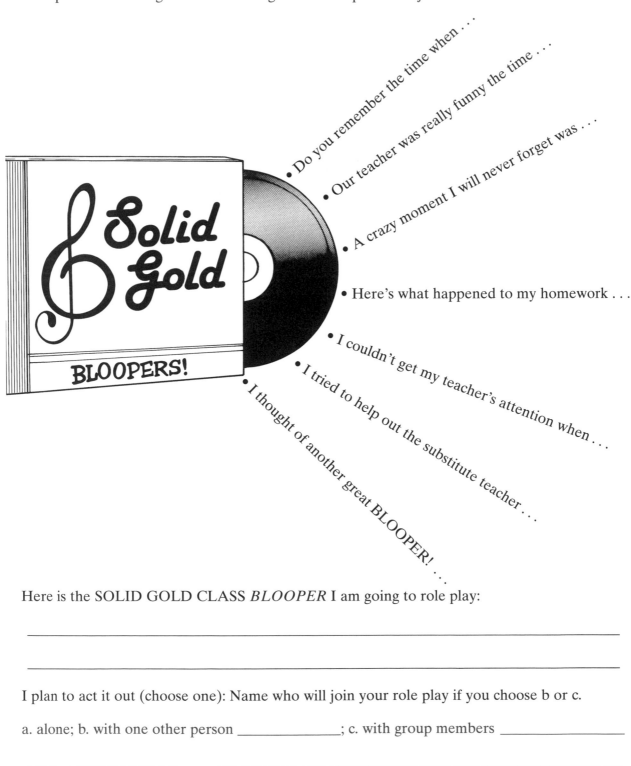

- Do you remember the time when . . .
- Our teacher was really funny the time . . .
- A crazy moment I will never forget was . . .
- Here's what happened to my homework . . .
- I couldn't get my teacher's attention when . . .
- I tried to help out the substitute teacher . . .
- I thought of another great BLOOPER! . . .

Here is the SOLID GOLD CLASS *BLOOPER* I am going to role play:

_____

_____

I plan to act it out (choose one): Name who will join your role play if you choose b or c.

a. alone; b. with one other person _____; c. with group members _____

_____

2–12. YOU ARE MY SUNSHINE AND 2–13. I'M KEYED!

Acknowledging the people who are special in their lives is an essential element in forming a feeling of security in children. The intended outcome for students upon completion of these activities is that they can identify and show their appreciation to the people in their lives to whom they feel closest. Also acknowledged are those in their lives who may not be as close as parents or best friends, but may be special in their lives in other ways, such as teachers, coaches, and other friends or relatives.

Materials Needed:

- "You Are My Sunshine" activity sheet
- "I'm Keyed!" activity sheet
- Colored pencils

Directions ("You Are My Sunshine"):

1. Discuss with your students what the phrase "You are my sunshine" means to them. *Responses:* "You make my days bright." "You light up my life."
2. Ask students to think of the people in their lives to whom they feel closest. Elicit the feelings the children have for these special people and how the special people show their feelings to them.
3. Explain that sometimes people who are very special to us are not necessarily those we spend time with daily. They may influence us greatly and may be significant in our lives even though we only see one another periodically. Ask the students if anyone in their lives fits this description. *Response:* "I'm still in touch with my good friend who moved away." "I'm only with my cousin twice a year but we always have good talks together."
4. Distribute the activity sheets. Ask students to write the names or draw pictures of people who bring them "sunshine." The names of those *closest* to them go inside the sunshine. Other special people are placed inside the points around the sunshine.

Directions ("I'm Keyed!"):

1. After passing out the activity sheets, ask students if they are "keyed up" about this activity. If they answer "yes," ask them what it means to be "keyed." *Response:* "I'm tuned in, ready, and raring to go!" Explain that we need to "tune in" to acknowledging people who are special to us.
2. As a follow-up to "You Are My Sunshine" activity sheets, discuss with your students ways in which we can let these special people know how much they mean to us. *Responses:* "Do nice things for them." "Tell them why they are so special to you." "Give them a hug!"
3. Tell students that we will be concentrating on *verbal* words of appreciation in this activity sheet. Ask for positive comments they use when talking to those close to them. *Responses:* "I feel good when I'm with you because I can be myself." "I appreciate the extra help you gave me in Math."
4. After reading the comments *a – k* on the activity sheet, ask students to decide to whom they would like to give each of these comments. The name or picture of that special person is then placed in the appropriate keyboard letter that corresponds to the lettered comment.

YOU ARE MY SUNSHINE

Who are the special people in your life, those who bring you "sunshine" or happiness? Think about people at home, your mother and/or father or guardian, brothers, sisters, and relatives you feel close to. Who else makes a positive difference in your life? Remember to consider friends, teachers, coaches, and others. Place the names of those *closest to you* inside the sunshine. Place others special to you inside the points around the sunshine.

Extra!! Sunny Activity:

When you go home, tell the special people you chose above that you put their names on your "sunshine." Watch them *light up*!

I'M KEYED!

Tune in to people in your life who are special to you. Let them know how much they mean to you. Think about WHO you would like to tell they are special and what you would like to say to them. Draw a picture or write the name of the person inside each key on the keyboard, which has the letter of the comment you would like to make to that person. *Example:* If you want to write to a good friend who moved away, you may choose letter "j" and draw his or her picture inside the "j." If a special comment you would like to make is not listed below, make up your own comment and place it by letter "k."

Special People on My Keyboard

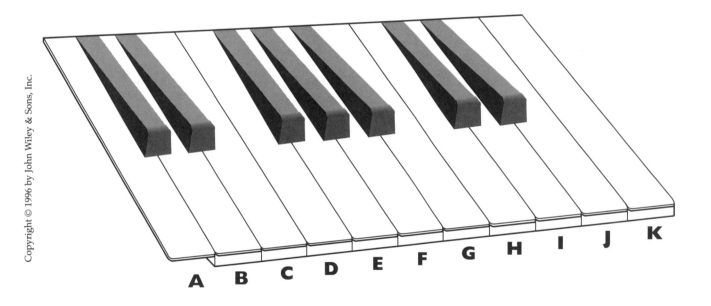

A. You are always there for me.

B. Thanks for helping me.

C. Your comments to me really encouraged me.

D. You showed me the right way.

E. Thanks for the love you always show me.

F. You cheered me up when I was down.

G. You are a lot of fun!

H. I enjoy your company whatever we do.

I. We share one special interest together.

J. I miss being with you and doing things together.

K. _____

2–14. WHAT A HOOT

This activity provides students with the opportunity to give their ideas about what they can do to improve their classrooms and their schools. This activity, if done by each classroom in the school, can all be combined to form a school foundation with the "brick" dittos (at the bottom of this activity page) that contain students' most practical ideas. The front school hall can then be filled with a foundation "built" of bricks made by the students.

Materials Needed:

- "What a Hoot" activity sheet
- Scissors, black markers
- Brown construction paper for individual student owls (*optional*)

Directions:

1. Pass out the activity sheets. Tell your students you hope to hear any ideas they have on how to make your classroom a better place. After a class discussion, ask for further suggestions to improve your school, making it a more positive place for kids and for educators. Tell them to consider the following areas: how to deal most effectively with bullies, gangs or any violence that occurs; new kids in the school; kids who need boosters; recognition of kids' and teachers' birthdays; Buddy Program of pairing older kids with younger kids . . . to name a few ideas to get started. Your kids should brainstorm other areas that need improvement. You may want to schedule several class discussions in order to cover the many areas and to have a recorder write the ideas on chart paper.

2. After having the class discussion, students should now be prepared to write out their own ideas for classroom/school improvement.

3. Ask the class to write their suggestions in the lines at the top of their sheets.

4. Ask each student to write his or her "best" (the most workable, fair idea) suggestion on the brick at the bottom of the activity sheet. If you prefer to make it a classroom-only ideas activity, make it clear to your class that they will only write suggestions that affect your classroom, not the entire school. Otherwise, they will need to focus on the entire school for their best ideas. You may choose to divide them into cooperative groups, with each group given one area to plan how to improve. After everyone has completed the bricks, they may then cut them from the activity sheet and hang them either in your classroom or, if you plan to integrate them into an all-school foundation, hang them all together in the front hall.

Bulletin Board Link:

A caption "Ideas to Hoot About" along with ideas for the school from each student could be hung on small owls or on one large owl hanging on the bulletin board or a large wall. If you choose to get the whole school involved, the caption could read (Name of school) "Has Built a Strong Foundation" with the bricks from each classroom hung together to form a school foundation. (The bricks may also be used for the chimney formation for Activity 2-2, "Our School Is a Warm Place.")

Name _____ Date _____

WHAT A HOOT

Write some ways you would like to make your classroom a positive place. HOWL would you go about it? Improving your school is something to *hoot* about!

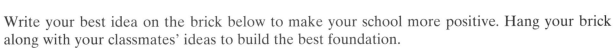

1. _____

2. _____

3. _____

4. _____

5. _____

Write your best idea on the brick below to make your school more positive. Hang your brick along with your classmates' ideas to build the best foundation.

Here's how I would like to build a better school. My idea is:

- -

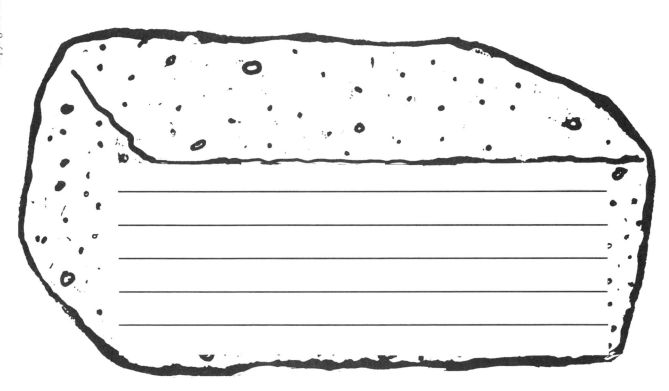

41

2–15. I'M A HIT ON OUR CLASS CHART AND 2–16. WOW

One of the most valuable activities we can give to children is the opportunity for them to hear their positive qualities from their peers. Looking at themselves through the eyes of kids their own ages makes a lasting impression on them and, if positive, remembered and treasured.

Materials Needed:

- "I'm a Hit on Our Class Chart" activity sheet
- "Wow" activity sheets, one for older and one for younger students.
- Colored pencils, markers
- Scissors
- Construction paper

Directions:

1. These activity sheets are completed in small groups of six members per group. The object of both sheets is to provide students with positive feedback about their strengths as their peers see them. The impact these validations can have on a student is tremendous, especially to a child who has never had a compliment. All students benefit from this exercise. However, it is a very teacher-directed activity, so it is best to do these activity sheets when it's a good day for you to be available to oversee the signing activity. The adverse effect of this activity if a child receives his or her paper back with one or more students "passing" or leaving a blank space cannot be underestimated. Therefore, it should be made clear before beginning that nobody is allowed to "pass." *Everyone* must sign a positive comment about the person whose paper he or she receives. Tell your class that everyone has something positive; sometimes they have to look to find it in others. Remind them how they would feel if they received their own papers back with some children in their group having left blank spaces, with nothing positive to say about them!

2. Distribute either "I'm a Hit on Our Class Chart" or "Wow" to your class. (The sheet you do not choose for this lesson can be done at a later time in the year with different groups formed. It is such a valuable exercise that it warrants doing twice!) Discuss what kinds of validations students are going to make on their sheets. Ask students what kinds of comments make them feel good. After hearing several responses, you could summarize by saying that specific compliments about something others like or admire about you are the best compliments—those that *boost you up on the inside!* Tell students the first thing to do after receiving their sheets is to put their names on the top. Ask, "Who can tell why it's so important to do this?" *Response:* "Because how else will the people in your group know whose paper they are signing when they're passed?" Right!

3. Once students' names are at the tops of their sheets, have them begin passing them to their left in their groups. It is important that you rotate around the classroom to make

sure everyone signs each sheet passed to him or her and to help children make specific compliments to one another.

4. When all groups have completed their sheets and each child receives his or her own sheet back, observe the looks on their faces as they receive compliments from their peers. Many of them will light up with pleasure as they make comments such as, "I didn't know anybody cared that I did that". "I tried so hard and I didn't think anyone noticed. Now I see that they did." "I feel good!" "Kids think there are some special things I can do."

5. If you are able, it will mean so much to your students if you sign a positive comment about each of them. If they want to give their sheets to other classmates, you may have to decide if some may feel left out if they have no friends to pass their sheets to. Some may want to take them home for signatures.

Bulletin Board or Hall Display Link:

Students can decorate finished "Wow" sheets and mount them on colorful paper, hanging them up with the caption "Here's How We WOW Each Other!"

"I'm a Hit on Our Class Chart" sheets could be hung with captions "I'm a Hit—Here's How!" or "OUR TOP (number of students in class) HITS!" Students could each receive old-fashioned black record outlines and copy his or her compliments from their activity sheets onto paper glued on the records. A large jukebox could be added to the display.

I'M A HIT ON OUR CLASS CHART

TUNE IN TO HEAR MY RECORDING!

Pass this sheet to five members in your group.
Each member will tell you why you are such a HIT! Examples: Good sport, fun, tries hard.

_____ is a HIT! Here's why:

1. _____

2. _____

3. _____

4. _____

5. _____

Name _____ Date _____

Form groups of six. Pass this sheet to your left to the five members in your group. Each person will sign a quality they admire about you (if they know you well) or a quality you have that has made a positive first impression (if you have just met). Nobody passes. You will receive your sheet back to see just how you "WOW" others!

Decorate, cut out and display your WOW's in your classroom!

Name _____ Date _____

Form a team of 5-6 students. Put your name on your sheet, then pass it to your left for each person to write inside your "WOW" one positive quality which "WOWS" them! Examples, you are kind, lots of fun, try hard at sports, help at home.

Decorate your Wows and Brighten up you classroom.

2-17. CRAZY CROSSWORD!

Let's all go crazy over our family roots and what we have learned about our ancestors. Fill in the Crazy Crossword Puzzle with answers to the numbered clues below. The answers are related to the "Dig It!" multicultural lesson. After you complete the puzzle, fit the phrase "GOIN' CRAZY" (GOIN' without the "G") into the puzzle.

Across:

1. A festive celebration
2. A group within a larger society that continues to speak a foreign language and share a way of life
3. Strong feelings of belonging to a place or group
4. The customs, beliefs and arts of a group of people
5. To get by looking for or studying

Down:

6. The practice of orally passing down stories, customs, and beliefs from one generation to the next
7. A large group of people with certain physical characteristics passed on from one generation to another
8. Something handed down from one's ancestors or the past, as a characteristic or tradition
9. A feeling of one's own worth or dignity
10. The study of family descent

Extra Crazy Activity:

Crazy Wilbert got his letters all mixed up when he tried to talk! He also forgot to finish his sentence! Find out what he is trying to say by making a sentence out of the letters and complete it with *your* choice of word(s).

_____ (Complete): _____

ANSWERS TO CRAZY CROSSWORD!

Here are the answers to the crossword puzzle, which provides a review of the terms learned in the activity sheet "Dig It!" The Extra Crazy Activity fits "crazy" to "genealogy."

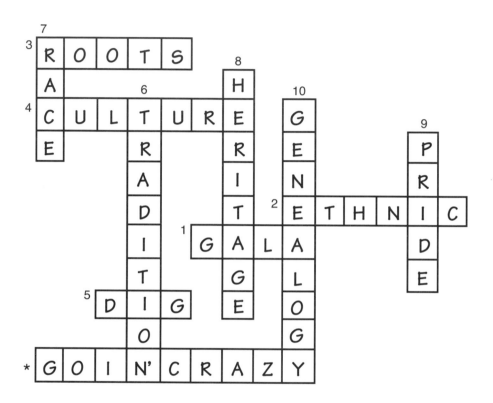

Extra Crazy Activity:

Below is the sentence formed by the "crazy" letters. Students may fill in their own completions.

I am crazy about _____

3

Positive Identity

A POSITIVE IDENTITY

Rationale:

During the Positive Identity phase, a student is forming a sense of individuality of what makes him or her special. Leading children to recognize their inner strengths and to accept their limitations is crucial at this stage. Encouraging those strengths and giving positive feedback will help lead to a positive identity. Students are taught that no one can make them feel low without their permission.

Goals:

- Teach students to take responsibility for their successes and failures.
- Provide opportunities for students to display positive qualities, to experience success at their own levels.
- Enable students to give and receive peer strength appraisals.
- Teach children that they are responsible for their own responses to events. E + R = O (EVENT + RESPONSE = OUTCOME). No one can make them feel low without their permission.
- Aid students in rescripting negative self-talk into positive self-talk.
- Enable students to recognize strengths of which they are unsure, giving extra time to children who cannot name *any strengths*.
- Demonstrate unconditional acceptance. Provide encouragement when limitations are evident.
- Provide positive feedback for efforts as well as achievements.
- Encourage students to be themselves. Bullies, class clowns, and show-offs cover up their true selves.

Intended Outcome Statements for Students:

- "I may not be the best artist, but I sure can write great stories."
- "I'm responsible for getting a low mark on my spelling test. I'm also responsible for getting all the problems right in math."
- "I will show my true self to others, not cover up what I feel inside by bragging, bullying, having an 'attitude.' "
- "Other kids told me good things about myself I never knew before!"
- "I know the strengths within myself that make me special."
- "When my old negative self-talk begins, I will replace it with positive self-talk. I'm responsible for my feelings about things happening involving me."

3–1. DIRECTIONS FOR THE POSITIVE IDENTITY QUIZ

This quiz may be used as a pre-test before the Positive Identity component is introduced in your classroom. After you feel your students have completed a sufficient number of positive identity building activities, the quiz may again be given and the results compared with the pre-test. Below are the Positive Identity components you are assessing. An abbreviation key is included beside each component.

Feelings of a positive identity to be instilled in students:

- Independent of Approval (from others)—Looks to self for intrinsic approval.
- Awareness of Strengths—Possesses knowledge of positive qualities.
- Positive Self-Talk—Has knowledge of how to encourage and boost oneself.
- Worthy of Praise—Feels entitled to boosters when deserved.
- Accepts Limitations—Is aware of shortcomings with aims for improvement.

Answer Key:

If a student answer differs from the answer key, it may be an indicator of weakness in that component and you will know specifically what his or her needs are.

1. YES; Awareness of Strengths, Positive Self-Talk
2. YES; Awareness of Strengths
3. NO; Independent of Approval, Accepts Limitations
4. NO; Independent of Approval, Awareness of Strengths, Accepts Limitations
5. NO; Independent of Approval, Awareness of Strengths, Accepts Limitations
6. YES; Worthy of Praise
7. YES; Awareness of Strengths, Accepts Limitations
8. YES; Positive Self-Talk
9. NO; Independent of Approval, Awareness of Strengths, Positive Self-Talk
10. NO; Awareness of Strengths, Positive Self-Talk, Accepts Limitations

- -

Teacher Evaluation—Notes on Weak Areas

Student:_____ Date: _____

Observed behavior in the area of: _____

_____

My plan to help to strengthen that area: _____

_____

_____

STUDENT POSITIVE IDENTITY QUIZ

Directions: Circle YES or NO depending how you *usually* feel about the statement. Your answers will not be shared with the rest of the class.

YES   NO   1. I can name at least two good things about myself. For example, "I am a good sport."

YES   NO   2. I usually get enough positive (good) attention without showing off or bullying.

YES   NO   3. I can't seem to please anyone so I usually just give up.

YES   NO   4. If I looked better, kids would like me more.

YES   NO   5. When someone in my classroom puts me down, I feel useless.

YES   NO   6. I usually feel I deserve a "booster" or compliment when someone in my class gives me one.

YES   NO   7. Kids in my class like me for myself. I don't need to "fake" it or do anything I don't feel is right in order to please them.

YES   NO   8. When I talk to myself, I usually say, "Hey I CAN handle this!" when I am facing a new or challenging situation.

YES   NO   9. I usually wait for someone else to tell me if I've done a good job.

YES   NO   10. Every time I make a mistake, I feel like a total failure!

Why I answered YES or NO on number(s):

_____

_____

_____

_____

_____

Here are some of my ideas to be more positive about myself:

_____

_____

_____

_____

_____

_____

3-2. THE TIFFANY SKIT

This activity helps students to realize that their self-esteem can be built up or torn down bit by bit daily.

Directions:

1. Tryouts for these roles are held at random. Choose the students for the role play. Perhaps a student who does not read well could be the alarm clock and/or telephone.

2. Players are assembled in front and a student is chosen to be "Tiffany" (or whatever name you may choose, or perhaps a boy may be chosen).

3. Each player—with the exception of the alarm clock, the telephone, Tiffany, and Tiffany's best friend—receives a small negative sign made out of construction paper or bristol board. Tiffany's best friend receives a positive sign. These should be large enough to fit onto two backpacks—one for negatives and one for positives—that Tiffany or the lead role in the play will wear. The backpacks should each be marked with a plus or minus. (Alternative to using backpacks: Tiffany could hold a paper heart and tear it off piece by piece as negative comments are made.)

4. After each statement is read, the player drops the minus sign into the minus backpack and Best Friend drops a plus sign into the plus backpack.

5. Choose a short class favorite song for playing in the skit and have the tape ready to play.

Class Discussion After the Play:

This role play is to be used as a stimulus to the question, "How many of you have negative days like this?" (Students raise hands.) "It's normal for us to have negative days. However, when people have many negative days over and over, what does that do to their feeling good about themselves?" *Responses:* "They feel sad, good-for-nothing, like not going out anymore, like your heart is shrinking."

If someone has many "negative backpack days" over a long period of time, what can he or she do to deal with that negativism? *Responses:* "No one can make you feel low unless you allow them." "Spread more positivism to others, more 'boosters' instead of 'put-downs.' " "Learn to love yourself; spread it to other people and it will come back to you."

THE TIFFANY SKIT

NARRATOR:	It was a bright sunny Monday morning. Tiffany's alarm clock went off.
ALARM CLOCK:	B-Z-Z-Z-Z!
NARRATOR:	Tiffany yawned and dropped back off to sleep until her big brother yelled . . .
BIG BROTHER:	Hey, Tiffany, get out of bed! You're going to be late for school. Didn't you get your homework finished again? You're so lazy! *(Minus Sign into Minus Backpack)*
NARRATOR:	At school her teacher, Mr. Butterbea Quiet said . . .
MR. BUTTERBEA QUIET:	Class! Be quiet! Tiffany, you did not hand in your Math again today! That's the third time in two weeks. Stay after school to see me! You will miss soccer. *(Minus Sign into Minus Backpack)*
NARRATOR:	Tiffany's eyes dropped. She had forgotten it at home when she overslept. On the way to recess when her head was down, she banged into the door just opening. Tiffany cried . . .
TIFFANY:	Ouch! That hurt!
GILMORE:	What a hoot! Did you see Tiffany walk right into that door? A real space cadet! *(Minus Sign into Minus Backpack)*
NARRATOR:	Then out in the playground, Tiffany made the strikeout for the last out of the baseball game.
SUE:	That strikeout lost the game for us, Tiffany! Thanks a lot, loser! *(Minus Sign into Minus Backpack)*
NARRATOR:	Tiffany goes to her bedroom when she arrives home from school and puts on her favorite tape. *(Tiffany's favorite tape can be heard playing.)* Tiffany hears the front door open and footsteps approaching her bedroom.
TIFFANY'S MOM:	Tiffany, I've had a long day at work. I had asked you to start dinner. Here you sit listening to tapes! Turn that junk you call music off, please! *(Minus Sign into Minus Backpack)*
TIFFANY:	I feel like such a loser!
NARRATOR:	Just then the telephone rang. It was Tiffany's best friend:
TELEPHONE:	R-R-R-I-N-G!
TIFFANY'S BEST FRIEND:	Hey, Tiff, come on over. We're renting a video. You're always lots of fun. Hope you can come! *(Plus Sign into Plus Backpack)*

3–3. LET'S GET PUMPED!

Discussion for this activity could follow the Tiffany skit by asking students, "What happens to your feelings about yourself when you have a lot of negative days, receiving many put-downs?" Explain that everyone has bad days; however, this question refers to a child who has one negative day after the other, receiving no positivism.

Materials Needed:

- "Let's Get Pumped!" activity sheet
- Pencils
- Five or six small paper hearts (to pass during the circle heart talk)

Directions:

1. After the Tiffany skit, ask students to show by raising their hands how many have days that are full of negatives. (After the play, students will be familiar with the terms "negative" and "positive.") Most hands will probably be raised to this question. Acknowledge that everyone has bad days; however, some people receive no positive encouragement in their lives.

2. Ask the students how a person who receives no positive comments and only negative comments over a long period of time would begin to feel about himself or herself. *Response:* "They feel stupid, good-for-nothing, that no one cares, they don't want to try anymore, they might want to die."

3. Explain that one child responded to this question by explaining, "My heart feels like it is shrinking." Ask if students feel this is a good description of a child who has one negative day after another. *Response:* "Yes, because you don't feel you are loved so your heart feels like it is shrinking."

4. If you are going to do the "Heart to Heart" circle talks, form groups before passing out the activity sheets and have each group go through the questions together in small groups.

5. Distribute activity sheets to your class. Ask students to think of a time when they felt their hearts were shrinking. A few students may volunteer personal examples of themselves or of people they have known who had negative days. After you have heard several responses, ask the students "How could you pump it up again?" In other words, "What could you do to make yourself feel better about your negative experience?" *Response:* "Realize others do not make you feel low about yourself; you do." "If you spread love and Boosters to others, they will return them to you." "Learn how to love yourself."

Bulletin Board Link:

The bulletin board caption is "We're Pumped!" or "Our Class Is All Heart!" A large heart could be hung, filled in with a collage of pictures (either drawn by students or collected from magazines) of:

- Photos of students feeling good about themselves.
- Pictures that depict people "pumping up" someone else, showing a lot of heart.

3-3. LET'S GET PUMPED (cont'd)

Cooperative Learning Activity:

Form "Heart to Heart" circle groups of five to six students each. Small paper hearts are given to each group. The hearts are passed to the left and the student holding the heart speaks in response to the questions on the activity sheet. Questions should be visible on the board or a chart for students to refer to. Only the child holding the heart speaks. Nobody else in the circle interrupts, offers suggestions, or judges—NO PUT-DOWNS! Anyone may "pass" if they choose not to share a personal experience. However, everyone is gently encouraged to participate. If a child decides to "pass," no one in the group may criticize. Perhaps the teacher may privately suggest having a private heart talk with that child.

Music Link:

"Have a Heart" by Bonnie Raitt, Celine Dion, or Duke Ellington

Name _____ Date _____

LET'S GET PUMPED!

What happens to your feelings about yourself when you have a lot of days with negative (bad) comments? *Examples:* "You're a loser." "You're a geek." "You will never amount to anything." "You can't do it." "You're a slow learner." One reply from a third-grade student was, "Your heart shrinks."

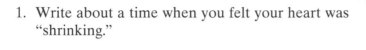

1. Write about a time when you felt your heart was "shrinking."

   _____

   _____

   _____

   _____

   _____

2. How could you pump it up again?

   _____

   _____

   _____

   _____

   _____

3. How could you help someone else who needs encouragement?

   _____

   _____

   _____

   _____

   _____

3-4. ANY WAY YOU SLICE IT, I'M DELUXE!

This activity of seeing several different positive qualities as pizza toppings is a method of giving students a taste of their own deluxe strengths.

Materials Needed:

- "Any Way You Slice It, I'm Deluxe!" activity sheet
- Scissors and paste
- Gold and light brown bristol board
- Red, green, white, and brown construction paper
- Colored pencils or markers

Directions:

1. Write on the board or a chart each adjective shown on the pizza toppings: smart, happy, athletic, humorous, artistic, studious, kind. Ask the students to give a synonym for each word on the board or chart to show that they grasp the meanings. Ask them to think of adjectives that were not mentioned and add them to the list.

2. Ask students to think about which "toppings" apply to them as they explain the meaning of the adjectives.

3. Explain that in order to choose each topping, students do not have to show that description *all* the time. For example, nobody is *always* humorous, smart, or kind.

4. Have students cut out five to six toppings from the activity sheet that best describe themselves. Encourage them to fill out the "other" toppings with other positive qualities that describe themselves. Be aware of students slower to recognize few or any toppings applicable to them. Help them individually by pointing out some qualities you feel they display. Paste the toppings on the pizza. Students should save their pizzas as a reminder of what makes them special.

Bulletin Board Link:

Make one large pizza of light brown or gold bristol board. Each student may trace a topping and choose his or her deluxe quality to go on the topping with his or her name. Heading may read: "Any Way You Slice It, Our Class Is Deluxe!" or "Our Class Is Incredible!" or "Try to Top Our Class!"

Cooperative Art Activity:

Instead of individual worksheets, students may be divided into groups of five. "Pizzas" are cut out of bristol board large enough to hold five toppings. (Trace shapes of pepperoni, green peppers, onions, and bacon onto bristol or construction paper.) Each topping with a student's name can be passed to team members for a deluxe topping or students can choose their own. Team pizzas may then be hung around the classroom or on a classroom bulletin board. *Note:* Instead of pizza, ice cream, hot dogs and hamburgers can be used with their special toppings.

ANY WAY YOU SLICE IT . . .
I'm Deluxe!

Cut out and place the "toppings"—your deluxe qualities you feel you have—on your pizza. Add some other toppings of your own.

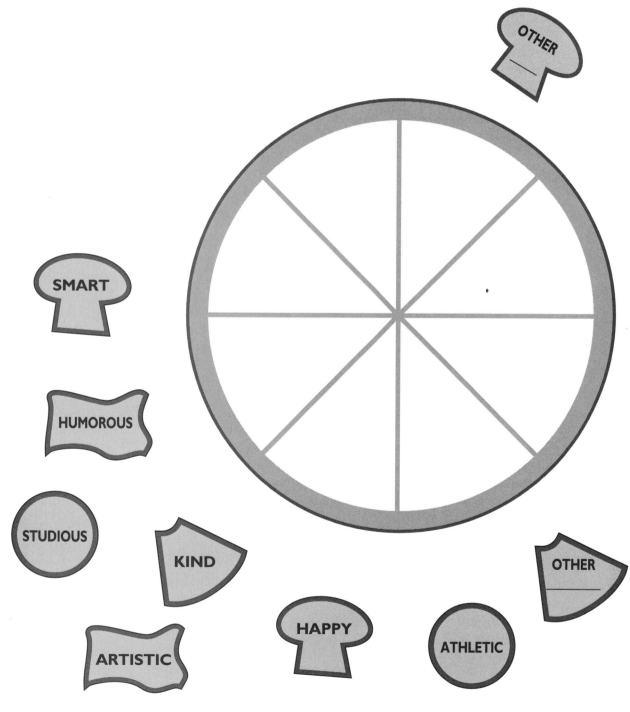

OTHER

SMART

HUMOROUS

STUDIOUS

KIND

OTHER

ARTISTIC

HAPPY

ATHLETIC

3–5. AN AVALANCHE OF QUALITIES YOU WOULD LIKE TO HAVE

Students are asked to explore the qualities they *would like* to develop. This activity gives students who are having difficulty recognizing their strengths the opportunity to get in touch with some of the strengths discussed during the previous pizza activity.

Materials Needed:

- "An Avalanche" activity sheet
- Pencils, pens

Directions:

1. Review some of the qualities discussed on the "Any Way You Slice It" activity sheet. Ask the students to think if there was a quality or qualities they would have liked as toppings for their pizzas, but did not feel they really had.

2. After students have silently chosen the qualities they would like to have, ask them to think about what they need to do to develop those qualities. For example, if they want other kids to see them as more thoughtful, they will have to begin to listen to others' interests and problems more closely. In other words, they will have to learn the qualities they want to develop.

3. Write "avalanche" on a chart or the board and ask the students for its meaning. *Response:* "A fall or slide of a large mass of snow or rock down a mountainside." Ask why this activity is called an "avalanche" of strengths. *Responses:* "Ideas that are falling forward." "An overwhelming amount of strength to overcome obstacles in the way."

4. Ask the students if they have ever watched anyone ski or snowboard. Mention that each time they overcome an obstacle, they get closer to the finish line and closer to being a peak performer. Tell students to think about each strength they would like to develop as they take an imaginary run down the mountain.

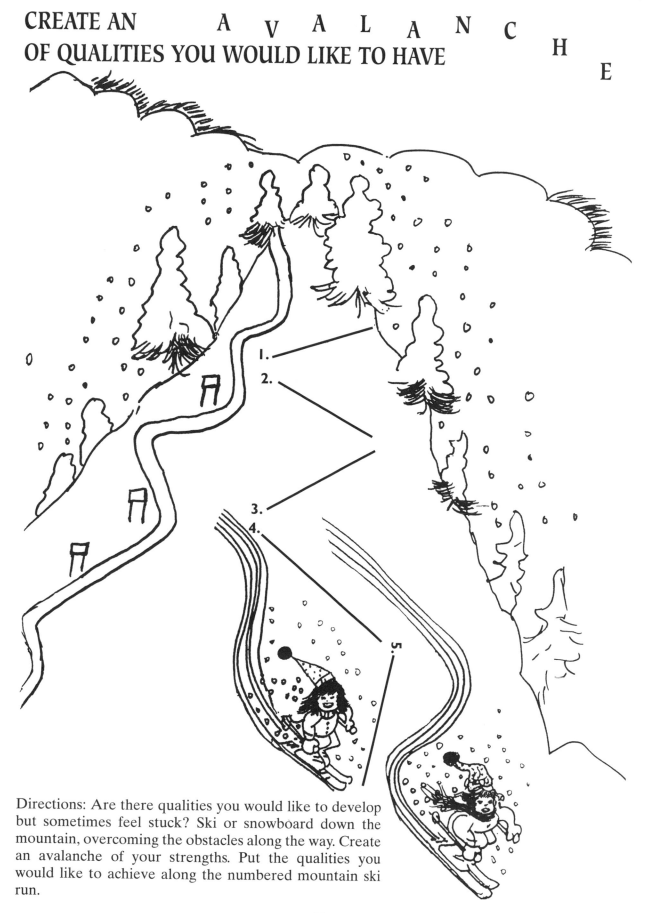

CREATE AN AVALANCHE
OF QUALITIES YOU WOULD LIKE TO HAVE

1.

2.

3.

4.

5.

Directions: Are there qualities you would like to develop but sometimes feel stuck? Ski or snowboard down the mountain, overcoming the obstacles along the way. Create an avalanche of your strengths. Put the qualities you would like to achieve along the numbered mountain ski run.

61

3–6. PIÑATAS EXPLODE WITH GOODIES

Geography and art are combined in this activity, which culminates in students finding the positive qualities within themselves—just as "good things" are found inside the piñatas. The Spanish custom of piñatas introduces a cultural element that can be explored more fully, if desired.

Materials Needed:

- "Piñatas Explode with Goodies" activity sheet
- Map of South America
- Papier-mâché materials *(optional)*: 1 cup of flour, 1 cup of water, pot for mixing on stove; *or* 1 teaspoon wallpaper paste mixed with 1 1/2 cups of water
- Balloon (inflated)
- Paint, paintbrush
- Multicolored crepe or tissue paper
- Buttons, rhinestones, decorating items
- Glue
- Newspaper strips

Directions:

1. Display a map of South America. Explain that Spanish is a predominant language in that country.

2. Write the word "custom" on a chart or the board and ask students its meaning. *Response:* "A custom is a practice followed by people of a particular group or region." Ask the students for some customs they know of that are practiced in North America. *Responses:* "Easter egg rolling and dyeing." "Christmas trees and lights." "Hanukkah candles." Encourage students who may be shy to share their customs with the class.

3. Explain that in South American countries (also Mexico and some Spanish-speaking states in the U.S.) a piñata (PEE-NYA-TA) is a decorated container covered with frilly, colored crepe paper. Piñatas come in every shape and size—from animals to clowns and starbursts with fringes and streamers. They are filled inside with candy, nuts, fruits, and little toys. They are strung overhead for children to break with a stick so that all the "goodies" fall out.

4. Distribute the activity sheets and ask students to draw a piñata outline in whatever shape they choose.

5. Inside the outline they should write three "good things" about themselves. Some examples of qualities to look for inside themselves should be written on a chart or the board. *Examples:* kindness, loyalty, good sense of humor, fair player.

6. Have students fill in the outlines with bits of crepe or tissue paper, buttons, rhinestones, or other materials.

7. If papier-mâché piñatas are desired, follow these steps:

   (a) Soak squares of strips of brightly colored tissue paper in water, then wring them out. Do the same with strips of newspaper.

   (b) *Paste mixture:* Mix 1 cup of flour and 1 cup of water on the stove until a smooth paste forms; *or* mix 1 teaspoon wallpaper paste with 1 1/2 cups of water.

   (c) Paste the damp squares of paper or strips of newspaper to an inflated balloon, alternating tissue paper layers with newspaper layers.

   (d) Place one piece over the other to cover your balloon evenly until about seven layers are covered.

   (e) Cardboard cutouts or other materials can be glued to the last layer and left to dry.

   (f) After the layers have dried (overnight), the hard surface may be painted, then decorated with charcoal, markers, curled ribbon, yarn, rhinestones, buttons, etc.

   (g) Finished papier-mâché piñatas can be hung by string, yarn, or wire from the ceiling. Students may write their three good qualities on tiny papers and attach them to the yarn, wire, or string as if they are falling out of their papier-mâché models.[1]

---

[1]*I Did It!* by Harlow Rockwell. New York: Macmillan Publishing Co., 1974.

PIÑATAS EXPLODE WITH GOODIES

Do you know what a "piñata" is? It is a decorated container used in South American countries suspended from a height and filled with good things. When children break it with their sticks, the good things fall out.

Directions: Draw the outline of an animal for a piñata. Inside your outline put three of your "good qualities."

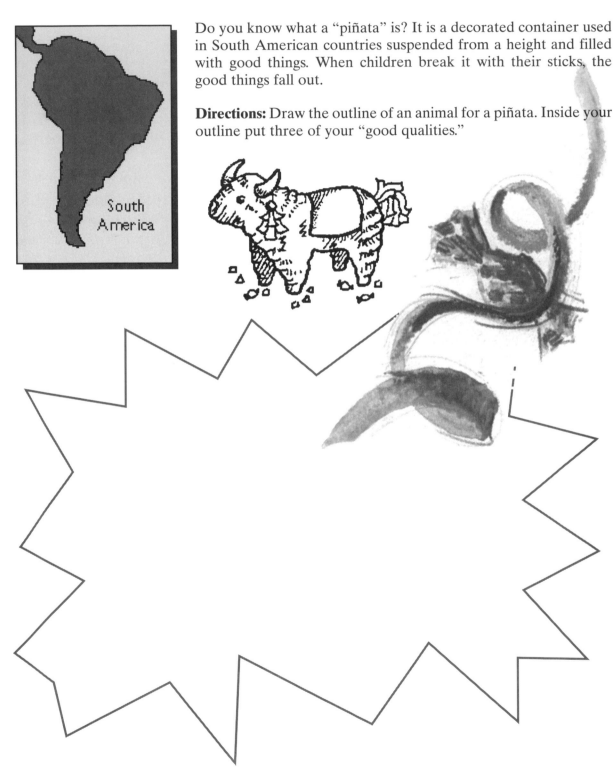

South America

3-7. WHAT MAKES ME POP

One of the main aims of the self-esteem component, Positive Identity, is for the children to recognize positive qualities in themselves. In this activity, they look for the good things they do and the strengths they have that make them *sizzle*!

Materials Needed:

- "What Makes Me Pop" activity sheet
- Colored markers, pencils

Directions:

1. Tell students you are going to pass them each a box of popcorn, on which they are to fill in the kernels with the qualities they feel make them sizzle. Then pass out the activity sheets.
2. Ask students for some examples of "sizzling qualities" and write them on a chart or the board. *Responses:* "Good sport." "Fair player." "Fun." "Kind."
3. Explain that if we do not develop our good qualities, they will remain as unpopped kernels of corn. Have students write in the kernels the positive qualities that come to mind most readily. Tell them not all of the kernels need to be filled in. It is important to monitor this activity closely and watch carefully for students who are not filling in any kernels of their boxes. Individually point out some examples of positive qualities you see in them. You may prompt them by asking, "Do you help with younger siblings? Are you kind to others? Do you help others sometimes? Are you fair when you play games? Do you try hard at school?"
4. Students may then color their popcorn activity sheets.

Bulletin Board Link:

The caption is "What Makes Us Pop!" or "Our Class Sizzles!" The decorated popcorn boxes can make a very colorful addition to the classroom, either placed around the room or on a bulletin board.

Cooperative Art Activity:

The class can be divided into cooperative learning groups of five or six students each. Each student receives a yellow popcorn kernel made out of bristol board and—after putting his or her name on the kernel—passes his or her kernel to the left until every member of the team has signed one "sizzling" quality about that student on the kernel. Each group makes one popcorn box made of white bristol board with a slit in which all five or six kernels are placed so that each one is displayed either in the slit or taped or glued coming down the side of the box. Students can decorate their boxes.

WHAT MAKES ME P⬭P!

In the kernels write the qualities you feel you have that make you *SIZZLE! Examples:* good sport, fun, smart, witty.

If we do not develop our good qualities, they will remain as unpopped kernels of corn!

3–8. IT'S WHAT'S INSIDE THAT COUNTS

For this activity, students will learn that people arc not always on the inside what they appear to be on the outside. They are led to see the importance of getting to know the inner person, not just what that person appears to be on the outside.

Materials Needed:

- "It's What's Inside that Counts" activity sheet
- Scissors; tape, glue, or stapler
- Construction paper

Directions:

1. Begin discussion by asking students if they know someone who they feel puts on an act by showing off, bullying, or excessive clowning to cover up what he or she really is inside. *No names are to be mentioned; only the behavior the person has displayed.* Ask students what they think that person was trying to cover up. *Responses:* "They wanted to fit in." "They didn't feel they would be good enough so they tried to cover up." "Sometimes kids become loners and stop trying to fit in for fear of being rejected."

2. After passing out the activity sheets, have students write something about themselves on the inside of the tuxedo (which you may need to explain is a fancy suit) that they would like to show more often. Give some examples, such as, "I feel shy sometimes and unsure of myself." "I really care about my grades but don't show it because I'm embarrassed they're so low."

3. Ask students to write on the outside of the tuxedo some behavior they show to others. Some examples you can put on a chart or the board may be: "I act really cool and confident." "I act like I don't care about the grades I get and say I didn't study."

4. Ask the students, "Did anyone have the same feelings on the inside as the behavior they showed to others on the outside?" Responses should lead to a discussion on showing others our true inner feelings.

5. Ask, "What do you feel you need to do in order to show others the way you really are inside?" *Responses:* "Be more confident that others will accept me the way I really am." "Nobody really likes a bully, a show-off, or a class clown."

6. Have the students cut out the tuxedo base and flaps and staple, tape or glue so that the flaps open and close. For fun, heads or class pictures and legs may be added.

Bulletin Board Link:

Under the caption "It's What's Inside that Counts," draw a large version of a tuxedo base with the stapled flaps opening to the most frequently mentioned "inside" and "outside" qualities on the individual students' tuxedos. Alternatively, the class could dictate the qualities they most frequently observe others behaving on the "outside" and how they believe they really feel on the "inside."

Music Link:

- "It Doesn't Matter, It's What's Inside that Counts" by Crosby, Stills and Nash
- "The Great Pretender" by The Platters or Freddie Mercury

IT'S WHAT'S INSIDE THAT COUNTS

People are not always on the inside what they appear to be on the outside. Some buy expensive, fancy clothes to "cover up" their low self-images. Try to see inside the real person, not just what he or she appears to be.

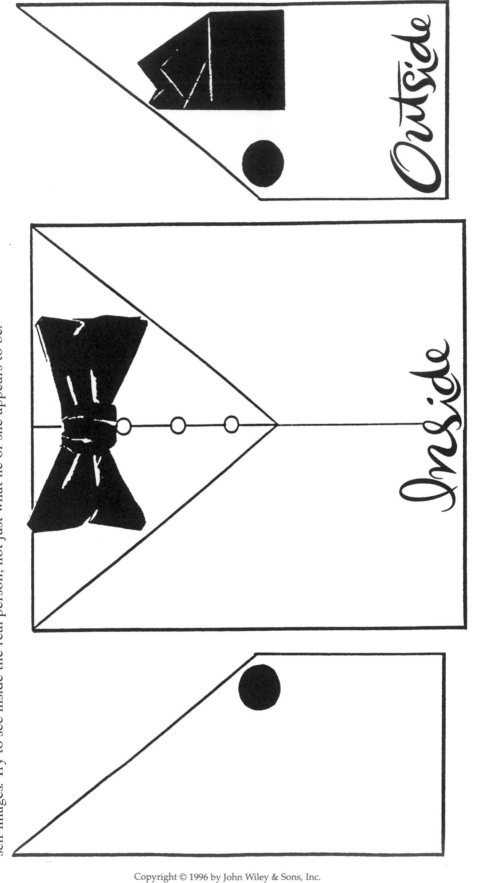

Cut out the two "outside" flaps and attach them to the tuxedo. On the "inside" write at least three feelings you have that you cover up by your outside behavior. On the "outside" flaps, write what your behavior will be, showing these feelings honestly. **Example:** (*Outside*) I'll show others I do care and ask for help. (*Inside*) I'm feeling sad about my low grades and cover up by acting like I don't care.

3–9. DIG FOR YOUR POT OF GOLD

In this activity, students will be encouraged to search for positive "treasures" within themselves. Because many students are not aware of their inner treasures, they will have to go on a treasure hunt. An intended student outcome is that students will "dig" this activity as a way of getting in touch with their good qualities.

Materials Needed:

- "Dig for Your Pot of Gold" activity sheet
- Colored pencils
- Black, gold, and yellow bristol board
- Shiny gold foil paper *(optional)*
- Small class photos *(optional)*

Directions:

1. Write "treasure" on the board or a chart. Ask students for synonyms. *Response:* "A treasure is a valuable or precious possession."
2. Ask students if they can describe their positive qualities as "treasures." *Response:* "Yes. Positive qualities are valuable and precious possessions, so they can be called 'treasures.' "
3. Ask students what happens if we cannot easily identify these treasures. *Response:* "We have to search for them." Tell students to begin their search with some examples by thinking to themselves, "Am I a loyal friend? Am I a student who tries hard? Do I help at home? Am I a good sport? What are some other treasures I have?"
4. Pass activity sheets to your students to fill in their "golden treasures" in each pot of gold.

Bulletin Board Link:

Display the caption "Find Me and You'll Find a Treasure." Draw a large pot and its handle out of black paper lined with gold foil. Class photos could go inside and appear pouring out of the pot. "We Dig It!" or "Our Class Treasures" may also be captions. Make a large treasure chest that opens out of bristol board or cut a large slit in which children's golden bricks or nuggets with students' names may be placed inside the slit and pouring down over the chest. Each gold coin, pot or brick can contain one golden quality chosen by each child. A rainbow made with pastel chalk or pastel markers can be included in the background of the bulletin board.

Cooperative Group Activities:

Students may form groups of five or six members each and choose one of the following two cooperative activities:

1. A small group could create a booklet on "The Qualities that Pioneers Needed Who Participated in the Gold Rush." They should include obstacles the pioneers had to overcome in their quest for gold.
2. A group might do a creative activity by telling a newly invented story about the pot of gold and how it came to be believed as existing at the end of a rainbow. The group should then tell the qualities of a person who would try to find the pot of gold at the end of the rainbow and any obstacles that person would have to overcome.

DIG FOR YOUR POT OF GOLD

What treasures of positive qualities would you find about yourself if you searched? Write your "golden treasures" in each pot of gold.

3–10. BE YOUR OWN BEST AMIGO

Before children can be friends to others, they first have to see themselves as being lovable and capable. Getting in touch with the qualities admired in their own friends, they can examine whether or not they possess those same qualities themselves.

Materials Needed:

- "Be Your Own Best Amigo" activity sheet
- Pencils

Directions:

1. Ask the class to define the Spanish word "amigo." *Response:* " 'Amigo' is a Spanish word meaning friend."

2. Elicit from the students why they feel they should be their own best "amigos." *Responses:* "If you don't like yourself, you act in ways that will turn off others." "Other kids won't like to be around you." "If you like yourself, you won't try to cover up and act like someone else." "It's important to accept your weaknesses as well as your strengths and still be your own best friend."

3. Ask students what qualities they feel they have to develop so that others will enjoy them as their "amigos." Tell students to imagine they are going to others for some advice. Ask what they feel they have to do to be liked more. Give students an example of a girl named Kyla who always wants to be the one to choose the videos she and her friends watch. Ask what advice would they give to Kyla that would make her friends want to include her more often when they get together.

4. Pass the activity sheets to your class. Ask a volunteer to read the introduction to the activity. Ask students to list in the first column qualities of a best "amigo." In the second column, they are to list qualities they need to develop to have more friends.

Extra!!

Ask students to look up in other languages different terms for "friend." How many can they find? In which countries or states would you find people calling friends "amigos"? *Responses:* "Central America, South America, Mexico, Spain, New Mexico, Florida, Arizona, California, Texas." Have students come up with other words for "friend" in the English language. *Responses:* "Buddy." "Pal." "Chum."

BE YOUR OWN BEST "AMIGO"

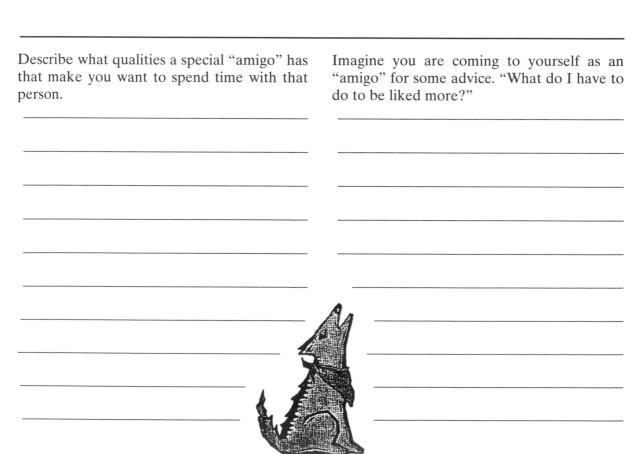

"Amigo" is a Spanish word meaning friend. If anyone should be your friend, it should first be YOU. If you don't like yourself, you act in ways that will "turn off" others toward enjoying being with you. Accept yourself as you are with your weaknesses as well as your strengths. Don't try to be someone else.

Describe what qualities a special "amigo" has that make you want to spend time with that person.

_____

_____

_____

_____

_____

_____

_____

_____

Imagine you are coming to yourself as an "amigo" for some advice. "What do I have to do to be liked more?"

_____

_____

_____

_____

_____

_____

_____

_____

3–11. REALITY CHECK

The purpose of this activity is to enable students to realize that the way they describe themselves is not always the way they act outwardly for others (publicly). Nor is it their ideal description. This is true in many cases for most of us. However, when we constantly cover up the "A" (Actual Self) and always show the "P" (Public Self) as being different from "A," then we are not showing others our true selves most of the time. If the "I" (Ideal Self) coincides with the Actual and the Public Selves most of the time, you have a person confident in showing his or her qualities to others. This person is usually aware of limitations as well as strengths and feels no need to disguise the fact he or she does have such limitations. It is important to make clear to students that very few people are able to integrate the "A-I-P" *all* the time!

Materials Needed:

- "Reality Check" activity sheet
- Pencils, colored pencils
- Bristol board in various colors
- CD (compact disc) holder and various covers (chosen at teacher's discretion!)

Directions:

1. Introduce the lesson by telling students this is an opportunity for them to go AIP over their CD's (their *c*haracter *d*escriptions and their *c*ompact *d*iscs)! Ask them to look at the three CD's at the top of the page. The first CD "A" correlates with Number 1. How will I describe my actual or real self? The next CD "I" correlates with Number 2. How would I describe my ideal self or the self I wish I were? The third CD "P" correlates with Number 3. How would I describe my public self or the self I show the world?

2. Give examples for each of the three initials starting with "A." An example could be "I'm afraid I won't make it—my grades, my goals in sports, etc." To follow the example in Number 2, the "I": "I want to show that I do care and that I am trying my best even if my efforts do not always succeed." An example for the "P": "I display an 'I don't care' attitude towards my marks, sports, and whether or not I am liked in general."

3. Tell students that if each of their descriptions in the CD's is similar, they are living up to and acting out the positive or negative image they think of themselves. If their "public" self differs from their "actual" self, then they are putting on a mask or a "front" for others. Remember that it is not always easy for a person's "public" self to match the "ideal" self. However, the "ideal" self should not always be hidden. It should begin to emerge more and more often publicly.

4. Ask the students to fill in their worksheets for numbers 1, 2, and 3.

5. Ask the students: "How do you feel about your descriptions? Is your ideal or public self always or sometimes different from your actual self?" They should write their answers at the bottom of the worksheet.

3–11. REALITY CHECK (cont'd)

Literature Link:

***The APE Inside Me* by Kim Platt** (Philadelphia: J.B. Lippincott Co., 1979): Full of discussion possibilities, this valuable book, written in the first-person narrative, is recommended to be read by the entire class. It appeals to a wide range of adolescent concerns such as controlling one's anger (described in the book as "Kong" the ape), aggression, and peer relationships.

Music/Art Link:

Character Descriptions (CD's): Define "character" together. *Responses may include:* "The combination of qualities that make a person stand out from someone else." Students enjoy making their own CD's. Trace a plastic CD holder onto bristol board. The smaller square made one thumb smaller can be taped or stapled inside the larger square so that the CD opens. On the outside cover write "CD by" (the name of the student). A cover is created by the student. The inside of the CD contains a student's character description that may (but need not) be written in song form.

Optional activity: A popular song may be used as the tune for the CD with new words created by the student (and performed, if desired).

REALITY CHECK

Look at how you see yourself in each of these CD's. Go AIP over yourself!

1. "A"—How would I describe my actual or real self?

_____

_____

_____

2. "I"—How would I describe my ideal self or the self I wish I were?

_____

_____

_____

3. "P"—How would I describe my public self or the self I show the world?

_____

_____

_____

Is the self you show others different from your real self or from your ideal self? If so, how can you change it?

_____

_____

_____

3–12. HERO

The purpose of this activity is to enable students to realize that their inner strengths, their "heroes," lie within themselves.

Materials Needed:

- "Hero" activity sheet
- The song "Hero" by Mariah Carey
- Biographies and autobiographies of "heroes"

Directions:

1. Play the song "Hero" for the class. This song is a favorite to which students can relate among educators and students! It's a worthwhile investment to your classroom music selections, to be played and sung along as an adjunct to difficult periods, visualizations, circle talks or restless, rainy days, in addition to this lesson. Ask your class what "hero" means to them. *Response:* "A person who helps another overcome a problem." (**Usage Note:** According to *The American Heritage Dictionary*, "The word *hero* should no longer be regarded as restricted to men.")

2. Ask students what "the hero lies within" means. *Response:* "Strength comes from inside a person when the need arises." Ask students for examples of times they have called upon their own inner strengths; discuss together as a class.

3. Distribute the activity sheets to your class to give their answers about inner strengths.

Literature Link:

The Once in a While Hero **by Carole S. Adler** (New York: Coward, McCann & Geoghegan, Inc., 1982): Readers have examples of courage and strength of character as a seventh grader struggles with a bully to defend a peer.

Kid Heroes: True Stories of Rescuers, Survivors and Achievers **by Neal Shusterman** (New York: Tom Doherty Ass's. Inc., 1991): This is a collection of true accounts of ordinary kids who have done heroic deeds.

Language Arts Link:

Assign students to read a biography or an autobiography about a person they consider a hero and to write why they consider that person's actions heroic. Students may also write their own autobiographies including their own real or imaginary heroic successes and/or efforts.

HERO

1. Listen to the song "Hero" by Mariah Carey. Where does the song tell you to look for your hero?

   _____

   _____

   _____

   _____

2. Do you feel your hero is within yourself? Why or why not?

   _____

   _____

   _____

3. If you have trouble finding your Hero within yourself, what's stopping you? Negative self-talk or put-downs you say to yourself might get in your way of thinking of yourself as a hero. What are some of the negative things you say to yourself?

   _____

   _____

   _____

4. Now turn the negative statements you say to yourself into positive statements you're going to say to yourself from now on.

   _____

   _____

   _____

5. Think about a time when you called on nobody else but yourself to solve a problem. It was an experience when you felt you had strength within yourself you never knew you had before. Write about your experience. If you haven't had an experience like this, write about an experience in which you see yourself being strong and solving a problem. Write about the hero inside yourself. Use the back of this sheet for your answers.

3–13. SHADES OF BLUE

The poem "Shades of Blue" may be used as a catalyst to a discussion about covering up one's true inner feelings. Students are able to identify with times in their lives they have disguised their own true feelings.

Materials Needed:

- "Shades of Blue" activity sheet
- Dictionary *(optional)*

Directions:

1. Pass activity sheets to your class. Ask students to read the poem silently to themselves. A volunteer may then read the poem aloud to the class.

2. Discuss together the meanings of the following terms:

   Norm—*Response:* "Standard or pattern regarded as typical."

   Disguise—*Response:* "Misrepresent or false show."

   Inner core—*Response:* "The basic or most important part."

   Pact—*Response:* "An agreement or a bargain."

3. Ask the students to think of a time in their lives when they covered up the way they were really feeling behind a "disguise" of behavior. Ask them to recall a time they acted in a way different than they were feeling. Experiences may be shared in small groups or by volunteers as a class-sharing experience. Assure students that it is normal to disguise our feelings sometimes; it is when true feelings are constantly covered up by our behavior that we need to look at what true feelings are being hidden and why they are being hidden.

4. Ask students why they feel the poem is entitled "Shades of Blue." *Response:* " 'Blue' means someone is feeling sad. 'Shades' can be a cover-up, so someone who covers up is often sad inside. Those who feel good about themselves do not feel the need to cover up."

5. Instruct students to answer the questions on the activity sheet. Answers are given below. The "Extras" are for older students who have been introduced to rhyme schemes and syllable counting.

Answers to "Shades of Blue" Activity:

1. Sad, depressed, unhappy.
2. Bragging, bullying.
3. When someone seeks to know him or her more and to love his or her real self.
4. The ways he or she differs from others; the true inner self.
5. When someone loves him or her unconditionally—no matter what the true self shows.
   EXTRA!! abab, cdcd, efef

   Eight syllables

Bulletin Board Link:

Captions could be: "Virtual Reality," "Reality Check," "Don't Play Cool—Play Real," "A Blue Daze," or "Shades of Blue—Our Poems." A huge pair of "shades" or sunglasses may be made of blue bristol board with silver foil placed inside the glasses. Class poems (see "Language Arts Link") could be hung around the sunglasses. (It is important to include all attempts in writing this poem so that no student feels left out. Non-readers may dictate their thoughts to another student to write out so they will be included.)

Language Arts Link:

Offer the opportunity for students to write their own poems that depict "masked or covered up" behavior. Poems should be encouraged for their content rather than form, which may be difficult for some younger students. Syllabic count and rhyming patterns should not be required, but may be an option for older students.

SHADES OF BLUE

Cover-ups in every form—
Bragging, bullying sure do hide
the ways I differ from the "norm."
Just do not ever look inside.

Safe I am behind the disguise—
it helps protect the inner core.
Who will be anymore the wise?
The one who seeks to know me more.

Maybe then I will drop the act
if only there is hope to be
accepted in a lasting pact
of, please, loving just the *REAL ME!*

—*Beth Teolis*

Answer the following questions:

1. Can you describe how someone is feeling if he or she is "blue"?

   _____

   _____

2. What are some ways in the poem people have of covering up?

   _____

   _____

3. When will the person who is covering up feel safe to show his or her REAL self?

   _____

   _____

4. What are the disguises hiding?

   _____

   _____

5. What are some examples of "masks" or "cover ups" you or someone you know has sometimes worn to hide the feelings inside?

   _____

   _____

EXTRA!! What is the rhyming pattern of this poem? _____

How many syllables are in each line of the poem? _____

3–14. PLANT A POSITIVE TREE

The goal of this lesson is to make **younger students** aware of put-down statements they make silently to themselves, known as *negative self-talk*. This negative self-talk can grow, as small acorns grow into oak trees, until it limits the student. The first step in eliminating self-doubt before it becomes a fully grown oak tree full of limiting beliefs is to make students aware of their negative self-talk. They need to realize in which areas of their lives they are limited as a result of their negative self-talk. The next step is for students to learn how to change those negative thoughts into positive thoughts or *positive self-talk*. Students can adorn their own trees with their new positive self-talk statements written on their leaves.

Materials Needed:

- "Plant a Positive Tree" activity sheet
- Paste, scissors, crayons

Directions:

1. Write the words "positive" and "negative" on a board or chart. Ask students for their meanings of the terms. *Responses:* "Positive means good, smart, or winning." "Negative means bad, stupid, or losing."

2. Discuss positive thoughts we have about ourselves. Ask students for some examples of what they say to encourage themselves when they are going to a birthday party and feeling shy, when they are learning something new in school, or trying out for a sports team.

3. Explain that we also have negative thoughts about ourselves. As with positive thoughts, they are a result of past failures to please ourselves or others; or discouraging or negative comments or gestures such as frowns, sighs of disappointment, angry scowls made to us by others since we were very small. Ask students to volunteer to share some of the negative things they say to themselves.

4. Explain to your class that talking to themselves about their bad and good thoughts is called self-talk. Self-talk may be positive or it may be negative. Tell students it is important to catch themselves when they are talking to themselves and to become aware whether their self-talk is positive or negative. It has been shown that our body energy follows the mind's energy, be it positive or negative. If we expect to succeed or expect to fail, we usually fulfill those expectations.

5. To further illustrate the concept of self-talk to students, ask them what are their favorite songs. After several have responded with the titles of their favorites, ask them if they can each sing their favorite songs silently to themselves so that nobody else can hear. Explain this is how our self-talk "plays" for each of us. Nobody else hears what is being said except ourselves. Self-talk is like a song or tape that plays when we face a situation that calls upon past negative or positive comments.

3–14. PLANT A POSITIVE TREE (cont'd)

6. Ask students to think of some thoughts they have that sometimes hold them back from doing something or from performing as well as they would like. Give them an example of negative self-talk: "I am a poor catcher in baseball." Ask for responses from students who are willing to share their negative self-talk with the rest of the class.

7. Ask the student who shared his or her negative self-talk experience to now change the self-talk into positive self-talk. In order to explain how to form this new positive self-talk, an example of the negative self-talk in step 6 would be: "I will practice my catching every day and I will catch the ball the next time I play baseball."

8. Distribute the activity sheets. Discuss why the title of this activity is "Plant a Positive Tree." Explain to the students that a small acorn of self-doubt can grow into a big oak tree of self-doubts. Our little negative or bad thoughts can keep growing until we hold ourselves back in certain areas—sports, school subjects, music, and making friends.

9. Ask students to decide which little negative "acorns" of negative self-talk they would like to change. They can put each new positive thought onto their leaves on the worksheets, cut out their leaves, and paste them into their oak trees to create a positive tree!

Bulletin Board Link:

A class "Positive Tree" may be drawn onto bulletin board background paper. To follow the above activity, you may choose to make an oak tree for students to fill in oak leaves with one new positive self-talk statement. Using the same idea, apple, pear or other fruit trees could be used. Perhaps a rose bush with thorns representing the old negative self-talk could be drawn, with students filling in roses with their positive thoughts. Captions might be: "Our Class Plants Positive Thoughts" or "Our Class Positive Tree" or, if roses are used, "Everything's Coming Up Roses!" Student leaves, fruit, or flowers may be hung on the large class tree.

Name _____ Date _____

PLANT A POSITIVE TREE

From a little acorn of self-doubt, a mighty oak tree of "I can'ts" or "I'm not good enough" can grow. Just like we listen to tapes on headsets, our thoughts can encourage us to do well **(positive self-talk)** or they can hold us back **(negative self-talk)** *Example:* "I'm going to mess up on this math test just like I did last time. I am not good at solving math problems" **(negative self-talk)**. You can change that negative self-talk "tape" playing in your mind by turning it into positive self-talk. "I studied hard for this math test and I feel ready for it. I CAN solve math problems well."

Write two examples of **negative self-talk**:

1. _____

   _____

2. _____

   _____

Now turn the two **negative self-talk** examples into **positive self-talk** on the two oak leaves below. Cut them out, color, and paste them to a big class oak tree, making a Positive Tree.

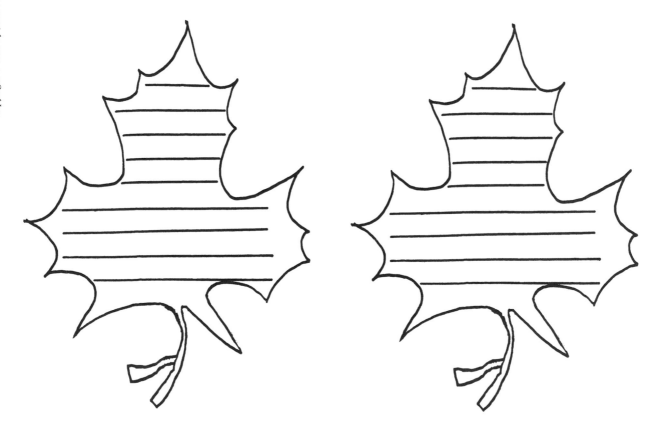

83

3–15. COOL VIBES

The goal of this lesson for **older students** is to make them aware of put-down statements they make silently to themselves, known as *negative self-talk*. This negative self-talk can grow until it limits the student. The first step in eliminating self-doubt is to make students aware of their negative self-talk. Next, children need to learn in which areas of their lives they are limited as a result of their negative self-talk. Knowing they are limiting themselves in some areas, they want to learn how to change those negative thoughts into positive thoughts or *positive self-talk*. Students relate to giving themselves "cool vibes" or positive self-talk.

Materials Needed:

- "Cool Vibes" activity sheet
- Pens, pencils

Directions:

1. Write the words "positive" and "negative" on a chart or board. Ask students for their meanings of the terms. *Responses:* "Positive means good, smart, or winning." "The definition for negative is bad or losing."

2. Discuss positive thoughts we have about ourselves. Ask students for some examples of what they say to encourage themselves when they are going to a party and feeling shy, when they are learning something new in school, or trying out for a sports team.

3. Explain that we also have negative thoughts about ourselves. As with positive thoughts, they are a result of past failures to please ourselves or others. Others may have given us discouraging or negative comments or gestures such as frowns, sighs of disappointment, or angry scowls that were made to us since we were very small. Ask students who would like to volunteer to share some of the negative things they say to themselves. You may want to lead with a revelation of your own negative self-talk. *For example:* "I'm all thumbs. I'll never be any good at sewing." Another name for having bad and good thoughts "talking to us" is called *self-talk*. Self-talk may be positive or it may be negative. Tell students it is important to catch themselves when they are talking to themselves and to become aware whether their self-talk is positive or negative. Tell students that another way of expressing positive self-talk is to say we are giving ourselves "cool vibes" that encourage us to let go of the "bad vibes" that limit us.

4. Explain to students that our body's energy follows the mind's energy, be it positive or negative. If we expect to succeed or expect to fail, we usually fulfill those expectations.

5. To further illustrate the concept of self-talk to students, ask them what are their favorite songs. After several have responded with the titles of their favorites, ask them if they can each sing silently so that nobody else can hear them. Explain that this is how our self-talk "plays" for each of us. Nobody else hears what is being said except ourselves. Self-talk is like a song or tape playing for us when we face a situation that calls upon past positive or negative comments related to the events we are facing.

6. Ask students to think of some thoughts they have that sometimes hold them back from doing something or from performing as well as they would like. Give them an example of negative self-talk or bad vibes: "I'm no good at sports." Ask for responses from students who are willing to share their bad vibes with the rest of the class.

7. Ask for a volunteer to share his or her bad vibes and to change them into cool vibes. In order to explain how to form these new cool vibes, an example from step 6 above would be: "I'll practice my favorite sport every day until I'm ready to try out for the team. I'll make it."

8. Pass the activity sheets to your class. Allow some quiet time for students to privately recall some negativism they play over and over to themselves, limiting them in things they would like to do. Then ask the students to change the negative statements they make into positive, cool vibes on their activity sheets.

Bulletin Board Link:

A large "guitar person" may be made with the heading, "Cool Class Vibes." The most common examples of new positive vibes students have written on their activity sheets can be compiled and written inside the "guitar person."

COOL VIBES
AND ALL THAT JAZZ

ONLY *YOU* CAN CHANGE THE NEGATIVE THINGS YOU SAY TO YOURSELF INTO POSITIVE OR COOL VIBES.

Directions: Change any bad vibes you play on your private headset into cool vibes. What are the new, positive self-talk statements you will give yourself? Write them in the guitar.

1. _____
2. _____
3. _____
4. _____
5. _____

3–16. LOOK FOR WINNING "WEIGHS"
—ON THE INSIDE!

The purpose of this activity sheet is to enable students to increase their feelings of self-worth in ways other than "measuring down" to societal pressure to look attractive by achieving a certain "model" body image. Less than one percent of the population is diagnosed with eating disorders; however, many girls do feel the need to conform to our culture's standards of attractiveness in movies, music videos, magazines, TV programs and ads—all of which give the message, *"Thin is in!"*

It is important to give students another message, *"Beauty lies within oneself."* If positive qualities are explored so that girls and boys become aware of their strengths, they will be less likely to depend on their appearances for acceptance and approval. The majority of young female adolescents concerned with body image and approval are more likely to develop eating disorders. Although young boys may also be concerned with "model" athletic body images, only about 5 to 10 percent of boys go on to develop eating disorders.

The purpose of this activity is to give students the opportunity to critically explore our culture's treatment of women and body image and to appraise their personal expectations of themselves in relationship to societal expectations. Point out to students that those whose answers from the "Winning Weighs Self-Quiz" differ from the answer key should *not* assume the results indicate they may have an eating disorder. For your information, some eating disorder information is briefly highlighted here. You may notice a student who has warning symptoms that you feel are more serious than simply dieting, purging, or binging *on occasion* in order to gain peer acceptance. Some eating disorders symptoms given by Health ResponseAbility Systems (1993) that may indicate the need for a doctor's diagnosis may include:

1. A refusal to eat
2. Large weight loss
3. A bizarre preoccupation with food
4. Hyperactivity
5. A distorted body image
6. Cessation of menstruation

A child who displays these symptoms may indicate one of the following eating disorders:

- **Anorexia nervosa**, defined as: "A condition of self-starvation."
- **Bulimia nervosa**, defined as: "Binge eating" or uncontrolled bouts of overeating with or without self-induced vomiting.

In most cases, both eating disorders are separate from one another. Most bulimics are not anorexic and a minority of anorexics are bulimic. There are, however, two commonalities between the two illnesses. Both anorexics and bulimics:

1. Overvalue bodily thinness, with an exaggerated fear of fatness
2. Have an obsession with food

3–16. LOOK FOR WINNING "WEIGHS" —ON THE INSIDE! (cont'd)

"People who are especially susceptible—those who never developed a healthy sense of self-esteem—will go to extreme lengths to avoid ostracism and rejection. They will sabotage their own bodies for the sake of an artificial, unnatural concept." This quotation by Russell Marx, M.D., found in *It's Not Your Fault*, goes on to point out that by no means is the sole causal factor in complex eating disorders so simplistic as having low self-esteem.

There are many contributing factors in developing an eating disorder. These causes may include: a desire to control one basic element in their lives, changing interactions within the family, and the societal pressure our culture places on young women to "be everything to everyone." If your students are interested in further reading about eating disorders, a reading list is included for students. This is a collection of books written for young adolescents concerned with their body images and peer approval. Included is an Eating Disorders Bibliography for your information, located in the Bibliography section of this book, if you would like further information about this topic.

Materials Needed:

- "Look for Winning 'Weighs'—On the Inside!" activity sheet
- Reading list for students
- Books and literature on eating disorders *(optional)*
- Collection of teen and women's magazines
- Edited collection of pictures of male and female models from magazines

Directions:

1. Ask students to bring to class:
   - fashion and movie advertisements featuring male and female photos from two newspapers
   - written descriptions of male and female actors or performers from one movie and three TV shows
   - collection of diet articles from three women's magazines
2. In groups of six, lead group sharing and discussion of the above collections. Do the "models" in these photos have a certain body image? Do their body shapes appear to be in keeping with the unspoken message "Thin is in"? Responses and discussion may be held within each group, to be shared later as a whole-class discussion.
3. Have each group compile their pictures and diet articles into a group collage, gluing the collection onto a background so that, when completed, a message is seen at a glance.
4. Ask the groups upon completion of the collages, "What message does your collage give?" *Responses will include:* "All the models, actors, and diet articles have one thing in common: looking good is looking thin!" "There are no overweight models and few overweight actors. People prefer to look at people who are thin."
5. Lead small-group discussions to later be shared with the whole class: "How do you feel our society's choice of people to be shown as models by the media *should* be chosen?" *Responses may include:* "By levels of fitness and achievements made along with their contributions to society, regardless of their body weight."

6. After students receive their "Winning 'Weighs' " activity sheets, read and discuss together the information at the top of the sheet. Assure students that less than one percent of thc population is diagnosed with eating disorders. If their self-quizzes contain several answers differing from the key, in addition to feeling upset about the lack of control they may have over certain situations as well as feeling a need to live up to a "model" body image, they do not necessarily qualify as having an eating disorder. Remind boys and girls that their answers will not be shared with the class. Discussion in small groups or as a class activity could follow, asking volunteers to share some of their answers at the bottom of the page regarding *control* and pressure they feel *living up to "model" body images.*

A Guided "Winning 'Weighs' " Fantasy:

Lead your class on a guided fantasy in which they appear to themselves as their *ideal* images. Play some soothing music as students are asked to relax. Lights may be turned off. Students may close their eyes or leave them open, depending upon how they can better visualize. Ask students to picture themselves arriving for a group activity. They can imagine who the group members are and what the activity will be, while picturing how they would appear with their "ideal" or most wished-for physical features.

Questions to ask students *to reflect upon* (to be discussed together after relaxation time):

1. What do you look like in your ideal state?
2. How are others besides those in the group you are imagining relating to you: family? friends? coaches? teachers? strangers? others?
3. Are these people (from #2) relating to you any differently than before you had a new "look"?
4. Are you different on the *inside* now with your new appearance?
5. Return to your normal appearance in your imagined group activity. How are those same people reacting to you now?
6. Do you think your outer appearance makes a difference in the way others relate to you? If so, why?
7. What do you think is the most important quality that influences others to treat you well? Tell students that if they answered, "The way you look is the most important quality that influcnccs people to treat others well," ask them to think about whether these people are those they want to impress, those who are only concerned with outer appearance? Tell the students to slowly open their eyes (if closed) and stretch. (Turning on bright fluorescent lights following a relaxation exercise should be delayed a few moments.)
8. Ask for volunteers who would like to share their ideal image experiences with the class.
9. Ask those students who did not change their appearances during the exercise to share why they chose to remain as they are.
10. Discuss together the questions you gave to your class during the relaxation exercise.

GREAT BOOKS FOR KIDS WHO WANT TO *GO BANANAS* ON SELF-IMAGE AND EATING HABITS

The Pig Out Blues by Jan Greenburg

An overweight teenager learns it is up to her to make her own decisions. She realizes she has been eating as a way to assert her independence from her mother. (Farrar, Straus and Giroux, Inc., 1982. Ages 12 and up.)

Beanpole by Barbara Park

Lillian, the tallest girl in Grade 7, learns to put her height in perspective. This first-person narrative deals with being concerned about having an imperfect body. The hurt feelings and consequences of name-calling on one's self-image are explored. Lillian discovers that she alone has the power to make her own dreams a reality. (Alfred A. Knopf, Inc., 1983. Ages 10–13.)

Fat Glenda's Summer Romance by Lila Perl

Glenda's weight problem troubles her when she is tempted by an abundance of food in her summer waitressing job. Glenda's self-doubts and her difficulty with friends are highlighted in this first-person narrative. (Clarion Books, 1986. Ages 9–12.)

The Jell-O Syndrome by Winifred Morris

This book looks at the scorn a young woman feels for beauty competition and the "dating game." She sorts out her search for her own individuality while having a relationship with a boy and realizes that one need not be sacrificed for the other. (Atheneum Publishers, 1986. Ages 12 and up.)

Blubber by Judy Blume

The feelings of a fifth-grade girl are explored when she is ridiculed for her weight. (Yearling, 1974. Ages 9 and up.)

Jelly Belly by Robert K. Smith

An overweight eleven-year-old boy is determined to win a coveted camping trip. The hitch? He has to lose 30 pounds!! Find out whether or not he succeeds and if so, how. (Delacorte Press, 1981. Ages 10–12.)

A Girl Called Al by Constance Clarke Greene

An overweight girl tries to overcome her feelings of rejection by treating herself to sweets while assuming an "I don't really care" attitude. As Al's self-concept improves, so does her ability to control her eating habits. (Viking Press, Inc., 1977. Ages 11 and up.)

I Was a 98-Pound Duckling by Jean Van Leeuwen

This book deals with the problems a young girl faces when her body image does not match the stereotypes displayed in the media. She finally discovers that she can be accepted and liked for herself. She realizes the problem was not her thin, tall body but her own poor self-image that held her back in her peer relationships. (Dial Press, Inc., 1972. Ages 11 and up.)

LOOK FOR WINNING "WEIGHS"— ON THE INSIDE!

Knowing the positive qualities you have inside yourself makes it less important to depend on your outer appearance to win approval. Magazines, movies, and TV programs often feature girls who are very thin, sending a message to viewers that "Thin is in!" The desire to be attractive and win approval may become more important than eating regular, nutritious meals. Also, sometimes you may feel you cannot control what's going on around you; however, you CAN control what you eat. A result of this may be eating too much or eating too little. If this eating pattern becomes a habit and you experience a large weight loss, you may need to learn more about eating disorders and how you can learn to help yourself.

Anorexia nervosa and **bulimia nervosa** are eating disorders that involve the way you feel about yourself. Regular binging, purging, or not eating are symptoms of these illnesses. However, if you feel you may have a problem or someone else thinks you do, talk to someone who can help you, such as your school counselor or doctor.

If you're interested in reading some books that deal with problems facing kids who are struggling with their self-images and their eating habits, a <u>Go Bananas!</u> reading list is available from your teacher.

WINNING "WEIGHS" SELF-QUIZ

Answer the following questions by circling the answer as to how you *usually* feel. Your answers will not be shared with the class. The answers can be found at the bottom of the page.

YES   NO   1. I usually only eat when I feel hungry.

YES   NO   2. I often binge on food (bags of chips, cookies, a carton of ice cream or other "good stuff"), then I feel guilty and worry about gaining weight.

YES   NO   3. I attract others only by my appearance.

YES   NO   4. I see myself as too fat, even though others tell me I have lost weight and look thin.

YES   NO   5. Although it's cool to look good, what really counts is what I'm like on the inside.

Activity:

"Sometimes I feel upset when I can't do anything to control what's going on around me." Can you relate to this statement? Write why you agree or disagree.

_____

_____

_____

"I often feel pressured to look like models on TV and in magazines." Do you agree or disagree? Why?

_____

_____

_____

Answers: 1. YES; 2. NO; 3. NO; 4. NO; 5. YES

3–17. NO ONE CAN MAKE YOU FEEL INFERIOR WITHOUT YOUR CONSENT

The quotation "No one can make you feel inferior without your consent," by Eleanor Roosevelt, is an important component of building positive self-esteem. Following up this lesson with a classroom banner will further reinforce this concept in your classroom.

Materials Needed:

- "No One Can Make You Feel Inferior Without Your Consent" activity sheet
- Computer paper (long section) or butcher paper
- Dictionaries *(optional)*

Directions:

1. Elicit from students their meanings of the term "inferior." If not using dictionaries, give students an example: If Michael Jordan were to walk in the room, what would he mean by saying, "Hey, you are all *inferior* in size to me!" *Response:* "Small or low." These responses may be written on the board or a chart.
2. Students enjoy discussing current movies they either have seen or would like to see. Ask them what is a recent movie they have been to or would like to go see. Then ask if they usually have to check the rating of the movie and get the *consent* from someone at home. Ask for synonyms for the word "consent." *Responses:* "Permission." "Allow."
3. Ask the students to look at the quotation written on a chart or the board. Ask who would like to repeat this quotation in their own words. *Response:* "No one can make you feel low if you don't allow it." The quotation now has more meaning to the students because they can relate to the wording.
4. Ask students to give examples of times when they have felt low because of something someone else said or did to them. After hearing their responses, distribute the activity sheets. Have students fill in the definitions of "inferior" and "consent" and ask them to rewrite the quotation in their own words. If the class has agreed on, for example, "No one can make you feel low if you don't allow it," then everyone in the class may write that on their activity sheets; *or* they can use their own words, as long as it has the same meaning as the quotation.
5. Go through the thinking experience at the bottom of the activity sheet with the students. Those who would like to share their experiences orally may be given the opportunity or they may be written individually.

Activity Links:

Ask for volunteers to make a banner out of the quotation, either the original quotation or the one the class has chosen to rewrite in their own words. The banner may be made on the computer or by hand and hung in a visible place in the classroom.

Eleanor Roosevelt had many accomplishments besides being the wife of a U.S. President (Franklin D. Roosevelt). Find out what her other accomplishments were and what positive qualities she needed to possess in order to hold such a number of high offices in the United States (an American diplomat and delegate to the United Nations, 1945–1950 and 1961–1962). She was a human rights advocate and author of *This I Remember* (1949).

In order to fulfill these responsible obligations, Eleanor Roosevelt must have possessed the positive qualities of self-confidence for public speaking, courage, kindness, and compassion, to name a few.

"No one can make you feel inferior without your consent."

—ELEANOR ROOSEVELT

Look up in the dictionary the definitions of:

Inferior:

_____

_____

_____

_____

Consent:

_____

_____

_____

_____

Now rewrite the above quotation in your own words.

_____

_____

_____

_____

Think about an experience when you allowed yourself to feel low about something you did. If you purposely hurt someone or caused some difficulty, you should feel responsible and resolve to improve. If you feel you were treated unfairly and allowed yourself to feel low, you must realize that you and you alone are responsible for the way you react. No one controls your reaction but *you*.

3–18. HERE'S THE SCOOP: E + R = O

We are responsible for our reactions to an event. We determine our own outcomes. When we are tempted to blame someone else or external events for our bad moods, anger toward others or violent behavior, we need to stop and remember that we alone are responsible for how we are feeling at any given moment:

E + R = O (EVENT + RESPONSES = OUTCOME)

Materials Needed:

- "Here's the Scoop" activity sheet
- Colored pencils

Directions:

1. Approach a student you know is a "good sport" and tell the student that he or she has green hair! (Response will be laughter.) Ask the student why there is laughter instead of a frown. *Response:* "Because I know I don't have green hair."

2. Now tell the same "good sport" student that you noticed he or she was walking into the classroom looking a little "clumsy." Note that the response may not be laughter. Explain to the class that this student is really not clumsy, but this was just an example used to demonstrate a point. Ask the class why the student did not laugh when he or she was accused of being clumsy. *Response:* "(S)he knew that the green hair was a joke because there was no doubt about having green hair; there *was* a doubt about being clumsy."

3. Enable the students to realize that if they have any inner doubts about themselves, comments made to them will result in hurt feelings. On the other hand, if they do not have doubts about themselves, they will not be so likely to be hurt by comments made to them. Explain that this is why it is so important for students to get in touch with their positive qualities. It is also important to be aware of their limitations and to be realistic about them.

4. Pass the activity sheets to your class. Explain that students' responses to an event determine the outcome. Say, "Everyone loves vanilla ice cream." Then ask students how many agree with the statement. *Response:* Not all hands will be raised. Explain that everyone has a different response to vanilla ice cream. People have different responses to an event and those responses determine the outcome. Tell students to answer the questions on the activity sheet and color their favorite flavors on the ice cream sundaes.

Cooperative Learning Activity:

Form small groups of five or six students. Have the students follow the activities on the activity sheet and share their favorite ice cream flavors among members of their groups. Ask, "Did everyone in the group choose vanilla ice cream?" Responses will be "no" from a number of students. Ask, "What does that tell you about the E + R = O formula?" *Response:* "Everyone has different responses to the same event. The outcomes are all different because each person in the group has his or her own responses; not everyone has vanilla ice cream as a favorite flavor." Tell students their responses are up to them. "Your reactions determine the outcomes you will get." Tell the groups to use "You didn't make the soccer team" as an example for an event and discuss possible responses. Discuss your own possible responses as well as the ones on the activity sheet and your own possible outcomes as well as the ones on the activity sheet. For the bottom of the activity sheet, students should move to their own desks and complete the activity individually, giving an example of an E + R = O experience they have had.

HERE'S THE *Scoop*

E + R = O

"*EVERYONE* LOVES VANILLA ICE CREAM!" Color your favorite flavor on the sundae. Ask several classmates for their favorite ice cream flavors. How many responses did you receive? Do you agree with the above statement about vanilla ice cream?

The Scoop:

People may see or hear the same thing but have a different response or reaction. This is because how you respond is up to you. *Example:* Which response would you choose for this event?

Event (E): You didn't make the soccer team.

Possible Responses (R):
1. Give up soccer.
2. Practice harder for next tryouts.
3. Take your disappointment out in the form of anger on those around you.

Outcomes (O):

If you chose #1, you will not play soccer again.

If you chose #2, you will continue to play and try out for soccer again.

If you chose #3, those around you will probably be hurt by your behavior.

Give an example of an E + R = O you have had:

Event (E): _____

Response you chose (R): _____

Outcomes (O): _____

Name two responses you did not choose.

_____

_____

What would the outcomes have been for each?

_____

_____

95

3–19. GIVE A GIFT, GIVE A BOOSTER

This activity sheet provides practice giving boosters to one another. Recognizing positive qualities in others is needed in order to form boosters for group members. Students realize the good feelings that come as a result of both giving and receiving compliments.

Materials Needed:

- "Give a Gift, Give a Booster" activity sheet
- Colored pencils or markers, pens
- Small gift wrapped in several layers of different gift wrap *(optional)*

Directions:

1. Because this activity depends upon groups of six students, decide how you are going to form your groups. If you have regular cooperative groups and feel the students work comfortably together, you may choose to use those groups. If you are forming new groups for this activity only, be sensitive to the groups you place together. The aim of this sheet is to give one another specific boosters, so care must be given in choosing which students to include in groups together.

2. This is a teacher-directed activity, so keep the following points in mind while preparing your students:
   - Every group member must fill in a booster for each member's activity sheet in the group; no one may leave a blank space on any of the sheets.
   - No put-downs are allowed to be written.
   - Boosters referring to clothing or physical assets are not allowed; boosters must refer to positive inner qualities or admirable behavior displayed by students.
   - Students new to the classroom may have difficulty giving boosters and their groups may have difficulty not knowing the new student well enough to offer compliments. Perhaps you could have a private session among yourself, the new student, and one or more children with whom he or she has been in contact since arriving at school. Perhaps you could place him or her with a group of sensitive students you feel would give a pupil new to the school their *positive first impressions.*

3. Pass out the activity sheets. Ask for a volunteer to read the introduction. Remind your class that *boosters* should be *specific positive comments about an inner quality or behavior displayed by the person.* Compliments about clothing, jewelry, and physical assets are empty boosters and do not produce the feeling of accomplishment we like to receive. Go through some personal experiences with the class, asking for examples from them of superficial boosters that didn't really make them feel as rewarded as boosters given to them about qualities such as kindness, fairness, and loyalty they have displayed.

4. Spend some time discussing *empathic feelings*, the ability to share in another's feelings or emotions. Ask students how they think they will feel when they receive their activity sheets back, filled with specific boosters about their good points. *Responses:* "It will mean a lot to me because the boosters will come from kids my own age." "I hope I'll learn what good things others see in me." "I'll see things about myself honestly from someone else's viewpoint." After you listen to their responses, ask them how they will feel if they receive their sheets back with one or more blank lines even though all members of the group are present. *Responses:* "I would feel like the person who passed on a comment about me could not think of one good thing about me!" "I'd be embarrassed and hurt." Remind the class to remember how they would feel if they are tempted to leave a student's sheet blank, saying they cannot think of a positive quality about the student or that they "don't like" the student. Explain that they should keep in mind, when filling out group members' sheets, *their own feelings* and how they would feel if they receive sheets back with blank lines. Tell your class you expect them to, and *know that they can*, find one good thing about each group member!

5. Remind students to write their names on their activity sheets where shown. Once the sheets are passed among the groups, it is the only way of identifying the owner of the sheet.

6. Direct the students into groups of six members per group. (After passing their sheets within their groups, each student will receive five signed boosters back with their sheets.)

7. Sheets may be passed to the left as students fill in boosters for the person whose name is on the page. As the sheets are being passed, rotate among the students to monitor the activity. Reminders should be given to students to write a positive comment about each person in their groups. Remind your class that any comments that may be intended as funny but viewed as put-downs are unacceptable.

8. When sheets are returned to their owners, notice the looks on the students' faces. They will be absorbed in reading what their peers have written about them. After giving them a few moments to read their boosters, process this activity by discussing their feelings upon reading what their classmates had to say about them. Ask for volunteers who would like to share their reactions. *Responses:* Smiles. "I didn't think anybody noticed I am artistic!" "Other kids like and respect me. They think I try really hard in school." "I didn't realize I made that kind of good impression on others."

9. If you write a booster at the bottom of each student's activity sheet, some of your children may treasure your positive comments for a long time. Of course, signing one or a few will necessitate signing sheets for the entire class to avoid any hurt feelings!

Booster Exercise: Pass the Present, Give a Booster:

A booster or validation exercise to do on an ongoing basis with your class is, "Pass the Present, Give a Booster." The goal of this exercise is to give students the opportunity *to give* oral boosters to one another as well as the ability *to receive boosters* with the feeling, "Yes, I did deserve that booster. I worked hard!" Many of us do not feel worthy of praise we receive, even when it is well deserved.

3–19. GIVE A GIFT, GIVE A BOOSTER (cont'd)

1. Wrap a small gift, such as a tiny mirror, in several different layers of gift wrapping paper. Begin by passing it to a student you feel needs or deserves a booster. He or she then passes the gift to a classmate to whom he or she feels most deserves a compliment about something positive that student has done in the classroom, on the playground, in the halls, or at home. The booster is to be given while looking directly at the student who receives the booster. The receiver then thanks the giver and unwraps a layer of gift wrap. The process continues until all the layers are unwrapped. The child who takes off the last layer of wrap keeps the gift.

2. *Reminders to be stressed with your class each time you do this booster exercise:*
   - Pass the gift to students deserving praise for an act or quality you noticed them display.
   - Remember to pick the kids who are often overlooked for praise, *those who succeed in quiet ways.*
   - The gift is not intended to be passed from friend to friend. The entire class must be included. The aim is that the gift is passed to those whose efforts, although not always successful, or acts of kindness toward others often go unnoticed.
   - Make sure the gift goes to different kids each time you have the exercise.
   - After doing this several times as a class exercise, students will not only be better able to both give and receive boosters, they will also be sensitive to whom the gift needs to be passed. You will see the gift will be passed *into the hands that need it the most.*

GIVE A GIFT, GIVE A BOOSTER

Here's a chance for you to practice giving and to enjoy receiving boosters! Form **groups of six kids**. After writing your name below, pass this sheet to your left to the other five people in your group. They will each give you a booster. You will sign five boosters and get back five. **A thoughtful reminder:** How would you feel if you received your sheet back with one or more kids who did not sign anything on your sheet? Sad? For sure! Write to everyone in your group about something you've noticed about them that will make them feel good inside!

Name _____

1. _____

2. _____

3. _____

4. _____

5. _____

3–20. BUBBLEGUM BLOWOUT!

Color the gumball letters of words you have seen in your self-esteem activities. All the letters of each different word should be the same color. If a letter is used for two words, both words must be the same color. Beware! Five words are sdrawkcab (backwards). **EXTRA!** The unused letters form a self-esteem message. When you have figured out the correct message, look below (upside down) to check.

FIND THESE WORDS:

bananas	image
dig	popcorn
pizza	tape
self	amigo
deluxe	pot
shades	hero
cool	gold
tuxedo	hit
blue	scoop
love	wow
vibes	

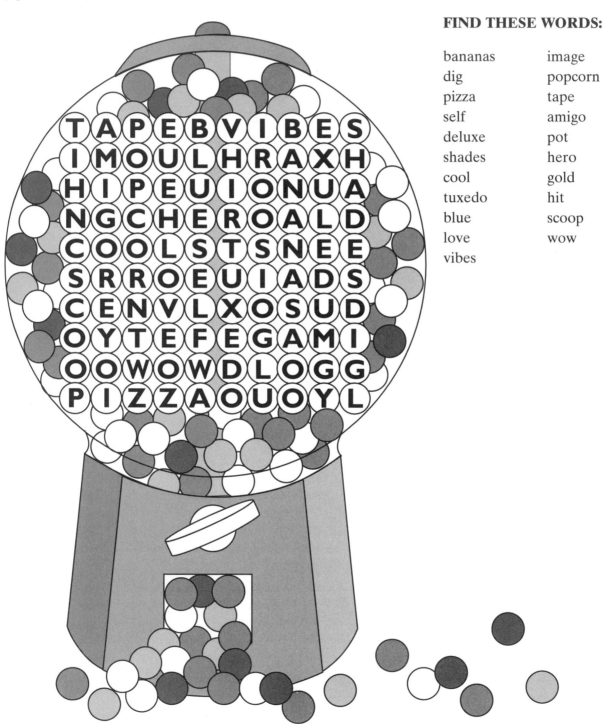

EXTRA! Your hero lies in you.

4

Friendship Building

FRIENDSHIP BUILDING

Rationale:

An important skill for life is the ability to develop an awareness of the qualities that attract others as friends. In this section students work on activities that help them develop qualities such as showing empathy for others when they are feeling low and recognizing the hurt that can result from put-downs. Affiliating with friends with similar good values and interests fulfills a young person's needs of belonging, lessening the need to affiliate with friends or gangs who may have a different set of morals.

Goals:

- To recognize and develop the qualities that attract and maintain friendships.
- To teach students how to give boosters to others as well as how to receive boosters.
- To be aware of the importance of thoughtful, empathic feelings toward others.
- To understand the varying relationships of different friends—some are closer than others.
- To realize the importance of choosing friends with similar values and interests.

Intended Outcome Statements for Students:

- "Others like the same things about me that I like about them!"
- "I know I need some work on taking turns and not wanting my own way so much."
- "I'm aware now of things I do that are turnoffs to others. I'm improving!"
- "If I choose friends who have the same interests and values as I have, I can be myself and not worry about peer pressure to do things I don't want to do."
- "I need to stop and realize that my jokes sometimes turn into put-downs that really hurt others."
- "I used to attract friends easily but lose them quickly. Now I know what it takes *to keep* friends."

4-1. DIRECTIONS FOR THE FRIENDSHIP-BUILDING QUIZ

This quiz may be used as a pre-test before the Friendship component is introduced in your classroom. After you feel your students have completed a sufficient number of friendship-building activities, the quiz may again be given and the results compared with the pre-test.

Below are the Friendship components you are assessing. Friendship-building components encourage students to:

- **Give Boosters**—Form specific validations to give to others.
- **Respond to Needs of Others**—Listen, share interests, and cooperate with others.
- **Affiliate with Peers**—Feel sense of belonging with at least a few friends or a group of friends.
- **Maintain Values**—Avoid pressure to go against own values in order to feel they belong.
- **Display Empathy**—Feel the hurt another experiences and make efforts to boost him or her up.

Answer Key:

If a student's answer differs from the answer key, it may be an indicator of weakness in one of the friendship-building components and you will know specifically what his or her needs are.

1. NO; All areas
2. YES; Give Boosters
3. NO; Affiliate with Peers
4. YES; Respond to Needs of Others
5. NO; Respond to Needs of Others
6. YES; Affiliate with Peers
7. YES; Maintain Values
8. YES; Display Empathy
9. NO; Affiliation with Peers
10. YES; All areas.

- -

Teacher Evaluation—Notes on Weak Areas

Student: _____ Date: _____

Observed behavior in the area of: _____

My plan to help to strengthen that area: _____

_____

_____

_____

_____

STUDENT FRIENDSHIP-BUILDING QUIZ

Directions: Circle YES or NO depending how you *usually* feel about the statement. Your answers will not be shared with the rest of the class.

YES	NO	**1.**	I lose my friends as soon as I make them.
YES	NO	**2.**	I give compliments to friends to let them know they're special to me.
YES	NO	**3.**	I often feel like I have no friends and don't belong anywhere.
YES	NO	**4.**	I am a good listener to a friend.
YES	NO	**5.**	I'm the one who always decides which video to watch, where we're going to hang out, or which video game we play.
YES	NO	**6.**	When I want to make a new friend, I go for it! I ask to do something together.
YES	NO	**7.**	When someone asks me to try something I don't feel is right, I say "no."
YES	NO	**8.**	I can feel the hurt when I watch someone get put down, so I try to build him or her up.
YES	NO	**9.**	There are lots of different kinds of friends. Some are closer than others.
YES	NO	**10.**	If I want to feel less lonely and have more friends, I need to develop qualities so that others will want to be friends with me.

Why I answered YES or NO on number(s):

_____

_____

_____

_____

Here are some of my ideas for making and keeping friends:

_____

_____

_____

_____

_____

4–2. FRIENDS

The aim of this activity is to explore friendships and the characteristics we look for in a friend. In focusing on what makes others appealing as friends, students realize these qualities are ones they themselves will want to adopt in order to make and keep friends. Some suggestions for beginning a **buddies program** to assist some of your students who are going through a difficult period and have few friends are given in these teacher directions.

Materials Needed:

- "Friends" activity sheet
- Scissors, colored pencils, crayons or markers
- Construction paper in various colors
- Fingerpaints in red, yellow and green, and brown butcher or art paper *(optional art activity)*

Directions:

1. Pass out the activity sheets. Ask students to fill in each letter in FRIENDS with the sentence-stem completions listed.

2. After completing their sentence stems, students can then decorate and cut out their FRIENDS, mounting them on colored background paper along with photos or drawings of friends. Be sensitive to students who do not have many—or any—friends. These students could draw pictures of kids they admire or of relatives close to them. Subsequent activities in this section will guide these children in making new friends.

A Buddies Program:

1. *If there isn't one in your school, why not start one up?* You may want to plan now or in the future to start a pairing of older/younger students together as buddies.

2. *When to use a pairing between older/younger students?* For a younger student new to the school who is feeling insecure or a child having difficulty in the home due to: divorce, separation, alcoholism, drugs, a parent out of work, abuse, death in the family or other turmoil. Or the pairing may be planned *to help the older buddy* through one of the previous difficulties he or she may be going through. The pairing helps the older buddy by giving him or her a sense of responsibility (if there has been turmoil in the home, the buddies program is something over which he or she has control when things at home seem out of control) and pride felt in helping a younger child.

3. *What do the buddies do together?* They may go on an outing each month along with other Superbuddies from other classes. The outing should be supervised and funded by the school. They should have get-togethers for "chill-out time" once a week. They may have lunch together; however, it's not always possible to schedule times for lunch-

4–2. FRIENDS (cont'd)

es together. If lunch is not possible to schedule, time (about 10 or 15 minutes) from the school day should be given for both buddies to leave their classrooms. This time should be spent airing out anything the younger child would like to discuss with the older buddy. If the older buddy enjoys art, they could do an art activity together or another planned hobby or craft activity. They could meet near or in the office area where supervision is close by, in a quiet part of the library, or in the faculty room, if few teachers are using it at the time.

4. *What to call the buddies?* Big Dudes/Little Dudes; Superbuddies or Superbuds; Amigos; Amis; Superpals; or Big Heroes/Little Heroes. This program will help a discouraged younger child feel more secure and look forward to something at school. The older buddy will gain a positive sense of accomplishment knowing he or she has helped a younger child.

Bulletin Board Link:

The bulletin board caption might read "That's What Friends Are For" or "A Friend Is Special" with the decorated FRIENDS displayed. If you begin a buddies program in your school, the FRIENDS could be written and decorated for each set of buddies to give to each other and all hung together in the front hall with the caption "Superbuddies" or the name they have chosen.

Art Activity:

Younger students enjoy creating colorful treetops by fingerpainting using red, green, and yellow fingerpaints. The treetops are attached to the trunk made from brown butcher or art paper. Students' names are written on the trunks along with the names of two friends or— if the child has no friends to name—relatives. Names could be drawn from a bag and each child could add to the trunks the name he or she drew for her or his "tree friends." Trees are hung together to create a forest with the caption "Our Forest of Friends" along with the statement: **A tree on its own will wither. Trees need one another. When they blend together, they create a beautiful forest. Aren't trees a lot like friends?**

Name _____ Date _____

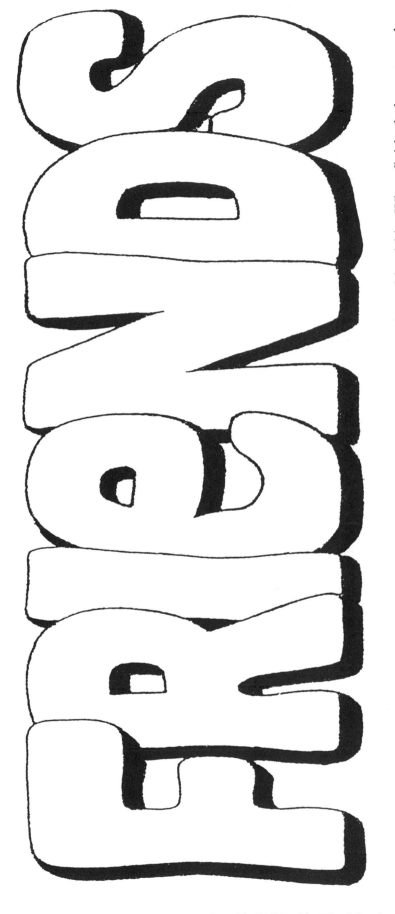

Inside each letter of "friends" write the way you want to complete the sentence stems about friendship. When finished, decorate and mount on paper with photos or illustrations of your friends.

F – My favorite thing to do with a friend is to . . .

R – When my friend is upset I . . .

I – To make a new friend I . . .

E – When I find out I've hurt a friend I . . .

N – If a friend asks for help and I'm busy I . . .

D – When I'm doing something with my friend I feel . . .

S – To keep my friends I . . .

4–3. YO, DUDE! IT'S A ROUND-UP

This activity enables students to focus on the positive relationships they have formed in their lives. They then explore the qualities they need to develop to build more positive relationships.

Materials Needed:

- "Yo, Dude! It's a Round-up" activity sheet
- Pencils, pens

Directions:

1. Pass out the activity sheets to your class. A volunteer can explain the meaning of the term "round-up." *Responses:* "A gathering together of anything." "In *cowboy* terms, it refers to driving cattle together and collecting them in a herd." Announce that in this activity, students are going to have a "round-up" of all the good relationships they have with people in their lives!

2. Ask for a student to read the introduction at the top of the activity sheet, which explains what goes into the formation of a positive relationship. Explain to students that a positive relationship is one in which the people involved get along well together, sharing both good and bad times. The positive relationships may be with one or both parents, relatives, teachers, friends, and other people with whom they feel comfortable and enjoy spending time.

3. Tell the class they are going to have a "round-up" of the special people they already have positive relationships with. Students should go down the list on the left side of the sheet, *checking off people they have positive or good relationships with now*. This list is intended to act as a reminder of all the different relationships in their lives. Then the *names* of those people can be written **inside the first lasso**. The *names of people they want to develop good or positive relationships* with can be written **inside the second lasso**.

4. After students have completed their lists and their names in the lassos, ask students what they feel they need to develop in order to build new positive relationships with the people in their second lassos. *Example:* If they want to build a friendship with someone who just moved into the neighborhood, perhaps they could develop some skills by helping the newcomer meet other kids in the neighborhood and include him or her in some activities. Ask the class to volunteer other examples of relationships they want to develop but aren't sure how to go about it. The class can brainstorm some of the skills that may be needed to help the students develop some new relationships.

5. The students are now ready to complete the bottom portion of the activity sheet. Ask how they are going to *spur themselves on* or get going to develop qualities for better relationships with the names in the second lasso. Referring to the chart, instruct them to write the names of people from their second lassos under "person" and beside each person, the qualities (patience, loyalty, ability to take turns, etc.) they need to develop better relationships.

Name _____ Date _____

YO, DUDE! IT'S A ROUND-UP

Have a **round-up** of people you already have positive relationships with and others you want to have positive relationships with. Put a check in front of the people listed below you *already have positive relationships with*. Write the **names** of those people you checked off *inside the first lasso*. Write the names of others you *want to develop positive relationships with* but have not up until now, *inside the second lasso* below.

_____ parent(s)
_____ guardian
_____ brother
_____ sister
_____ relative
_____ teacher
_____ coach
_____ other instructor
_____ friend
_____ other

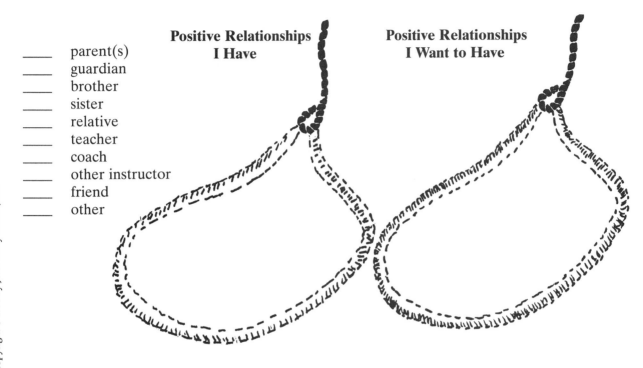

**Positive Relationships
I Have**

**Positive Relationships
I Want to Have**

How can I SPUR ON positive relationships with each of the people in my second lasso?

Person: **Qualities I need to develop:**

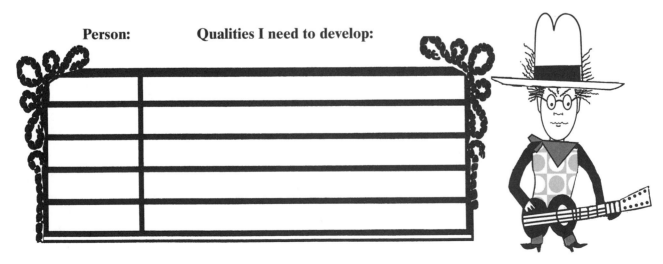

4–4. FIRST IMPRESSIONS:
WHICH ONES GET YOUR STAMP OF APPROVAL?

What impresses you most when you meet someone for the first time? What kind of first impression do *you* make? Becoming aware of qualities that impress others motivates students to develop similar ones themselves, thus giving these qualities their stamps of approval.

Materials Needed:

- "First Impressions" activity sheet
- Paste, scissors

Directions:

1. Introduce this activity by leading your class in a discussion on first impressions when people meet. Ask if they usually know right away whether they would enjoy getting together with that person again. Inquire about behavior that *impresses or makes a lasting (favorable) impression* and also behavior that turns them off. Tell students the activity sheets they are going to receive will make them more aware of qualities that attract them to others. Explain that if they develop attractive characteristics in themselves, they will make not only good first impressions but also favorable *lasting* impressions.

2. Distribute the activity sheets to your students. Announce that this will be an opportunity for them to give their *stamps of approval* on qualities in others that leave them with a good first impression.

3. Choose a volunteer to read orally the introduction to the activity. Use the following questions to discuss together as a class:
   - What kind of first impression do you make?
   - When you meet someone for the first time, what are some of the things he or she does that make you want to see that person again?
   - What makes you want to become friends with that person?

4. Direct students' attention to the list of qualities on the activity sheet. Ask, "Do these qualities make a positive impression when you first meet the person?" If students are impressed with a quality on the list, tell them to cut out a rubber stamp from the bottom of the page and paste it in front of the quality that impresses them. Tell your students that they will be giving their stamps of approval to qualities that leave appealing first impressions!

Name _____ Date _____

FIRST IMPRESSIONS—YOUR STAMP OF APPROVAL

When you meet someone for the first time, what are some of the things they do that make you want to see that person again? What makes you want to become friends with that person? Below are some qualities people show to others. If you think a quality helps yourself and others make a good first impression, cut out a stamp from the bottom of the page and paste it beside what attracts you as a good first impression. You will give it your stamp of approval!

Do these qualities make a positive impression when you first meet the person?

makes eye contact with you	does anything to please the crowd
is interested in you	is sincere and real, not a fake
looks down or away	always wants own way
makes fun of others	frowns a lot
swears	has a positive, "up" attitude
has a sense of humor	interrupts conversation with own ideas

4–5. A COOL MIX

This "menu" provides the *natural ingredients* needed for attracting friends. Developing a mix of positive qualities in the friendship recipe is discussed as a desirable menu plan!

Materials Needed:

- "A Cool Mix" activity sheet
- Pencils, pens
- Natural Recipe written on a chart, the board, or a menu made of colorful bristol board or art paper to leave up for classroom display *(optional)*

Directions:

1. Ask, "If you were to receive a formula or plan for attracting others, would you follow the points offered?" *Responses:* "I'd like some direction in making friends because I seem to attract them, then I lose them. I'm not sure what I'm doing wrong." "I'm always the one left out. What positive qualities can I develop to make friends?" Following the discussion, tell your students you are going to offer them an appetizing *menu* of desirable qualities.

2. Pass out the activity menus to your class. Ask for a volunteer to read orally the Natural Recipe and the directions below the recipe. Hold a class discussion about the ingredients and whether students agree or disagree with each of the ingredients in making a good friend. The discussion should encourage any additional positive qualities students want to contribute to the recipe.

3. The activity questions may each be discussed together as a class before asking students to fill in their answers. Or you may prefer to ask them to fill in their answers and then hold a class discussion about their answers.

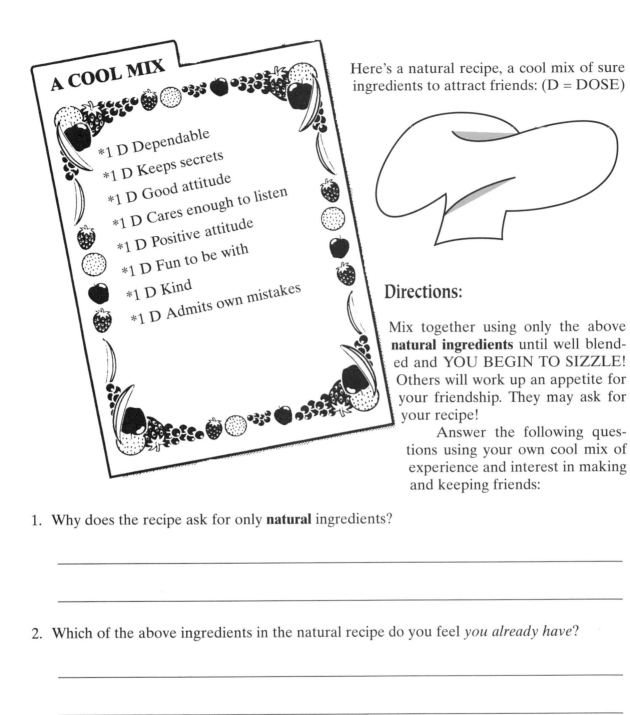

A COOL MIX

*1 D Dependable
*1 D Keeps secrets
*1 D Good attitude
*1 D Cares enough to listen
*1 D Positive attitude
*1 D Fun to be with
*1 D Kind
*1 D Admits own mistakes

Here's a natural recipe, a cool mix of sure ingredients to attract friends: (D = DOSE)

Directions:

Mix together using only the above **natural ingredients** until well blended and YOU BEGIN TO SIZZLE! Others will work up an appetite for your friendship. They may ask for your recipe!

Answer the following questions using your own cool mix of experience and interest in making and keeping friends:

1. Why does the recipe ask for only **natural** ingredients?

   _____

   _____

2. Which of the above ingredients in the natural recipe do you feel *you already have*?

   _____

   _____

3. Which of the above ingredients in the natural recipe would *you* like to develop?

   _____

   _____

4. Do you feel this recipe measures up to qualities *you* look for in a friend? _____ Why? Why not?

   _____

   _____

4–6. MAKE A SPLASH WITH OTHERS

In this activity, students are taught that qualities they admire in others are desirable qualities that they themselves need to develop in order to attract friends. Choosing friends with similar interests and values and avoiding peer pressure are discussed.

Materials Needed:

- "Make a Splash with Others" activity sheet
- Colored pencils or markers, pens

Directions:

1. Pass the activity sheets to your class, announcing that this will give them the chance to learn how they can *make a splash* or *develop qualities to attract others*. Tell students their answers need not be shared with the rest of the class unless they want to during the class discussion. Choose a volunteer to orally read the introduction to the activity at the top of the sheet.

2. Hold a class discussion about the statement, "Others will be attracted to many of the same qualities in you as you admire in others." (Write this on a chart or the board.) Tell volunteers to state whether they agree or disagree with the statement and why. *Responses:* "Friends usually share a lot of the same qualities—someone who is kind likes to be around thoughtful friends." "People need to develop in themselves the things they like about others."

3. Point out to older students that an exception to this development of qualities that attract others would be the following example: kids who want to belong to a group that is doing things considered "cool" but that go against their own beliefs and values. Depending upon the age group in your class, you may want to lead a discussion on drugs, alcohol, smoking, and the peer pressure to belong to a group. If they would like to belong to that group, they begin to feel they need to adopt the same qualities in order to be accepted by the group. Stress to your students that giving up their own values and morals in order to feel a sense of belonging with others is **not** the way to make friends. Remind students to choose friends with values and interests that are much the same as their own so that they will not feel the pressure to impress others. Ask how many of them like to feel they can be comfortable just being themselves when they are with others. *Responses:* "I'm a lot more relaxed when I don't feel like I have to impress anybody." "I like to be myself."

4. Direct your students' attention to their activity sheets. Tell them to circle the three qualities they most admire in others and to write those qualities on the three lines under the rafts.

5. The activity below the rafts calls for some introspection about friends. Tell them to answer YES or NO to questions asking if they choose friends with the same interests as themselves and whether they feel comfortable with their friends. They are then to write what they could do to feel comfortable with friends if they answered NO to num-

ber one. *Responses:* "I could assert my need to have a turn doing what I like more often." "We don't share many interests. Maybe it's time to look for friends who share what I like!" If they answered NO to feeling comfortable with their friends, instruct students to write what they could do to feel more comfortable. *Responses:* "I am always trying to be what I think my friend wants me to be; I can't just be myself. I am going to make friends with whom I can be myself." A class discussion should follow this activity. Students who are involved with others who pressure them to conform to their ways should be aware of alternatives they have to feel a sense of belonging.

6. Ask your class to choose three favorite things they like to share with friends and to write them on the numbered lines on the activity sheet. The following list may be copied onto a chart or the board or read orally. It will give students some ideas of activities they may choose from in addition to other favorites they may have: renting videos, playing sports, talking on the phone, going to the mall, sharing favorite books, telling each other problems, sharing good news, going to parties, etc.

Name _____ Date _____

MAKE A *SPLASH* WITH OTHERS

Circle the three qualities you most admire in others, then write them *under* the rafts. If you start using these qualities, *you* will soon be making a SPLASH attracting others!

honest	**listens to me**	**sense of humor**	**kind**	**takes turns**
good attitude	**loyal**	**reliable**	**keeps secrets**	**positive**

_____   _____   _____

1. Do you choose friends with the same interests you have? _____

2. If you answered "no," what could you do to share the same interests with friends?

_____

3. Do you feel comfortable with friends you have now? _____

4. If you answered "no," what could you do to feel comfortable with friends?

_____

Write below *three favorite activities* you like to share with a friend:

_____

_____

_____

4–7. HEARTFELT FRIENDS

This activity provides an opportunity for students to assess current friendships. After identifying friends in their lives, they can then think about skills they need to work on to maintain those relationships and qualities needed to develop new ones.

Materials Needed:

- "Heartfelt Friends" activity sheet
- Pencils, pens
- Journals or writing paper

Directions:

1. Pass out the activity sheets to your class. Ask the students to think about (*not* to raise hands, as some students may be embarrassed by their answers if they have no—or only one—friend) how many friends they have. Ask them if more than one friend comes to their minds. If so, ask if they had some difficulty deciding who they should count as "friends." Explain that there are different levels of closeness of friends, depending upon how much they enjoy being with that friend, how often they get together, and how they are getting along together now. Explain that the diagram on this activity sheet will help them identify their friends and how close they feel those friends are to them.

2. Volunteers may orally read each of the descriptions of friends and place the symbol for each description on a chart or the board for a further visual reference as students fill in their sheets. A few oral examples for each description may be given until students have the idea. Give your class directions for filling in the hearts on their diagrams. Instruct them to write the name of a friend who fits the description inside the heart that contains the matching symbol. If they cannot think of a friend to fill a particular description, they can leave it blank.

3. After the students have filled in their hearts, referring to the description in which a child *wants to become better friends* with another child, discuss the qualities (good listener, sense of humor, honesty, loyalty, dependability, to name a few) that will attract that person so that he or she will want to be friends. As a follow-up activity, have students role play favorite things friends do for them or say to them that make them feel good. They should refer to the names in their hearts and identify the friendship qualities they need to work on for each friend in their diagrams.

Heart-to-Heart Link:

Pass heart shapes to children to write about themselves with the heading "I am a loving person. I'd like to be friends with me because . . . " Children complete the sentence stem with some of the qualities they see in themselves that they feel would attract friends.

Music Link:

"Heart of the Matter" by Don Henley (This song talks about forgiveness among friends.)

HEARTFELT FRIENDS

Fill in the hearts surrounding the "Me" with *names of those friends who fit the descriptions* at the bottom of the page. The symbols in each heart will correspond to the symbols you find in front of the descriptions. The diagram will then give you a chance to look at all your current friendships. You can then think about ways you can improve your friendship-making skills with each of the people you choose for your hearts!

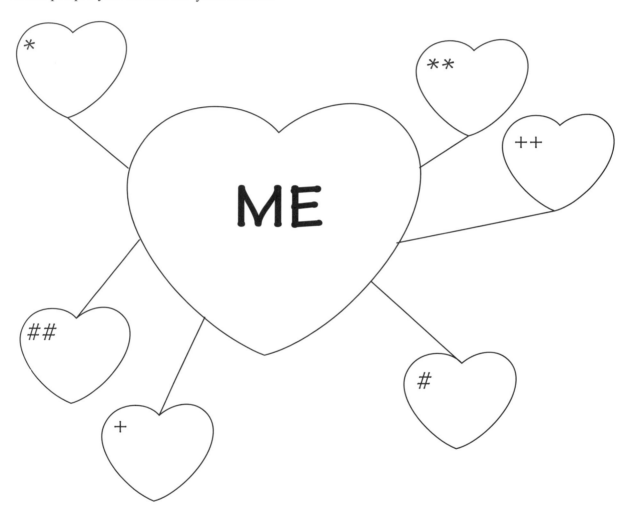

**This is my very best friend.

*This person is not my very best friend, but we have fun sometimes doing things outside of school together.

++This person is an old friend, but we don't get together much anymore. We have good memories, but that's about all.

+This is a friend who lives far away. We only see one another once in awhile, but we get along well. We write to each other a lot.

##I am not getting along with this friend right now. I don't want to lose our friendship, but I feel we're not so close as we used to be.

#I really want to be better friends with this person I admire. I have fun when I'm with him/her at school. I'd like to do things together outside of school also. I want to develop this into a great friendship!

4–8. STARS

The meaning of friendship is reviewed in this activity. Students are given the opportunity to give written boosters to friends, letting them know they are special as well as why they shine. The activity provides a lesson in *giving* to others we care about.

Materials Needed:

- "Stars" activity sheet
- Colored pencils or markers
- Yellow bristol board or construction paper
- Scissors, paste *(optional)*
- Glitter *(optional)*

Directions:

1. Pass out activity sheets to your class. Ask for a volunteer to read orally about the tale of the Starcatcher. After the Starcatcher story is read, tell your students they are all going to be starcatchers for this activity!

2. Ask students if they have friends who brighten up their days when they are sad. *Responses:* "The people who are really my friends help me feel better when I'm down." "A lot of kids are just worried about their own problems. I know I have REAL friends when they take the time to tell me something positive to brighten me up." "A good friend knows how to get my mind off my troubles and onto something totally different—a distraction! It works!" Explain to your class that these friends are valuable. They do not ask for boosters, they *give* because they *care*. It is thoughtful, however, to tell them you appreciate their helping you out when you feel low.

3. Ask a student to read orally the activity directions. Direct your students' attention to the stars on their sheets. Remind them to fill in the name of a special friend and why that friend shines to them. Advise them to give some thought to which special friends they will choose for their stars. When the stars have been completed, the students may then cut out the stars and present them to the recipients! Here are some alternative ideas for presenting the stars:

   - Stars are mounted on yellow bristol board with added wands (for younger students).
   - Personal cards are made from folded colored paper with the stars pasted on the cover. Inside the card, students could include either a poem written to the friends or a personal written recollection of special times in which the friends brightened them up (for older students).
   - Cooperative groups of six students pass activity sheets to one another after students have written their names on their sheets. Each star on each group member's sheet will be filled in with shining qualities others have noticed.

Bulletin Board Link:

The bulletin board caption may read "Here's How We Sparkle!" "Put a Twinkle in Someone's Eyes!" "Our Shining Stars," or "We Glitter in Grade ___." Any of the above uses of the stars may be mounted under one of these captions. For fun and sparkle, add some glitter to the stars!

STARS

There is an old tale about a Starcatcher who wanted to give something special to all her friends. She looked up at the shining stars winking back at her, giving her an idea. The stars lit up the dark sky just as her friends brightened her up when she felt sad. The Starcatcher grinned and whispered a plan, "I'll catch all those sparkling stars and give them to my friends to show them how they brighten my days!"

Do you have friends who brighten your days when you feel sad or lonely? If so, you may not be able to catch any real stars to give them like the Starcatcher did, but you can let them know how much their friendship means to you. In the stars below, fill in the names of three friends and how they shine! Cut out the stars and give them to your friends.

120

4–9. WHO'S THE BIG CHEESE?

Students who do not receive validations or boosters in their lives find it difficult to give them to others. Instead they give put-downs to others. This activity teaches students not only how to give boosters, but also the importance of giving them to others.

Materials Needed:

- "Who's the Big Cheese?" activity sheet
- Colored pencils or markers, pens

Directions:

1. Ask your class who is familiar with the phrase, "You're the big cheese!" *Responses:* "The phrase refers to someone you look up to, someone important to you." "It could refer to a friend, a mentor, a coach, a parent, a teacher, or anyone else you admire or hold in high esteem."

2. Review the term "booster" with students. The meanings, given to you by volunteers, could be written on a chart or the board. *Responses:* "A compliment." "A positive validation." "A comment given to a person that lifts him or her up." "Telling others something specific you admire." Remind students that boosters which tell people something positive about themselves on the *inside*, an admired *inner quality*, mean more than superficial compliments such as, "I like your basketball jersey." Ask how many students would prefer the booster, "I noticed how hard you worked on the used skates drive. You did a good job!" *Responses:* "I feel more proud when I get a specific booster than when I get compliments on what I'm wearing." Ask them how they feel when they *give a booster* to others. *Responses:* "I feel proud." "It feels good to give *and* to receive compliments."

3. Ask students for their meanings of the term "put-down." *Responses:* "A negative comment made to bring someone down." "To make fun of another person." "A statement made with the intention of hurting another person." Ask students to volunteer how they feel when they *receive* a put-down. *Responses:* "I feel hurt." "I feel like a loser." Ask them how they feel when they *give* a put-down to others. *Responses:* "I sometimes put someone else down because I want to look cool. But I don't usually end up feeling cool when I see how hurt the other person is." "I give put-downs to others when I feel a little jealous of them. Afterwards, I realize the put-down didn't help me by hurting others." A class discussion could follow on the topic "Reasons People Have for Putting Others Down."

4. Pass out the activity sheets. Ask for a volunteer to read the introduction at the top of the sheet and the booster examples. Ask if, while reading through the booster examples, students can think of names of people they know to put with each of the boosters. Some students may volunteer some of their names to share with the class. Ask if these names would be considered "Big Cheeses" to the students. *Response:* "Yes. These are important people to me whom I admire."

5. Direct your class to the directions at the bottom of the activity sheet. Ask them to think of four "Big Cheeses" (friends, parent[s], teacher or others they admire) to whom they would like to give boosters. Tell students to then write the booster—a positive statement about something *specific* they admire about that person—on the line next to the name of the person.

Name _____ Date _____

WHO'S THE
"BIG CHEESE?"
...YOU ARE!

Do you enjoy receiving put-downs? Not many people do. Why not give **boosters** to others instead of **put-downs**? Make others feel the way you like to feel. Make them feel special! Read the following boosters. How would each booster make *you* feel if you received one?

Boosters:

"You always take time to listen to me."
"You're a loyal friend to me."
"I've noticed how kind you are to others."
"You were such a good sport when your team lost."

Activity:

A fun way of describing someone you admire who means a lot to you is to say he or she is the **Big Cheese**. Choose four people you consider "Big Cheeses"—friends, parents, teachers, or others in your life to whom you would like to give more boosters. What would your boosters be?

PERSON: BOOSTERS:

1. _____

2. _____

3. _____

4. _____

4-10. GET IN ON THE MAGIC OF MAKING FRIENDS

There's no magic about being popular, about attracting a wide number of friends. The attractive qualities people possess are those that anyone can strive to develop. This activity points out the "magical powers" others *appear* to have that are, in reality, characteristics such as loyalty, ability to listen, sense of humor, honesty, and compatibility, to name a few. You may not be able to wave a magic wand to empower all your students to develop endearing qualities, but you can help them be aware of some desirable traits they can develop in themselves.

Materials Needed:

- "Get in on the Magic of Making Friends" activity sheet
- Pencils, pens

Directions:

1. Pass out the activity sheets to your class, telling them they are going to take an imaginary carpet ride with—guess who? *Response:* "Wilbert!" Seeing Wilbert dressed up like a magician, they will ask what he's up to now. To satisfy their amused curiosity, have them read the introduction to the activity, which explains why Wilbert has put on a magician's outfit. Wilbert had hoped to learn the magical powers to become more popular. Ask students if people who have lots of friends have hidden magic. *Responses:* "Some well-liked kids have a certain draw, almost like a magnetic attraction. It's sort of like magic, but not really, of course." "Something is different about popular kids. They almost always seem to know the right things to do and say. I know it's not magic, but sometimes it seems like they cast a magic spell!"

2. Ask the students to review some of the traits that attract them to others. As they dictate, positive traits may be written on the chalkboard. *Some responses:* "Honest, dependable, fun to be with, loyal, good listener, trustworthy, responsible, goal setter."

3. As students become aware that *anyone* can develop the positive qualities it takes to attract friends, and if they receive your encouragement, they will have taken the first step to striving for worthwhile traits that not only attract others but also make them happier within themselves. Explain that the act of being happy with yourself, by trying to do the right thing when others sometimes try to encourage the opposite, will in itself attract others to seek your company.

4. Instruct your class to choose three of the qualities or traits they feel most attracts them to others and to write these on the lines below the magic carpet. Remind students that those same traits that attract them to others will "work the same magic" attracting others to themselves!

GET IN ON THE *MAGIC* OF MAKING FRIENDS

Do you sometimes ask yourself about certain people who have lots of friends, "What magical powers do they have to attract all those friends?" There really is no magic in being a person others want as a friend. What seems like magic is their ability to know just what to do so we like to be around them a lot! Wilbert got all dressed up to learn the magical powers to be more popular. Let's explain to him what it really takes to be a good friend with no magic involved. He has the desire, so he has already begun his goal!

   Fill in the lines below the magic carpet with qualities that attract you to others, which make you want that person to be your friend. If you start to use the same qualities, **presto,** you'll have lots of friends—and so will Wilbert!

4-11. WAS MY FACE RED!

Students are able to relate to real-life situations in this activity as they role play giving boosters to victims who have been put down. Most children are able to recall times when their own faces were red from embarrassment, which is the subject for the put-down scenarios. *Empathy* or compassion for the feelings of others is an intended outcome of this activity.

Materials Needed:

- "Was My Face Red!" activity sheet
- Props for role playing *(optional)*
- Pens, pencils

Directions:

1. Ask your class to recall an experience in which they were so embarrassed their faces turned red. You may want to begin the revelations with some "Was My Face Red!" stories of your own! Those who are willing to share these experiences can then be called upon to relate them to the class. These situations will probably be more humorous than hurtful or many students may not volunteer to share them with their peers. Tell your students that in addition to humorous tales of embarrassment, there are times when people are very hurt by comments made by others. Explain that when put-downs are given that leave their victim feeling embarrassed, hurt, isolated and sad, they are certainly not humorous. Ask your class what they feel are some of the reasons people may have in putting others down. *Responses:* "People who feel good about themselves usually don't put others down." "Some people think they look 'cool' by putting others down."

2. Before you pass out the activity sheets, decide how you are going to divide your class into groups of about five or six students for the role plays. As well, plan how you will allocate the scenarios to the groups. A simple way to decide which groups perform which role plays is to give numbers to each group that correspond to the numbers of the scenarios on the activity sheets; or have students pick out colored cards.

3. **Procedure for the Role Plays:** Groups make up their own lines to include the one put-down line given on the activity sheet. The role of the student who plays the "victim" of the put-downs will be to express his or her feelings aloud to the audience after the put-downs have been given in ACT I. In ACT II, players make up all their lines, which are aimed at encouraging and boosting up the "victim." As in ACT I, the "victim" voices her or his reactions to the boosters to the audience.

4. Prepare your students for the role playing by explaining that the sheets they are going to receive are going to give them scenarios they will act out in small groups. Instruct students how to form their groups and which scenarios each group will perform. Pass out the activity sheets to your class. Explain that the purpose of the role playing is to show *empathy* (term may be written on a chart or the board), putting themselves in another person's place and experiencing the emotional feelings from the "victim's" viewpoint. Ask for a volunteer to read the introduction to the activity.

4–11. WAS MY FACE RED! (cont'd)

5. Tell the class how long (about ten minutes) groups will have to rehearse their lines for the role plays. Divide them into groups with a time by which all will be ready to return to their seats, prepared to perform their role plays. After rehearsal, students may perform their role plays.

6. As a follow-up to each role play, call upon the audience to *process the empathy they felt* while watching the put-down scenarios. Ask students the following questions, which may be written on a chart or the board for reference:

   - Could you relate to the put-down scenario? Have you had or witnessed a similar experience?
   - What were your feelings about the students who gave the put-downs?
   - How do you think the "victim" felt after receiving the put-downs?
   - How did you feel for the "victim"?
   - What boosters would you have chosen to give the "victim"?
   - How do you think the "victim" felt after receiving the boosters?

7. After all role plays have been performed and processed together as a class follow-up discussion, students may be asked to individually fill out their activity sheets, giving the boosters they would have given to the "victim" in each scenario and making up or telling about a put-down scenario of their own for step 6.

WAS MY FACE RED!

Have you been a witness to a real-life scene in which others were put down and, as a result, their embarrassed faces turned red? Did you consider how you would have felt if it had been *you* who had been put down? These are questions to consider as you prepare for your role playing. Each group will perform for the class a scenario from the real-life situations below (after rehearsal) following these instructions:

ACT I: Act out the **put-down** scenario first. Players will give put-downs to the student in the group who agrees to take the role of the "victim." After the put-downs have been given, the student faces the audience, saying how he or she feels. For example, a possible response to scenario #3: "I feel so out of it. I'm ashamed of the clothes I'm wearing. I feel hurt and all alone."

ACT II: Act out the **booster** scenario, in which several group members now give both *verbal* and *nonverbal* (a hug, a pat on the back, or an arm around the shoulders of a discouraged person works wonders!) boosters to the "victim" to make her or him feel better. After these statements and gestures have been given, the "victim" faces the audience, saying how he or she now feels. Possible responses: "I don't feel so down any more. Somebody cares about me."

After all the scenarios have been role played, fill in the boosters you would have given to the "victims" in the lines on the next page.

127

WAS MY FACE RED! (cont'd)

Put-down scenarios to role play:

1. A player is cut from a sports team. Several players who made the team say, "What a loser! You didn't even make the team!" What boosters would you give to make the "victim" feel better?

   _____

   _____

2. A student receives a "D" on a math test. Two kids at nearby desks say, "How many 'D's' does that make this term?" What would you say or do to boost up this student?

   _____

   _____

3. A group makes fun of a student who is wearing clothing that is too small, laughing and saying to the student, "You look like a GEEK in those clothes!" What could you say to boost up this student's spirits?

   _____

   _____

4. A group of kids is laughing and making rude comments to a student new to the school whose first language is not English. They say, "You're a HOOT when you try to speak English in class." What could you do to make the student feel more comfortable?

   _____

   _____

5. Make up your own real-life put-down scenario. Write how you would boost up the "victim." Use the back of this sheet for your scenario and boosters.

   _____

   _____

4–12. DO YOU EVER GET LONELY?

In this activity, students learn to accept responsibility for their feelings of exclusion and loneliness. The connection is made between their social skills and others choosing to be or not to be with them. Once they accept the fact that building friendships depends on a certain group of skills, they can begin to develop those skills.

Materials Needed:

- "Do You Ever Get Lonely?" activity sheet
- Pens, pencils

Directions:

1. Begin the discussion of loneliness by asking (without a show of hands) if students ever feel lonely. Assure them that everyone feels lonely at times; however, if they feel lonely to the point that they feel really down, they *can* do something to alleviate their loneliness. Tell students to ask themselves why others are choosing not to be with them while they go through this "checklist" of social skills.

2. Pass the activity sheets to your class. Explain to your students the difference between the need to be alone at times to relax, to listen to music, to read, to dream, etc., and the loneliness felt when they feel nobody cares or wants to be with them. Refer them to the "Check Out the Action Below" section on their sheets; these statements should be filled out individually. Tell students the results will not be shared with the rest of the class.

3. Processing the correct responses to these statements is an activity that could be best done as a whole-class activity. This way, the anonymity of individual answers could remain intact. Discuss each statement with volunteers contributing their comments about each one. The following points should be made about the statements that are *not checked* on the sheets:

    #2 and #4: Ask students why these are not friendship builders. *Responses:* "Kids won't really respect you if you don't have any values of your own and if you seem desperate to be part of the group." "If a group asks you to do something you don't believe in, do you really want to be part of it?"

    #6: Responses: "Overeating and too much passive entertainment just covers up my loneliness." "I need to get out and do the things I need to do to make friends instead of bingeing and vegging out."

    #7: Responses: "Finding out I do drugs isn't going to attract the kind of friends I want to be with." "Drugs are a way to avoid my real problem of attracting friends."

    #9: Responses: "Do I really want to be part of a group that makes fun of someone?" "If I have to do something I don't really believe in to be part of a group, I'd better rethink if it's worth it to me to be 'in' with them."

4. Students may enjoy making up role plays in small groups for each of the statements.

Do you ever get Lonely?

Do you ever feel lonely? Do you have times when you feel nobody really cares about you? Chances are, you gave an answer like, "Sort of." "Yes!" or "Too much!" Instead of lying around feeling sorry for yourself, why not pick yourself up and do something about your loneliness? How? First of all, understand the difference between loneliness and being alone. Kids need to be alone sometimes. If you are alone most of the time because you have no friends, it's time to *get started on building friendships.*

Put a *check* in front of the statements you **agree with**. (Check bottom of page for responses.)

_____ 1. Listen to what others are saying to you without thinking about whether or not they like you and what you're going to say next.

_____ 2. Do anything to please as long as you are accepted into the group.

_____ 3. Get involved with things you love to do and share your interests with others.

_____ 4. Kids may not like you if you don't try something new with them, even if you feel it's against some of your values.

_____ 5. Reach out to do things with others who share your interests. Maybe they're lonely, too.

_____ 6. When you feel lonely, eat plenty of junk food, watch endless hours of TV, videos and play video games to make you feel better.

_____ 7. Use drugs to ease the pain of loneliness.

_____ 8. Start a conversation with someone you've been wanting to get to know. Look for things you have in common for conversation starters.

_____ 9. Go along with an "in" group (you've been dying to join!) making fun of someone so you will have a laugh together. Then they might decide you're cool and accept you into their group.

_____10. Smile. Be positive. People are drawn to "up" people who are high on life—not drugs.

If you checked #'s 1, 3, 5, 8 and 10, *you checked out!* Others will be attracted to you, so you won't be lonely much longer! If you didn't check these numbers, decide if you want to develop the above ideas and, if you do, practice them.

4–13. BETWEEN FRIENDS

The aim of the following activities is to emphasize the importance of letting friends know they are special to you and *why*. Students also have the opportunity to role play various conflict situations that may arise between friends.

Materials Needed:

- "Between Friends" activity sheet
- Colored pencils, pens, crayons
- Photos of friends *(optional)*
- Props for role playing *(optional)*

Directions:

This activity sheet lends itself to several possible uses with students. Choose from the list below of suggestions for students. Instruct your students to:

- Fill the frame with photos or drawings of friends, including yourself, doing things together.
- Write a poem about friendship dedicated to a special friend.
- Compose a letter written to a chosen friend, recalling special times shared together.
- Write your solutions to the How Would *You* Handle "Between Friends" Scenarios?
- Form pairs of students, each of which will rehearse and perform a role play from the "Between Friends" Scenarios. Students should also be given the option of creating their own real-life situations, which should be written up in the format of the other situations for this activity and accepted by you before they rehearse and role play.

Music Link:

"Between Friends" by Richard Samuels

How Would *You* Handle "Between Friends" Scenarios?

1. Your friend shows up twenty minutes late to meet you to play wall ball. The week before, this same friend arrived late, causing you both to miss the movie you'd planned to see. You have to be home and now only have ten minutes left to play. How would you handle this situation?

2. You and your friend have been renting videos together every Friday afternoon for three weeks. The other two trips to the video store, your friend excitedly chose the video, saying you'd love it too. You split the cost of the video both times. On the third trip, you decide to choose the video you want. Instead, before you know it, you are going to the counter with your friend's choice again! How would you handle this situation?

4–13. BETWEEN FRIENDS (cont'd)

3. Your friend has been in a bad mood a lot lately and you appear to be the target! But you can't think of anything you have done to upset this friend. You've really tried to overlook the moods and negative reactions to anything you suggest doing together. How would you handle this situation?

4. You confided a family secret to your friend one day when you were feeling upset about your situation at home. Your single mom had just lost her job, but you didn't want anyone else to know all the details about it. When you arrive at school the next day, it turns out that several kids know all about it! How would you handle this situation?

5. Your best friend and a "sort-of" friend of yours have both gone to the mall together Saturday afternoon. *You* were NOT asked to go! Every other Saturday you and your best friend have hung out together. You spend the day all alone because you didn't make other plans. How would you handle this situation?

6. **EXTRA!** You loaned your friend money—$2.50—several weeks ago (three weeks and four days ago, but who's counting??). The money has not been paid back or even mentioned since then. You don't know whether to bring it up or not. You tell yourself it isn't a large amount of money and this is a very good friend. Then why do you keep thinking about it? How would you handle this situation?

4–14. FRAZZLED FRIES

Wilbert made a message on his fries with ketchup, then he dropped them! Can you put the message back together for him? *Hint:* The message is something Wilbert is trying to do to be a better friend. Write the message on Wilbert's sign. The answer is upside down at the bottom of the page.

HELP!

MY MESSAGE ABOUT
A FRIEND IS:

_____ _____ _____ _____ _____.

FRIES

A FRIEND LISTENS TO ME.

5

Goal Setting

GOAL SETTING

Rationale:

After students have formed foundations in the areas of security, positive identity and friendship building, they are ready to set aims for themselves—the skills involved in goal setting, the next building component of self-esteem.

Goals:

Goal setting enables students to:

- Set specific goals.
- Set measurable goals.
- Set realistic goals.
- Set achievable goals.
- Write goals.
- Visualize goals.
- Problem-solve roadblocks.

Intended Outcome Statements for Students:

- "It's possible to turn my dreams into reality. I can achieve them if I use my goal-setting skills."
- "If I write down my goals, I am much more likely to achieve them."
- "If roadblocks or problems get in my way, I'm ready for them! I can think of new, creative ways to solve them."
- "I put a picture of my goal next to my written goal so I can visualize myself reaching it."
- "I used to have a lot of good ideas but they never worked until I began to put them into specific, realistic goals I can achieve."
- "I set goals by which I can measure my progress."
- "Most of my goals are a bit out of my reach, but not so far that I can't reach them."
- "I know what my time wasters are now and how they can mess up my goal planning."
- "I break my long-term goals into short-term goals on a weekly plan."
- "I review how I did the past week reaching my goals, what I let get in my way, and what I'll do differently this week to reach my goals."
- "I thought about areas I never really tried to improve before that I will now set as goals."
- "I learned not to let anything get in the way of my doing the most important things on my daily goal schedule."
- "I know a new, inventive way to find solutions for problems after learning creative problem solving."

5–1. DIRECTIONS FOR THE GOAL-SETTING QUIZ

This quiz may be used as a pre-test before Goal Setting is introduced in your classroom. After you feel your students have completed a sufficient number of goal-setting activities, the quiz may again be given and the results compared with the pre-test.

Below are the goal-setting skills you are assessing. If a student answer differs from the list below, it may indicate a weakness in that area and you will know specifically how to strengthen his or her goal-setting skills.

Goal-setting Skills enable students to:

- **Set specific goals**
- **Set measurable goals**
- **Set realistic goals**
- **Set achievable goals**
- **Write goals**
- **Visualize goals**
- **Problem-solve roadblocks**

Answer Key:

1. NO; All areas
2. NO; Written-out goals
3. YES; All areas
4. NO; Problem-solve roadblocks
5. YES; Specific goals
6. YES; Problem-solve roadblocks
7. YES; Measurable goals
8. NO; Problem-solve roadblocks
9. YES; Realistic goals
10. YES; Visualized goals

- -

Teacher Evaluation—Notes on Weak Areas:

Student: _____ Date: _____

Observed behavior in the area of: _____

My plan to help strengthen that area: _____

_____

STUDENT GOAL-SETTING QUIZ

Directions: Circle YES or NO depending how you *usually* feel about the statement. Your answers will not be shared with the rest of the class.

YES NO 1. A good idea and a goal are the same thing.

YES NO 2. Writing down your goals is a waste of time.

YES NO 3. Goal setting will help me plan to buy a new headset.

YES NO 4. When I don't reach my goal right away, I give up and stop trying.

YES NO 5. Goals need to be specific or exactly what you want to achieve.

YES NO 6. I try to plan for problems that may get in the way of reaching my goal.

YES NO 7. I choose goals I can measure so I can check to see how I'm doing.

YES NO 8. If problems get in the way of my goal, I usually just give up on it.

YES NO 9. My goals are things I can really reach.

YES NO 10. When you set a goal, if you include a picture of what you look like reaching your goal, you will have a better chance of reaching it.

Why I answered YES or NO on number(s):

_____

_____

_____

_____

_____

_____

Here are some of my ideas that can help me set goals:

_____

_____

_____

_____

_____

_____

5–2. DREAM AND REACH FOR THE STARS!

Before teaching goal setting, students need to realize that goals begin with dreams they have about what they want to achieve. Students should be *encouraged to dream* and to believe that they *can* accomplish their dreams!

Materials Needed:

- "Dream and Reach for the Stars" activity sheet
- Pens, pencils

Directions:

1. Ask your students if they like to dream about things they would like to have and what they want to achieve. Encourage volunteers to share their dreams with the class. Write student responses on a chart or the board. Explain that dreaming is the first step in goal setting because without dreams we would not have reasons to form goals for ourselves. Ask your class about a child who is discouraged from dreaming by being told he or she can't possibly achieve the dream. Ask if the child should give up on his or her dream. *Responses:* "No. You can if YOU believe you can." "You shouldn't let anybody stop you from dreaming."

2. Distribute the activity sheets to your class. Encourage students to write out some of the dreams they feel they can reach. As an example, recall that Neil Armstrong, the first person to set foot on the moon, may have written his dream as "I want to be the first man on the moon." Would others have laughed at his dream? *Responses:* "A lot of people wouldn't have believed him. They would have told him he couldn't do it." Ask students if that should have stood in the way of Neil Armstrong setting his goal of being the first man on the moon. *Response:* "He went ahead and set his goal even when others did not believe he could accomplish it. And he did it!" Ask students whether he would have been the first man to set foot on the moon if he had not first had a dream.

Language Arts Link:

Paper cut in the shapes of large clouds could be used for students' poetry about dreaming. Ask your students to write a poem or story about their dreams and how they can reach for the stars. Or, ask them to write an "Act as if . . . " story about one of their dreams coming true. For example, if one of their dreams is of graduating from their present school with a certain average, say a "B," have them write about what it feels like to them to have achieved their dream, who is with them (if anyone), and how all of them are reacting to the accomplishment.

Bulletin Board Link:

Large clouds or stars with students' dreams are hung under the caption "Dare to Dream," "We Can Reach Our Dreams," or "We Reach for the Stars!" along with a large (smiling) star either containing each student's name in the class or decorated with glitter.

Dream and Reach for the Stars

Think of some dreams you have about things you would like to do. You create your own visions of what you want to accomplish. When planning goals for yourself, paint the best pictures you can! Below write three of your dreams that you would like to turn into goals. Remember, goals start out as dreams, so don't ever stop dreaming!

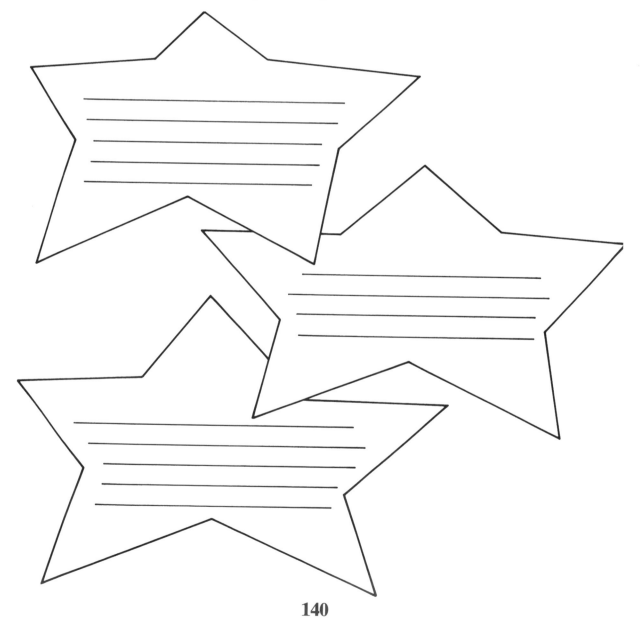

5–3. S–T–R–E–T–C–H YOURSELF

Becoming aware of our "comfort zones" that keep us from trying something new is the aim of this activity. We need to realize that we sometimes fear taking a risk, which may take us out of our comfort zones. Once we overcome this fear, which holds us back in certain areas of our lives, we can then set goals in areas in which we can expand our accomplishments.

Materials Needed:

- "S–T–R–E–T–C–H Yourself" activity sheet
- Pens, pencils

Directions:

1. Introduce this activity by telling your class they are going to do a hand activity. Ask students to clasp both their hands together. Ask them which thumb is on top. After noting their different responses, tell them to shake out their hands and then ask them to again fold their hands together—this time with the *thumb that had been on the top* now placed *under* the other thumb. The thumbs will simply be reversed from the first hand folding. Ask how the new hand folding feels. *Responses:* "Uncomfortable." "Weird. I liked it better the first time." Ask students why they felt weird the second time and liked the first time better. *Responses:* "It was comfortable because it's the way I've always done it." "I didn't like the change. I'd rather keep on doing it the comfortable way." If they were to continue folding their hands the new "uncomfortable" way for the rest of the day and for several more days, how would it begin to feel? *Response:* "Once you'd get used to folding your hands the new way, it would start to feel more comfortable." Explain that this activity is an example of how we all prefer to do things the comfortable way, the way we have always done them. We enjoy being in our comfort zones. We prefer not to get out of our comfort zones because it will take a while to get used to the new way. We feel comfortable with the old way!

2. Pass out the activity sheets to your class. They will spot Wilbert on a giraffe, looking pleased with himself. Their sheets include the explanation that Wilbert was told he needed to stretch himself, so he tried to do so by riding a giraffe! After having activity directions read, ask for volunteers who will tell about an area they would like *to go for* or to stretch. *Responses:* "I've always wanted to sing in a choir." "I didn't try out for the soccer team." Ask what has held the student back. If parental permission or health reasons have been a factor, explain that these are valid reasons for not trying. Otherwise, tell students that areas in which they would like to stretch, once identified, may then be set as goals to be achieved.

3. Instruct your class to check off the areas on the activity sheet they want to try as new activities or to improve. Encourage them to add other areas of interest if not already included on this list.

Name _____ Date _____

S-T-R-E-T-C-H YOURSELF

Are there things you would like to do but have never tried? Or given up when you didn't succeed the first time? Think of some areas of your life you would like to improve or learn something new, ways you can S-T-R-E-T-C-H yourself or grow in some way. Use the categories below to help you plan. This is the first step to goal setting. Once you know what you want to do, you can set specific goals to get there!

    Check off areas and then write what you would like to do in that area to improve or *stretch* yourself. Add your own if they don't appear below.

_____ Drama _____

_____ Music _____

_____ Art _____

_____ Reading _____

_____ Computer _____

_____ History _____

_____ Sports _____

_____ Collections _____

_____ Hobbies _____

_____ Science _____

_____ Social _____

_____ Family _____

_____ Personal Qualities _____

_____ (your choice) _____

_____ (your choice) _____

5–4. TIME TO GET SET

Deciding what will be the most important activities of their day, their *priorities*, and planning time accordingly are the aims of this activity. Time wasters that interfere with important activities are identified. Managing time for completion of important tasks is a life skill that will be useful to all students.

Materials Needed:

- "Time to Get Set" activity sheet
- Pencils, pens

Directions:

1. Ask students to identify what they can lose and know they will never get back. Give them the hint that the answer is something intangible, nothing they can physically hold. It may be several responses before you may receive the answer you are looking for, which is "time." Discuss with the class that although you can never get time back once you lose it, you can plan better so you don't continue to waste it.

2. Pass the activity sheets to your students. Ask a volunteer to read the top of the activity sheet.

3. Introduce the term *priority* by writing it on a chart or the board or, with younger students, you may prefer to use the term # ONE to describe the most important thing to do.

4. Copy the three columns shown on the activity sheet onto a chart or the board. The headings, as on the sheets, will read:

   - Here are the most important things I have to do today . . .
   - Here is what I'm planning to do today . . .
   - This is a good use of my time because . . .

   Fill in the columns with several students volunteering to have their plans used as examples. If plans for the most important things to be done do not coincide with what they are planning to do, ask them to change their plans to make the most important thing a **priority** or the **# ONE** thing that must be completed that day. "This is a good use of my time because . . . " should report the most important thing that has been completed. If it does not, ask the student what he or she *made* more important. Responsibility and choices may be discussed at this point. Nobody else made them go to a movie when they had planned to study for math—or playing video games instead of completing a task a parent asked them to do.

5. When you feel students have an understanding of what are the most important things they have to do and what they are *planning* to do, tell them to choose three things they consider the three most important things they want to do. To help them with this, say, "If you could only complete three things you really need to do, what would those three things be?" Tell them to then write what they plan to do and why it is a good use of their time. Ask them to evaluate their sheets the following day and observe whether they stuck to their three most important things. If not, ask them to do the activity sheet again and try not to *choose* to let other things get in their way.

TIME TO GET SET

If You Lose a Book, You May Get It Back—But . . . .
You Won't Get Back Time You Waste!

Learn how to use time so that you don't waste it. Every day make the best use of your time by asking yourself these questions:

- What are the most important things I have to do today?
- What am I planning to do today?

If your answers to these questions show you are not planning to do what's most important, stop and change your plans. Use this table to check if you are planning to use your time wisely:

Here are the most important things I have to do today	Here is what I'm planning to do today	This is a good use of my time because . . .

5–5. DON'T GET BOWLED OVER

Identifying time wasters is the aim of this activity. Time wasters can get in the way of achieving our goals. We sometimes put off something we need to do and instead choose another activity to take its place. Learning to eliminate time wasters will help students accomplish their goals.

Materials Needed:

- "Don't Get Bowled Over" activity sheet
- Pencils, pens

Directions:

1. Ask your students to raise their hands if they have ever put off something they needed to do by doing something else instead. Most likely, everyone will raise their hands. Assure them most people do put things off sometimes, especially when they prefer to be doing something more pleasant. As an example to students, if they have a history exam the next day and their favorite TV show comes on, they can choose to watch it *or* study for an hour. The key word here is "choose." Explain that they choose how to spend their time between the end of school and bedtime. Ask students if it would be okay to watch their favorite TV shows the night before an exam and, if so, under what conditions. *Response:* "Yes. If you have already studied history all week, reviewed it earlier that evening before the show and plan to review again after the show, so that you will be well prepared for the exam. The show could be planned as your relaxation hour."

2. Pass out the activity sheets to your class. Explain that they are to keep a log of their time after school for the next three days of school (if a weekend interrupts, have students continue the log on Monday.) This log will help them identify exactly how they spend their time between school and bedtime. Explain that you expect relaxation activities such as video games, TV, talking on the phone, etc., to be included in their logs; there is a difference between *relaxation time*, which everyone needs in order to work effectively, and procrastinating or *wasting time* by putting off what we need to do by doing something else. Advise students that time both for relaxation and for purposeful activities must be planned in their daily schedules.

3. After students have filled out their logs for three days, ask them to write their time wasters under the bowling pins at the bottom of the activity sheet. Tell them they will have completed the first step in ridding themselves of the time wasters, which is *identifying them.* You could suggest that if, for example, their time wasters seem to occur about the same time each day when they have planned to study, to choose that time period for relaxation instead of making it a study period. They could schedule their study time after they have relaxed. Ask what else they can do to avoid their time wasters. Discuss together students' suggestions for better use of their time after school. Write their responses on a chart or the board.

DON'T GET BOWLED OVER

When you put off something you need to do by doing something else, you are wasting your time. Time wasters can really mess up your schedule if you don't plan your time daily to include relaxation as well as steps toward goals you want to reach. After keeping a log for three days from the end of school to bedtime on the chart below, write your time wasters under the pins below. Instead of getting bowled over by them, **strike them out** of your future plans!

DAY ONE		**DAY TWO**		**DAY THREE**	
Time	Activity	Time	Activity	Time	Activity

END OF DAY!

My time wasters were:

_____

_____

_____

5–6. "COMPUTING MY GOALS" BOOK

The following pages may be bound together to make a personal goals book for each student. The books enable students to set specific, measurable, achievable goals and then keep track of daily, weekly, and monthly progress. Students also chart their past performances and evaluate changes that could improve their future efforts.

Materials Needed:

- Activity sheets: "Computing My Goals' Book Cover Page," "Compute Your Goals," "How Do You Compute?" "Computing My Goals for the Month," "Dazzling Discs," "Face the Fax," and "I'm Computing a Jam!"
- Stapler, paper clips, thumbtacks or other attachments to bind goal books; hole puncher for notebook placement, if preferred
- Colored pencils, markers, pens, pencils
- Magazines or newspapers for illustrations to be cut out; scissors

Directions for Goal Book Pages:

1. *COVER PAGE: Computing My Goals Book*—Names are filled in. Two cover choices are provided.

2. *PAGE ONE: Compute Your Goals*—This page serves as a handy reference included in students' goals books to provide a reminder of the goal-setting steps while they are completing their goal books.

3. *PAGE TWO: How Do You Compute?*—The difference between a *good idea* and a *goal* is the topic of this activity. A *good idea* may happen any time or it may not happen at all. A *goal*, on the other hand, is formed by turning a good idea into an aim that is measurable (progress must be determined), achievable (reaching it must be realistic), specific (achievement must be exact), a date by which they will achieve it, and who or what they need to help them reach their goals.

4. *PAGE THREE: Computing My Goals for the Month*—This monthly calendar provides students with goal planning for the entire month.

5. *PAGE FOUR: Dazzling Discs*—Students write out their weekly goals. If they are working toward a long-term goal, they may break it down into weekly goals. For example, if a goal is to graduate from the school they are now attending with grades one letter higher than they are now receiving, their weekly goals may include the extra time spent studying each day of the week as well as any extra help to be given, when and by whom in order to work toward that long-term goal. Or, the goal may be short term. For example, the students may have something they would like to buy so they may set a goal of how they are going to raise the money to buy the item. Under the discs, students write out their daily goals for one week. While forming their daily goals, students ask themselves the following questions, which are written on a chart or the board:
   - What will I do to reach my goal?
   - What or whom do I need to help me reach my goal?

5–6. "COMPUTING MY GOALS" BOOK (cont'd)

- What might get in the way of my getting my goal?
- What do I look like reaching my goal? Pictures of how you look and feel reaching your goals are drawn or an illustration cut out and placed inside the disc at the bottom of the page to be visualized daily.

At the end of each day, students may draw faces in the center of the discs to display their feelings toward the progress they have made that day (happy, so-so, unhappy). If the progress was not as they would have liked, students should ask themselves, "What could I have done differently?"

6. *PAGE FIVE: Face the Fax*—Students write goals they have completed or made progress toward completing the previous week. This provides a review of what may have gotten in the way of their achieving their goals, time wasters, and the opportunity to plan how to avoid them the following week.

7. *PAGE SIX: I'm Computing a Jam*—Students consider possible roadblocks or problems that may get in the way of achieving their goals and how they will deal with them.

"COMPUTING MY GOALS" BOOK

NAME: _____

"COMPUTING MY GOALS" BOOK

NAME:

_____

COMPUTE YOUR GOALS

Step 1. Decide *what you want to do or reach* and make it your GOAL. For example, you may want a new headset. What will you do to reach your goal?

Step 2. Make sure your goal is *realistic*. It may be a bit out of reach but it must be something you *can* reach. Don't get in over your head.

Step 3. There are two types of goals: *long-term goals*, like graduating from high school, and *short-term goals*, like improving your next report card by bringing each grade up one letter.

Step 4. Moving toward your goals is like climbing a ladder. Your goal is to get to the top of the ladder, but to get there you have to *climb one step at a time*.

Step 5. The most important thing you can do to reach your goals is to *write them out*.

Step 6. Your goal is where you are headed but you will never get anywhere unless you have *a plan* to get there.

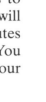

Step 7. Set *specific* goals you can *measure*. If your goal is to become a better reader, write out how much extra time you will spend each day to improve your reading. Will it be 15 minutes every weekday? Don't just say, "I'm going to read more." You won't be able to measure whether you are moving towards your goal.

Step 8. *Cut out an illustration* or *draw yourself reaching your goal* so that you have a *picture in your mind*. Remember, YOU CAN IF YOU BELIEVE YOU CAN!

Step 9. Nobody reaches his or her goal magically. Ask yourself daily, "Am I really working hard to reach my goal?"

Step 10. Write down what you did that got you closer to your goal. Don't worry if you make some mistakes. Learn from your mistakes by asking yourself what you are going to change to make sure the same problem doesn't come up again.

Step 11. Share your goals with friends who also have goals so you can encourage each other.

Step 12. Remember, setting goals will help you become the very best person you can be. Reach for the top of your abilities!

HOW DO YOU COMPUTE?

Do you have some good ideas you would like to achieve? Write three of your good ideas below. Choose one of them to turn into a goal. Put a check in front of the number you choose.

1. _____

2. _____

3. _____

Now get real about your goal by asking yourself if you will be able to reach it. Make sure you can check out your progress. In the lines corresponding to the letters below, answer the following questions:

A. What do you want to achieve?

B. By when do you plan to achieve it?

C. What or whom do you need to help you achieve it?

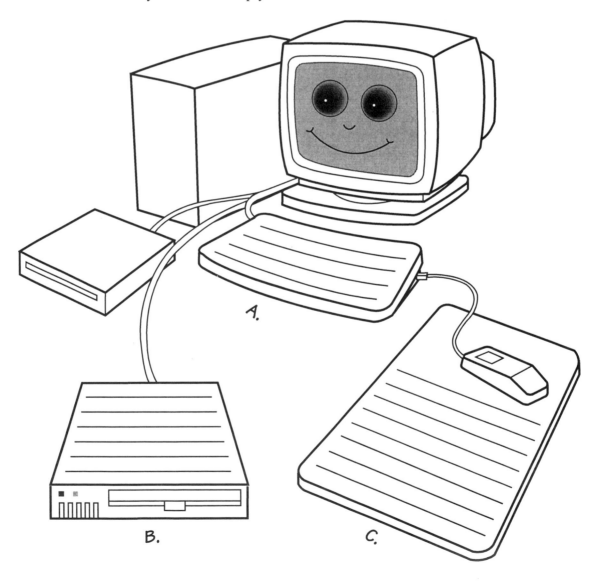

GOAL FOR IT !!!

Computing my goals for the month of _____

Sunday	Monday	Tuesday	Wednesday	Thursday	Friday	Saturday

DAZZLING DISCS

Below are some ROM (Right On the Mark) discs. Stay on your mark as you write your daily goals for one week. Draw or cut out an illustration to place in the disc at the bottom of the page of you dazzling yourself by achieving your goals for the week! At the end of each day, draw a small face showing how you feel about your daily progress in the center of that day's ROM disc. Before you form your daily goals, ask yourself:

- What will I do to get closer to my goal?
- How much time will I spend each day?
- What or whom will I need to help me?
- Will anything get in the way of reaching my goal? If so, how will I handle it?

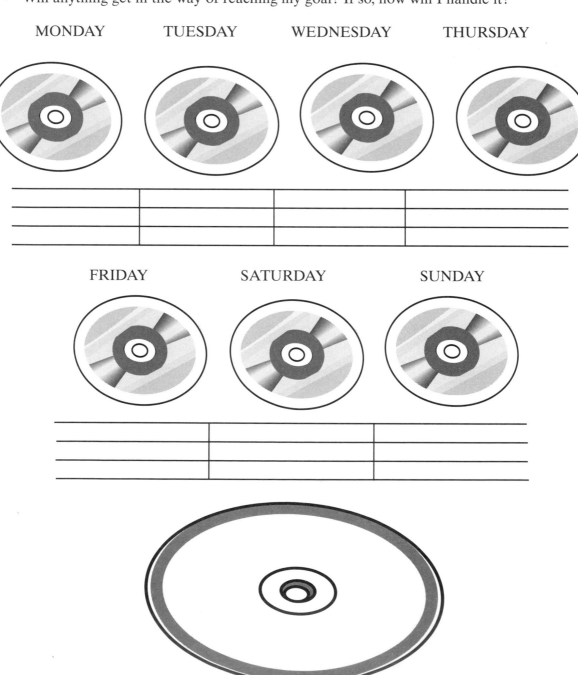

FACE THE FAX

Which of your goals did you make last week? Send a fax about your goals and take a look at how you can improve any days you fell short of making your goals. Face the fax and evaluate how you did.

Sunday _____

Monday _____

Tuesday _____

Wednesday _____

Thursday _____

Friday _____

Saturday _____

I'M COMPUTING A JAM!

Have you ever been working on a computer that jammed just before you finished your program? The computer jam was an obstacle or "roadblock" that got in your way. While working towards your goals, you may find things get in your way. The disc below is programmed for any jams that may come up when you are going for your goals. If you are experiencing a jam, follow the problem-solving steps below and write your solution in the spaces below, which correspond to each of the problem-solving steps.

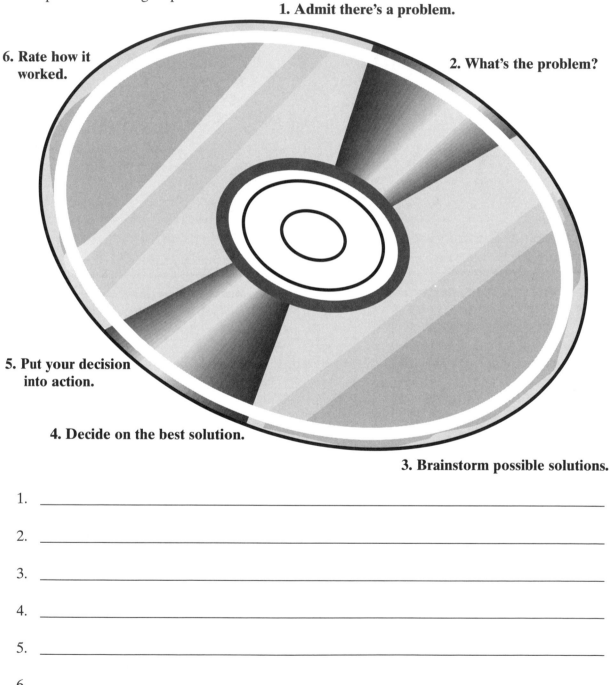

1. Admit there's a problem.

6. Rate how it worked.

2. What's the problem?

5. Put your decision into action.

4. Decide on the best solution.

3. Brainstorm possible solutions.

1. _____

2. _____

3. _____

4. _____

5. _____

6. _____

5-7. LOOK AT IT FROM A DIFFERENT ANGLE (PART I)

The quote, "Creativity is the ability to look at the same thing as everybody else but to see something different," by Charles Thompson, sums up the aim of this activity. Once students learn to stretch their minds to include inventive ways to solve problems, creative problem solving will be a life skill they will always have.

Materials Needed:

- "Look at It from a Different Angle (Part I)" activity sheet
- Pencils, pens
- The above quotation written on a chart or the board

Directions:

1. Discuss the above quotation with your class. Ask them for times when they thought of a new approach to solving a problem that nobody else thought of. Responses will vary. Announce that they are going to be thinking in a different way for this activity. Discuss the term "creative." Ask students for their meanings of the word. *Responses:* "New." "Original." "Inventors are creative because they create new things from ideas that weren't thought of before." The formal definition of the term is, "Stimulating the imagination and inventive powers."

2. Distribute the activity sheets to your students. Ask a volunteer to read the introduction to the activity. Assure them that the solutions that work show they are learning to think creatively, using a new approach to problem solving. If students' answers do not work, it does not mean they are wrong, just that they are on their way to finding a creative solution! Remind them that sometimes it takes several different "brainstorming" sessions to come up with a solution that works. Students may work on the problems individually or you may choose to have students form cooperative groups to brainstorm together possible solutions to the problems.

3. The solutions shown below are simply ones that have been most commonly given. There are many more possibilities creative minds will invent! If we, as educators, want students to begin to think creatively, we need to keep open minds to many different solutions. For example, item 2, the oats problem, was given to a group of students. A student replied, "A rat was added to the bag." The answer most frequently given is, "A hole." After being questioned how a rat could *subtract* five pounds from the bag of oats, the student explained that *the rat would have eaten five pounds of oats, making the bag five pounds lighter.* (Of course!) Thus, the following solutions are mentioned solely because of their frequency:

   1. Make applesauce (apple pie, cobbler, muffins, etc.).
   2. A hole.
   3. No days. You can't dig up a field that has already been dug up.
   4. They were each playing other partners, not each other.
   5. As long as the solutions creatively solve their problems, they work.

LOOK AT IT FROM A DIFFERENT ANGLE (PART I)

It's been said that once you begin to think *creatively*, your mind will continue to think up new ways for you to solve your problems. There are no wrong answers to the problems below *if your solution works!* For example, when you read the "apples" problem, like others who have just begun creative problem solving, you may try to give a mathematical solution. Don't! Look for a different way to solve it! Then go on to solve the other problems, letting your mind brainstorm possible solutions for creative problem solving.

1. Problem Situation:

How would you divide nine apples equally among ten nursery school kids you are entertaining at your little brother's birthday party? Each child is asking for an equal amount and you cannot disappoint any one of them, including your little brother (who also asks for his equal share.)

My Creative Solution Is: _____

_____

_____

2. Problem Situation:

A bag of flour weighed 20 pounds. After someone came along and put something into the bag, the bag weighed only 15 pounds. What was put into the bag?

My Creative Solution Is: _____

_____

_____

3. Problem Situation: (Is it getting easier to think in a new way?)

If it took five workers one day to dig up a field, how long will it take ten workers to dig up the same field?

My Creative Solution Is: _____

_____

_____

Name _____ Date _____

LOOK AT IT FROM A DIFFERENT ANGLE
(PART I) (cont'd)

4. Problem Situation:

Two kids were playing chess. They played five games and each of them won the same number. How could that be? (Nice try! There were no ties!!)

My Creative Solution Is: _____

_____

_____

5. Problem Situation: Your Choice!!

_____

_____

_____

_____

_____

My Creative Solution Is: _____

_____

_____

5–8. LOOK AT IT FROM A DIFFERENT ANGLE (PART II)

It has been said that once our mind is stretched to a new idea, it never quite goes back to the same dimensions. Now that students have had an opportunity to explore creative problem solving in Part I, they will enjoy further problems to solve in Part II.

Materials Needed:

- "Look at It from a Different Angle (Part II)" activity sheet
- Previously completed "Look at It from a Different Angle (Part I)" activity sheet
- Pens, pencils

Directions:

1. Pass out the activity sheets to your class. Announce to them that they will be doing more creative problem solving. Decide whether you will divide the class into cooperative groups or ask them to work on their problems on the activity sheet individually. As in the previous creative problem-solving activity, stress that it is the creative effort you are encouraging, not whether or not they necessarily arrive at an answer that works. Some students may quickly arrive at creative solutions that work; students who have done creative problem solving previously (in previous classes or at home with their families) will process solutions to these problems more quickly than those students who have had no experience in this area. Once they learn the process, however, they will then be at the same level. It is important that those with experience do not give away the solutions orally until the inexperienced children have had an opportunity to learn the process.

2. The following solutions are simply the most frequently given or most obvious. Be open to any solution that differs from those below by asking students to tell you more about why their solutions would work. You will enjoy some of the creative ideas they invent! Some possible solutions are:

    1. A snowman had melted and left behind in the yard two prunes (his eyes), five dates (his smile), the carrot (his nose), and the scarf he had worn. A person already living in the building or in the neighborhood would probably have noticed the snowman before and would not have wondered, as the visitor did, why these items were lying on the ground.

    2. How would the cab driver have known where to take the politician if he could not hear where he wanted to go?

    3. George and Georgia were goldfish in a pet store. The pet store owner closed the store at 9:00 P.M. and reopened it at 9:00 A.M. the next morning. The owner found them dead on the floor beside their broken goldfish bowl. Nearby was an empty cage that had been tipped over to let a puppy loose. In his excitement, the puppy knocked the bowl over and drank the water from the bowl.

    4. The man was flying alone in his plane when it exploded in the air. He had time to parachute out, but died of a heart attack on the way down. The cloth was his silk parachute.

    5. The emphasis here is that the students *think creatively*. Because this is a new process for most students, their problems may begin very simply. As long as they are creative and have reasonably workable solutions, students should be encouraged.

LOOK AT IT FROM A DIFFERENT ANGLE
(PART II)

Now that you are thinking in inventive ways, try some more creative problem solving. Remember, you are trying to reach a solution that works. Let your creativity go!

1. Problem Situation:

Two prunes, five dates, a carrot, and a scarf are lying in the yard in front of an apartment building. A visitor arrives at the building and wonders why these things are there. You know there is a reason for their being there. What do you tell the visitor?

My Creative Solution Is: _____

_____

_____

2. Problem Situation:

A New York cab driver picked up a politician whose political ideas he did not agree with. In order to avoid a huge argument, he pretended to be unable to hear. Arriving at his destination, the politician paid the driver, got out, and then realized the cab driver could not have been unable to hear or speak. How did he figure it out?

My Creative Solution Is: _____

_____

_____

3. Problem Situation:

George and Georgia are lying on the floor. They died 12 hours ago. Nobody was in the room when they died. Nine hours after they died, the person returned to find them dead. They were not poisoned and there were no marks on their bodies, although broken glass was found nearby.

My Creative Solution Is: _____

_____

_____

LOOK AT IT FROM A DIFFERENT ANGLE
(PART II) (cont'd)

4. Problem Situation:

A man was found dead in the forest with a piece of cloth beside him. He had not been murdered nor did he commit suicide. He had no broken bones, bruises, cuts, bites, or symptoms of disease. How did he die?

My Creative Solution Is: _____

_____

_____

5. Problem Situation: Your Choice!!

_____

_____

_____

_____

_____

My Creative Solution Is: _____

_____

_____

_____

GOAL
SETTING

FRIENDSHIP
BUILDING

CONFLICT
SOLVING

POSITIVE
IDENTITY

COMPET

SECURITY

6
Competence

COMPETENCE

Rationale:

Student are ready for building the self-esteem component of competence following the formation of security, positive identity, friendship building, and goal-setting skills. They have an "I can!" attitude and are then able, after having built a securely positive self-image, to look beyond their own needs toward the needs of others. They are more capable of making responsible decisions and avoiding peer pressure when it goes against their own values.

Goals:

Competence building enables students to develop the skills of:

- Responsible decision making
- Holding on to their own beliefs when faced with peer pressure
- Awareness of the importance of their values
- Looking outside themselves to helping others
- Reasonable risk taking
- Intrinsic reward system

Intended Outcome Statements for Students:

- "Hearing praise from others is great, but the important thing to me is that I feel good about myself on the inside when I know I've accomplished something."
- "I sought out some new kids to hang out with who share my values."
- "I've always wanted to play chess but never did because I was told I'd never understand the game. I now believe I *can* learn the game and have signed up for chess lessons."
- "Now that I feel good about myself, I am helping others in the school and I will also volunteer in the community."
- "I have a clearer sense of how important it is to stand by my own value system regardless of peer pressure."

6-1. DIRECTIONS FOR THE COMPETENCE QUIZ

This quiz may be used as a pre-test before Competence is introduced in your classroom. After you feel your students have completed a sufficient number of competence-building activities, the quiz may again be given and the results compared with the pre-test.

Below are the Competence skills you are assessing. If a student answer differs from the answers below, it may be an indicator of weakness in that area and you will know specifically what his or her needs are.

Competence skills enable students to:

- **Look outside selves to help others.**
- **Take risks in new areas.**
- **Develop awareness of capable decision making.**
- **Handle peer pressure responsibly.**
- **Develop critical-thinking skills.**

Answer Key:

1. YES; Look outside selves to help others
2. NO; Take risks in new areas
3. YES; Develop critical-thinking skills
4. NO; Develop awareness of capable decision making
5. YES; Develop awareness of capable decision making
6. NO; Handle peer pressure responsibly
7. YES; Take risks in new areas
8. YES; Handle peer pressure responsibly
9. YES; Develop awareness of capable decision making
10. YES; All areas

- -

Teacher Evaluation—Notes on Weak Areas

Student: _____ Date: _____

Observed behavior in the area of: _____

_____

My plan to help strengthen that area: _____

_____

_____

Name _____ Date _____

STUDENT COMPETENCE QUIZ

Directions: Circle YES or NO depending how you *usually* feel about the statement. Your answers will not be shared with the rest of the class.

YES	NO	1.	Now that I feel cool about myself, I'd like to help others.
YES	NO	2.	I'm afraid to try anything new for fear of not being able to do it.
YES	NO	3.	When facing a decision I need to make, I try to look at both sides.
YES	NO	4.	I look to others to make most of my decisions for me.
YES	NO	5.	If I make a mistake, I take the responsibility for it.
YES	NO	6.	When everybody in the group is doing something, I do it no matter whether I feel it is right or wrong.
YES	NO	7.	I've been told I'm not a good athlete but I'm still going to try out for the soccer team after practicing every day.
YES	NO	8.	I hang out with kids who have my kind of values so I don't get pressured into doing things I'm not into.
YES	NO	9.	I'm who I believe I am, NOT who someone else tells me I am.
YES	NO	10.	No matter what's happened in my past, my future is up to me.

Why I answered YES or NO on number(s):

_____

_____

_____

_____

_____

_____

Here are some ways I can be more competent:

_____

_____

_____

_____

_____

_____

_____

6-2. A GEEKY PLAY

The message students receive in this fun role play is that they are who they believe they are—not who someone else tells them they are. This is an enjoyable skit that leaves a lasting impression as students recall the humorous scenario between Wilbert and Granny.

Materials Needed:

- "A Geeky Play" activity sheet
- Role-play props: Large brimmed hat with a flower and yardstick to use as Granny's cane, "geeky" goggles or sunglasses, crazy scarf, tie or hat

Directions:

1. Decide who you would like to play the roles of "Granny" and "Wilbert" in the skit. Reversal of the male and female roles is recommended. Students find it lots of fun to see a boy play the role of "Granny." They laugh when he hobbles in wearing a big flowered hat! They also find it funny to see a girl play the role of "Wilbert." Wilbert enters wearing something "geeky," such as goggles atop his head or strange sunglasses along with a loud scarf, tie or hat. It's a good idea to privately ask the two students you choose to play the roles if they would enjoy taking the parts. Some children love the fun of playing a character of the opposite sex; others find it embarrassing.

2. Students who are chosen and have agreed to play the roles should take their props and practice their lines outside the classroom. This way, the whole skit will be a surprise to the rest of the class. It isn't necessary for students to memorize their lines. Reading their lines from their activity sheets, which may be given to them but not to the class before they have seen the skit, or from role-play cards as they present the skit works well. When they are ready, introduce the skit to your students by announcing you would like them to welcome a couple of visitors to your classroom, a Granny and her grandson, Wilbert! Students will recognize the name "Wilbert" from the comical recurring character they see on their activity sheets.

3. Because the skit ends on a more serious note than it began, it may be necessary for you to initiate the applause and keep the enthusiasm for the students who performed high by congratulating them on being "good sports" by changing their genders for the skit!

4. Pass out the activity sheets to your students to process the intended outcome of the skit. Review with them the following concepts:
   - Nobody can make you feel low if you don't let them.
   - You are in charge of your own reactions to an event:
     E + R = O (Event + Response = Outcome)
   - You are what you believe you are; not what someone else tells you you are.

The questions at the bottom of the activity sheet enable children to relate to a time they were put down and to express the way they felt. The aim is that their replies to the questions reveal the understanding of the concept that *they are in charge of who they believe they are; not who someone else tells them they are.* Ask students to fill out the bottom of their sheets individually. Discuss their answers together.

A GEEKY PLAY

Role play: Are You a Geek or a Lotus?

Granny enters first, hobbling in with her "cane" or "walker" in front of her, wearing a fancy hat. Wilbert follows, wearing goggles above his head or sunglasses and a crazy tie, scarf or hat. Granny speaks first.

GRANNY: "Why are you so upset, Wilbert?"

WILBERT: "Because Tony called me a geek and now I feel like such a geek!"

GRANNY: "Well, Wilbert, why don't you believe you're a Lotus?"

WILBERT: "Man! No offense, Granny, but I think you're losing it!! You think I'm a race car??"

GRANNY: "Wilbert, if you believe you're a geek just because Tony called you a geek, you might as well believe you are a shiny race car—a LOTUS."

WILBERT: "Hey, I'm getting it, Granny. I'm what *I* think I am—NOT what someone else tells me I am!"

GRANNY: "I'll remember that, Wilbert. I KNOW I'm not losing it, even though *I* was told I was losing it—by *somebody*!"

WILBERT: "Stay cool, Granny!"

Write your responses to the following questions:

1. Have you ever felt like Wilbert did when he was called a geek? If so, write about how you felt.

_____

_____

_____

_____

2. What did you think of the advice Granny gave Wilbert?

_____

_____

_____

_____

3. What's a good rule for how you're going to react now if someone puts you down?

_____

_____

_____

_____

6–3. GOOD RIDDANCE!

Henry Ford's quote, "Whether you think you can or you think you can't, you're right," is the stimulus for this activity. Our success or failure in what we do follows our positive or negative thinking. If we believe we are going to succeed and work very hard, we are more likely to achieve success than if we believe we are going to fail. In order to make room for positive "I can" beliefs, we need to throw out negative "I can't" beliefs.

Materials Needed:

- "Good Riddance!" activity sheet
- Pens

Directions:

1. Write the word "CAN'T" on the chalkboard. Before you ask your class the following question, request that if they have heard the question before and already know the answer, not to say the answer out loud. This way others will have the opportunity to think about the reply. Referring to the word "CAN'T," ask your students, "What can I do with this word?" Tell them to raise their hands when they know the answer. Students will slowly begin raising their hands as the reply occurs to them. Allow a short time for considering possible answers, then tell all the students with their hands raised to call out the correct answer, which is, "Make the word CAN!" or "Get rid of the 'T'!" Eliminating the word "can't" from their vocabulary is the idea. At this point, erase the "T" and introduce the quote also written out, "Whether you think you can or you think you can't, you're right." Hold a class discussion about the meaning of this statement along with students' examples of times they believed they would succeed or not and the success or failure that followed.

2. Pass the activity sheets to your class. The now-familiar quotation will appear at the top of their sheets. Ask a volunteer to read the introduction to the activity, which explains that in order to make room for the new, you must get rid of the old. Explain that before they choose areas in which they would like to succeed by using positive "I can" statements, they need to throw out or bury their old "I can't" statements.

3. Ask students to think about specific areas in which their negative "I can't" beliefs have held them back. *Responses:* "Reading, sports, sewing, making friends." Tell them to write out the "I can't" statements they say to themselves and to then turn them into "I can" statements on their activity sheets. When sheets are completed, ask students if they would like to say "good riddance" to the old to make way for the new. If so, tell them they can cut the "I can't" sentences from their sheets, say good riddance to them, and throw them into the garbage! The more often students focus on their "I can" statements, the more quickly they will leave their "I can'ts" far behind.

GOOD RIDDANCE!

"Whether you think you can or think you can't, you're right."
—HENRY FORD

Have you had times you succeeded because you believed you would? Times you didn't succeed because you believed you would fail? Replace your "I can'ts" with "I cans," which need to be about things you can make happen if you work hard. To make room for anything new—unless you want to get lots of clutter—you need to *get rid of the old*. Bury your "I can'ts." Replace them with "I cans"!

Here are the "I can'ts" I'm getting rid of   **I'm replacing "I can'ts" with these "I cans"**

I CAN'T: I CAN:

170

6-4. OPEN THE DOOR—LET THE SUNSHINE IN!

When you walk through a door, you can often create the way you are going to experience what will happen next. In many cases, it is up to you to look at a situation with a smile or a scowl, letting the sunshine in or the clouds in. Life can be seen as a series of doors we choose: to enter, not to enter, or we may *have* to enter regardless of our choices; however, *we can choose what we make of the situation.*

Materials Needed:

- "Open the Door—Let the Sunshine In" activity sheet
- Colored pencils, markers

Directions:

1. Ask your students who decides if they have a good day or a bad day. If responses point fingers at everyone else except the students, ask them what role they feel they play in deciding what kind of day they will have. If students continue to look to others to determine their good and bad days, review E + R = O (or your response to an event determines the outcome). Recall to students the fact that they are in charge of their own responses. At this stage of Competence, many students now feel secure in their positive identities and do not find it as difficult to overlook put-downs by others, knowing the strengths they have.

2. Distribute the activity sheets to your class. Explain that each day they may open the door either to a bright day or to a cloudy day—it's up to them. Ask them to illustrate themselves inside the door with the sunshine coming through (since we're stressing looking on the positive side of things) in a situation they don't usually enjoy, but this time they are making it a positive experience. Ask for volunteers to share what some of their illustrations will show before asking students to get started. *Response:* "I'll draw myself with a good attitude when I go to my cousin's house for dinner. He usually gets on my nerves because he starts fights, tells everyone that I started them, and then I get in trouble. This time we'll get along so well, he won't get bored and start a fight."

Bulletin Board Link:

Instead of placing themselves inside the door, students illustrate someone they are helping out. The caption could be "Let the Sunshine in for _____" and the child fills in the name of the person whose day he or she is brightening.

Music Link:

"Sunshine on My Shoulders" by John Denver

OPEN THE DOOR—LET THE SUNSHINE IN!

You can often *choose* whether you will be happy, mad, or sad. You can have a positive or negative attitude. Inside the door below, draw yourself doing something you are enjoying because of your positive attitude! Choose a situation you don't usually feel good about—but this time it's different because you've decided to change your response to it. Remember, you can let the sunshine in *or* the clouds in—it's up to you!

6-5. LIFE IS A HIGHWAY—AND YOU'RE THE DRIVER!

The objective of this activity is for students to realize it is up to them how they navigate their lives, particularly how they deal with peer pressure. It is unrealistic to tell students to avoid peer pressure because it will always be present. We need to offer choices to guide children in handling inevitable peer pressure in their lives.

Materials Needed:

- "Life Is a Highway—And You're the Driver!" activity sheet
- "Life Is a Highway" song by Tom Cochrane *(optional)*
- Props for role plays *(optional)*

Directions:

1. Students of all ages enjoy listening (with younger students often pretending to drive) as they sing along to the song "Life Is a Highway." The song can be used as a stimulus for a class discussion of the topic, "You alone are responsible for how you navigate your life." This statement could be written on a chart or the board and discussed together. *Response:* "The decisions I make are up to me." A whole-class or small-group discussion and role playing could follow on the following topics:

   - How to say "no" to your group of friends when you don't want to go along with what they are doing.
   - Some activities you've been uncomfortable doing in the past but didn't want to say "no."
   - Recall a time you were with a group and the group made fun of someone else. You didn't take part in making fun of the person but you didn't go against the group either. After the incident, you felt guilty, although you told yourself you didn't really do anything. You sure didn't!

   Ask students for examples of other situations that have made them feel uncomfortable but they were unsure how to handle. Provide time first for discussion, followed by having the role plays presented to the class.

2. Pass the activity sheets to your class, which may be completed individually or as small-group collaborations. The theme of the activity is the *highway of life* students will travel and the *detours* (times they might stumble from the right path), *roadblocks* (obstacles), and *danger zones* (temptations) they will meet along the way. They should be reminded to stop and proceed with caution when detours, roadblocks, and danger zones appear along their highways.

3. Instruct students to fill in their activity sheets, listing the danger zones or difficult peer (or other) situations they may encounter and how they will steer clear of them. Give as an example to your class the following scenario:

   BACKGROUND: The group of kids you are at a movie with want to sneak into a second movie in the same theatre complex. Although it looks as if you would not be caught, you refuse and leave. The rest of the kids go ahead and sneak into the second movie.

   DANGER ZONE: Movie with kids who want to sneak in.

   HOW I'LL STEER CLEAR: Ask students which of the following they would choose to do or what other action they would suggest. Refuse to sneak in without paying; go along with the group; don't go to another movie with that group; decide if these are the kinds of friends they want to spend time with. Other?

LIFE IS A HIGHWAY—AND YOU'RE THE DRIVER!

As you drive along life's highway, you will meet detours, roadblocks, and danger zones. List below some possible obstacles you may encounter and how you'll handle them.

Danger Zones	How I'll steer clear

6–6. A VALUES COAT OF ARMS

An important life skill to instill in children is the formation of values, the principles they adhere to when faced with choosing between right and wrong. Many of their values are formed from their families, the standards that are modeled and taught at home. Through role plays, whole-class and small-group discussions, and other value-affirming activities in the classroom, a child who is needy in the area of positive values formation may benefit from the value modeling and teaching you offer. You may feel discouraged if, with some children, it seems futile to try to reverse their previously formed negative value systems. But remember, *you can* make a difference to those children while they are in your classroom!

Materials Needed:

- "A Values Coat of Arms" activity sheet
- Pencils, pens
- Role-play props (*optional*)

Directions:

1. Write the term "value" on a chart or the board. Ask students what is meant by this statement: "Sam would not be part of that activity, even though his friends were doing it because it goes against his values." *Responses:* "Sam won't be part of something that goes against what he thinks is right." "Sam knows what he feels is right and wrong. Not participating in what he thought was wrong showed he had principles he stood by, no matter who else went ahead and did it." Ask students for examples of people they know (they may reveal their own personal examples) who stand by their values when faced with choosing between right and wrong.

2. Pass the activity sheets to your class. Ask a volunteer to read the introduction to the activity. The definition from the sheet may now be written beside your term "value" or you may choose to write the meaning given by students in their own words.

3. Ask if anyone knows what a coat of arms is. *Response:* "A light garment worn over armor decorated and arranged on a shield with a special emblem of identification." Tell students this activity can be compared to shields they wear—their values—that help protect them from harm. Go over the sheet's sentence-stem completions together to clarify any questions students have about values.

4. Students are asked to fill in their personal values coat of arms and the extra value questions at the bottom of the page. Depending upon the comfort level of small cooperative groups in your class, you may or may not choose to have students share their answers in their small groups. Otherwise, only volunteers would share their answers with the class.

A VALUES COAT OF ARMS

Your **values** are the principles you stand by when choosing what you feel is right and wrong. Fill in the sentence-stem completions inside your Values Coat of Arms. Your answers will reveal the values you hold important.

One thing I do well is . . . _____

Strongest value I hold is . . . _____

Family value most impressed on me is . . . _____

One valuable thing I want to achieve is . . . _____

The symbol that represents the way I would like others to think of me is . . . _____

Four words best describing me are . . . _____

_____ _____ _____

Extra Value!!!!

1. Do the values you have learned from your family affect many of the decisions you make when they involve making a choice between right and wrong? Why or why not?

_____

_____

_____

_____

2. Does the way you would like to be seen by others reflect your *true* values? Why or why not?

_____

_____

_____

_____

6–7. GIVE THE BOOT TO PEER PRESSURE

Students are faced with inevitable peer pressure, so it is not a question of just saying "no"; it is a matter of *how* to refuse situations with which they feel uncomfortable. This activity reinforces the need for students to have strength in their convictions as older students research harmful effects of succumbing to peer pressure.

Materials Needed:

- "Give the Boot to Peer Pressure" activity sheet
- Material for research on smoking, drug and alcohol abuse, sexually transmitted diseases, gangs (why kids join) and gang violence (*optional*)

Directions:

1. Pass the activity sheets to your class. Ask a student volunteer to read the introduction to the activity. Tell your students that, at one time or other, they will be faced with a situation in which they will feel pressure to do what the other kids in the group are doing. Students who don't want to try these activities but aren't sure how to say "no" need to explore ways they can get themselves out of the peer-pressure situation while "saving face." "Just say no" is the ideal phrase to use; however, it isn't realistic for kids in every peer-pressure situation. As a class, brainstorm situations that may arise and how to handle "no." (Situations will depend on the maturity of your students and their exposure to drugs, alcohol, and smoking. Give them the freedom to bring these subjects up; however if they don't and you feel they are ready for sex, drug and alcohol information, you may choose to introduce it.) *Brainstorming responses:* "If some of my friends don't want someone to come along with us and I do, I'll tell them I don't want to leave (him or her) out." "I'd tell my group I'm not cool with it and it's their decision if they want to go ahead; I'm not judging them." "If my friends are doing drugs, I might have to rethink hanging out with them."

2. Ask students to write on their activity sheets activities they will "boot out" of their lives. Activities will depend upon the maturity levels of your students. For example, younger students may not be mentioning drugs, alcohol, etc.

3. Older students are assigned individual or group projects for research on the following topics:
   - Harmful effects of drugs, alcohol, smoking
   - Sexually transmitted diseases
   - How joining gangs is influenced by peer pressure; why do kids join gangs?
   - Gang violence; why do groups do violent things the individuals in the group may not do alone?
   - Inhalants
   - Other

Name _____ Date _____

GIVE THE BOOT TO PEER PRESSURE

Choose an area below you'd like to research as to the harmful effects it could have on you. After you gather the information, you will be sure to "boot out" any temptation to ever give in to peer pressure to "try it"!

Check the area you choose to research:

_____ **Alcohol**

_____ **Drugs**

_____ **Inhalants**

_____ **Cigarettes**

_____ **Sexually transmitted diseases**

_____ **Gang violence**

Here are some facts I've found about my area. Some of the harmful effects are the following:

_____

_____

_____

_____

Here is how my area is linked to peer pressure:

_____

_____

_____

_____

This is why I'd walk away from pressure to "try it" (my research area)!

_____

_____

_____

_____

I'd refuse peer pressure by saying:

_____

_____

_____

_____

6–8. WEIGH BOTH SIDES

When children have reached the stage of Competence, they have developed a confidence in their own convictions. They find it easier to take a stand on their beliefs. The skills of critical thinking are practiced in this activity, in which students are encouraged to weigh both sides of an issue before making a final decision.

Materials Needed:

- Three controversial news articles (issues that have more than one side to be considered) brought in by each student
- "Weigh Both Sides" activity sheet
- Pens
- Critical-thinking steps written on a chart or the board
- Timer for game *Convince Me!*

Directions:

1. Ask students to look over their three controversial news articles and to choose one they would like to use for this critical-thinking activity. Be sure to have some extra articles on hand for any students who have no access to newspapers or news magazines. You may want to check the subjects of the news articles students have chosen. Certain moral issues may not be appropriate for this activity. Since the students were assigned three articles, together you could choose another article.

2. Pass the activity sheets to your students. Ask a volunteer to read both the introduction to the activity and the four critical-thinking steps, which should also be copied onto a chart or the board for student reference. The critical-thinking steps should be used when a student approaches a controversial topic or needs to make a decision in which both sides should be weighed.

3. Students probably have opinions about their controversial news topics. Remind them that the purpose of this activity is to look at both sides of the issue. When weighing both sides of their issues, ask students to go through the critical-thinking steps:
   - Ask the five W's: Who? What? Why? Where? When?
   - Gather as much information as possible about the topic.
   - Assess the information you gathered.
   - Make a decision. Weigh both, or all, sides carefully.

   Students then write their outcomes for both sides of their issues on their activity sheets. Remind them that looking at the other side of an issue does not mean they have to agree with the other side. Tell students they should stand by their convictions once they have gone through the critical-thinking steps and weighed both, or all, sides carefully.

6–8. WEIGH BOTH SIDES (cont'd)

4. Play the game *Convince Me!* Students form pairs consisting of a *convincer* and a *listener*. They will each have a turn to play both roles so it is just a matter of deciding which of the two will go first to be the convincer. The convincer chooses an issue from their articles to convince the other he or she agrees with *both* sides of the issue. The side genuinely agreed with is kept secret. The object of the game is to plead a good case for each side so convincingly that the partner should have a difficult time determining which side he or she is really for! After one minute is up, the partner playing the role of listener (whose role is to listen without comments or questions) again says "Convince me!" Time begins again for one minute of convincing, this time the *other side of the issue*. After the second minute is up, the partner guesses which side the other partner was really for and the convincer divulges his or her true beliefs. Then the roles are reversed and the partner who played the listener now has to be the convincer as the same procedure is repeated.

WEIGH BOTH SIDES

When you are faced with a controversial issue that has two sides, weigh both sides before you make your final decision about your opinion. The best way to do this is to go through the critical-thinking steps below.

Steps to critical thinking:

1. Ask the five W's—WHO? WHAT? WHY? WHERE? WHEN?
2. Gather as much information as you can about the topic.
3. Assess the information you gathered.
4. Make a decision. If a topic has two sides, remember to weigh both sides carefully.

Choose one of your news stories about a controversial issue, one that has two sides. Take a stand for your side but look at the other side also, and tell the facts about that side of the issue using the four critical-thinking steps.

_____

_____

_____

_____

_____

Recall a recent controversy you had with someone else—a parent, a friend, a coach or a teacher—and look at the issue from the other side. Present your side and also the other's side below, using the critical-thinking steps.

_____

_____

_____

_____

_____

6–9. COOL MOVES

Once children have formed feelings of security, positive identity, friendship-building, and goal-setting, they are then able to look outside themselves to see how they can help others. We can say they are outward bound!

Materials Needed:

- "Cool Moves" activity sheet
- Crayons, markers, pens

Directions:

1. Looking outward toward helping others may be a new concept to some students. A class discussion should precede the activity. If a class project is planned, brainstorm possible needy areas of your community to target. Or you may want to begin with a project right at your school. Ask if your students have any ideas, if they have noticed students in need of clothing, boots, skates, or books. Your class could sponsor a drive for the needed items. If your class would like to lend a helping hand to the community, an example may be performance of a class skit, songs, or poetry readings at a Senior Citizens Home.

2. Designate a "Random Acts of Kindness" week. A Bakersfield, California professor began this practice of committing random acts of kindness in retaliation for the numerous random acts of violence he so often heard and read about in the news. His college classes supported his efforts by collecting blankets for the homeless as well as other kind acts to help people. Their campaign attracted national attention. (For ideas for a class project on random acts of kindness, refer to *Random Kindness and Senseless Acts of Beauty* by Anne Herbert, published by Volcano Press/Kazan Books; or *Guerilla Kindness* by Gavin Whitsett, published by Impact Publishers.)

3. Pass the activity sheets to your students. Ask a volunteer to read the introduction to the activity. Decide whether you are going to plan a small-class activity or lead the school in a schoolwide or community project. You may want to have your students brainstorm ideas as a whole-class activity while a recorder writes ideas on a chart or the board; then have the class troubleshoot all the ideas. Or students may brainstorm in small cooperative groups and then have all their ideas recorded as a whole-class activity together. After brainstorming ideas are broken down to those plans the class commits to actually carrying out, Action Plans can then be made. The bottom portion of the activity sheet should then be filled in with the planned details of the project.

Bulletin Board or Hall Link:

If the class is to do a project together rather than individually, hang a large ice cream cone or sundae with a different flavor of ice cream scoop added each time a successful portion of the project is completed. A schoolwide project could be represented by a gigantic ice cream cone in the main hall with any of the following captions: "Our Random Acts of Senseless Kindness," "(Our School) Is Outward Bound," or "Here's the Scoop on What We're Doing." Remember, no flavor may be added that has already been used!

COOL MOVES!

Color a scoop of ice cream in your favorite flavor each time you do something kind for someone else. You may want to have a huge class ice cream cone (or a school ice cream cone displayed in the main hall with scoops represented by classes) and add scoops when individuals or teams complete their projects. No flavor may be used twice!

Who? Action Plan?

Here is who I plan to help in my community and my Action Plan. (This may also be a team or class activity.) *Example:* Skates, used books, or mitten drive for needy kids.

Community Need: _____

_____

_____

Action Plan: _____

_____

_____

Date to Complete Project: _____

Team Members and Responsibilities: _____

_____

_____

6-10. LET YOUR VALUES SHINE

For older students, recognizing not only their values but also how they arrived at their choices of values are the aims of this activity. There are six questions students may ask themselves when deciding how they arrived at their positions.

Materials Needed:

- "Let Your Values Shine" activity sheet
- Pens, pencils

Directions:

1. Review the term "values" with your students. *Response:* "Values are the beliefs you stick by when you're faced with a decision between right and wrong. What you believe is the right thing is your value."

2. Ask what *tests your values as being your own* and not simply a reflection of someone else's beliefs, such as a parent or someone in authority over you. *Responses:* "Standing by your values when you're tempted to go against them tests your values." "Doing what you believe is right when nobody else will ever know tests your values." "When everyone else is doing something that goes against what I believe in tests me to openly say and to act on my values." Tell students that the purpose of this activity is to see whether their values are freely chosen and acted upon repeatedly as their own.

3. Pass the activity sheets to your class. If they were to have a tug of war over their values, which three would they hold on to with all their strength? Assure them these answers will not be shared with the rest of the class. *Examples:* Honesty, compassion, empathy, sincerity, compassion. Ask students to write their three strongest-held values on the activity sheet.

4. Introduce the six questions, or facets, which, if answered YES, make their values shine. The object of the questions is that the more they answer YES, the more they truly believe and own the value. Read and discuss each question together. Ask students to go through each of their three values one at a time and answer each question with a YES or NO about that value. If they answer NO to some of the questions, talk over the reason for the NO and what they can do to aim for a YES for that value question. Ask volunteers to share their responses before the class is asked to answer their questions individually. *Responses may include examples similar to these:* "Integrity, doing the honest thing even when nobody else knows about it but me, is a value I hold strongly. It was modelled to me by my single mom, who has always showed integrity when it was difficult for us. Now it is my own value. I can say 'yes' to each of the six questions." "Not having sex before marriage is a value I hold strongly. My spiritual upbringing first taught me my value and it is now my own belief and I can answer 'yes' to each of the six questions."

5. Ask students to use the first value they had written on their sheets and go through each of the six questions. The next two values should then be used to go through the questions the same way. Your individual, private help with answers of NO may help students see how they could make that value more complete. For example, a child who has chosen honesty as a value, marks NO on his or her paper for "holds on over and over." Discuss with the child that honesty is a value that should be repeatedly held; however, everyone at times has lapses and it's important to try harder next time without getting discouraged. For students who have no role models in the home, their answers of YES to even a few of the questions should be encouraged. You could guide those students as to how they can add more YES answers to make their values shine.

LET YOUR VALUES SHINE!

Where did you receive your *values*, or beliefs in right and wrong, that you hold? Did you freely choose them? Do you truly believe in them? Write six values you treasure on the lines below. Then choose three of those values and answer the six questions below to see how you received the values and how strongly you hold them.

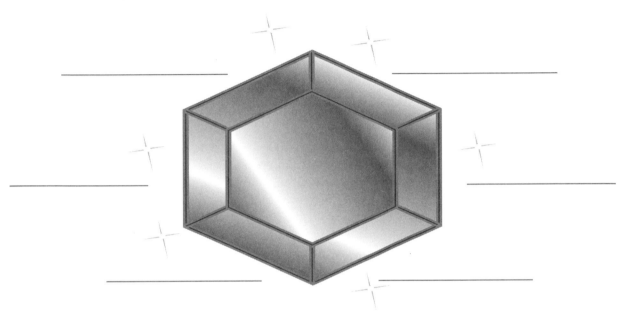

Name the three values you hold most strongly. For example, if you were to have a tug of war over this value, you'd hang on with all your strength! (*Examples:* honesty, fairness, kindness)

1. _____

2. _____

3. _____

Go through each of your three values above and ask each of the six questions below for each value. Write "Y" for YES or "N" for NO for each value. Your answers will tell you how you arrived at each value and how completely you hold it. If you answer NO, explore why you chose that reply and how you can turn it into a YES. For each question below, ask yourself, "How have I chosen each of my values?"

1. ____ 2. ____ 3. ____ Have you chosen this value from several different choices?

1. ____ 2. ____ 3. ____ Do you feel the value you've learned is now your very own?

1. ____ 2. ____ 3. ____ Are you proud of this value?

1. ____ 2. ____ 3. ____ Can you openly say this value in front of others?

1. ____ 2. ____ 3. ____ Have you acted on or done anything about this value?

1. ____ 2. ____ 3. ____ Do you hold on to this value over and over when it's put to the test?

185

6-11. DOMINOES

Character-building is an intended outcome of this activity. Standing by your values is sometimes tested when you want to make a good impression on peers or when you are the only one who knows whether or not you have committed a right or a wrong act. Will you still hold on to your values in the face of nobody else knowing if you have done right or wrong? These are dilemmas presented below.

Materials Needed:

- "Dominoes" activity sheet
- Scissors, paste

Directions:

1. Begin the discussion for this activity by asking students how they know someone has a strong character, a real sense of what is right and what is wrong. *Responses:* "When he or she does the right thing even if he or she is the only one who knows about it." "If a kid doesn't go along with what her friends are doing because she thinks what they are doing goes against what she believes is right, then she has a strong sense of right and wrong."

2. Have a personal example of a test of character volunteered by a student to share with the class. It may be a story about a time the child did the right thing that nobody ever knew about except the child. Or perhaps a student will have a story of character being tested in a moral dilemma, a "Should I? or Shouldn't I?" problem. If others wish to share similar stories, discuss two or three more.

3. Pass the activity sheets to your students. Have the introduction read and discuss together how people's decisions can either let others down or lift them up. Ask for some examples of times when students felt they had either built others up or let them down by their actions.

4. Tell students you are going to play a game of dominoes. The difference in this game is the numbers don't have to match to win. In fact, this isn't a game to win or lose. Instead, it's a game to see if there is any room for improvement. Tell students to cut out the half dominoes at the bottom of the sheet and paste what they feel is the best solution under the problems they refer to. You may choose to have students do the activity individually or in small cooperative groups, together deciding the best solutions.

5. All answers should be discussed together as a whole-class sharing activity when the dominoes are completed individually or in small groups. Have students add the total number of dots on their solution dominoes plus the dots on the problem dominoes. If the total matches the number at the bottom of the page, they have chosen the best solutions! This indicates they're on their way to forming a good sense of values. If the numbers differ, discuss which solutions could be better chosen. Go over each problem situation and the best solutions together, discussing why they were the best solutions and how other solutions chosen could be improved.

When the first domino in a row of dominoes falls, the rest of the row will fall. Have you ever felt your decisions have lifted others up or let them down? Cut out the best solutions on the half dominoes at the bottom of the page and paste them under their problems. Add the total number of dots on the problems and on their solutions for each domino. Check the bottom of the page (upside down) for the total number for each domino. If your totals check out, you chose the best solutions! If your number is different, think how you might change solutions.

Problem Situations:

1. You walked out of a store with an item you forgot you were holding and did not pay for. Nobody noticed you leaving with the item. You . . .

2. You were told by your mom to study while she worked late. You're tired of studying and your favorite TV show is on now. You . . .

3. A group of kids you've been wanting to "get in with" is laughing at someone's ethnic clothing. You're curious about different cultures, but you don't want to go against this group! You . . .

4. Your class has to stay after school because one student started a fight that involved several other kids in the class and the teacher didn't know who started it. After school a group plans to gang up on the one who started the fight. You . . .

Problem Solutions:

A. Let the person know privately the behavior wasn't appreciated.

B. Join the laughter so you won't upset the group.

C. Figure you'd better not go back to pay; if they didn't miss the item as you left, you're in the clear.

D. Join the group who is going to gang up on the kid or they might gang up on you!

E. Turn on your favorite TV show. Your mom won't know the difference.

F. Return to the store with the item and explain it was an honest mistake.

G. Keep on studying. Your mom won't know if you watch TV but *you* will. You'll negotiate TV time later!

H. Find out the student's name and ask to hear about his or her customs.

DOMINOES

1. Total Dots: _____

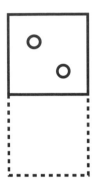

Letter of
Solution:_____

2. Total Dots: _____

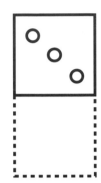

Letter of
Solution:_____

3. Total Dots: _____

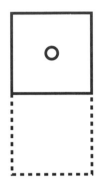

Letter of
Solution:_____

4. Total Dots: _____

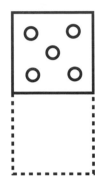

Letter of
Solution:_____

A

B

C

D

E

F

G

H

1. 3; 2. 6; 3. 6; 4. 9

188

Conflict Solving

7

CONFLICT SOLVING

Rationale:

Because conflict is inevitable in our lives, children need to learn creative and positive ways to handle it. If infused with role playing, music and language arts, a child's emotions, imagination and intuition are motivated. Conflict solving is best introduced after a child has built a foundation in the components of self-esteem: a feeling of trust and well-being with you and with classmates in your classroom, recognition of some of their inner strengths and a feeling of positive identity, the ability to form and maintain friendships, to set and attain goals, and opportunities to practice capable decision-making. With this positive base, the child is then ready to look outside of himself or herself to deal with anger within and anger directed toward others. Only then can he or she begin to learn successfully the skills of solving conflicts collaboratively.

Goals:

- To develop the ability to control behavior when angry, to stop to calm down, and to plan how to then best approach the conflict.
- To increase awareness that every person's inner peace contributes to peace in his or her home, school, neighborhood, and community.
- To teach the skills involved in collaborative conflict solving — both persons in the conflict win; nobody emerges as a *loser*. To handle a conflict with the TLC (Tender Loving Care) Approach.
- To develop appropriate problem-solving skills such as the ability to identify the problem, to brainstorm several possible solutions, and to choose one that best meets the needs of both involved in the conflict.
- To instill in students the ability to be a good listener, to be able to actively listen to the other's point of view and to repeat back his or her words to him or her.
- To recognize the different ways people express their anger.
- To assure students that anger is a natural emotion and in itself is not harmful; it is how they handle their *behavior* when they are angry, which can be harmful if it hurts themselves or someone else emotionally or physically.
- To teach children how to handle a conflict using a calm, assertive approach in stating their needs as opposed to a physically or verbally aggressive, pushy approach.

Intended Outcome Statements for Students:

- "Nobody is a loser here! We solved our conflict and we both feel like winners."
- "I use the TLC (Tender Loving Care) Recipe to help me solve conflicts. I tune in and listen so I can repeat the words back to the other person. Then we both choose the best solution to meet both our needs. It's a good recipe!"

- "I used to think I couldn't make a difference to peace. Now I think I *can make a difference* to my area and that will contribute to world peace."

- "If I stop (BBQ—Better Be Quiet Technique) to cool down, count to at least ten, then plan what to do next, both of us usually come out of the conflict feeling like winners."

- "Brainstorming together several possible ways of solving our problem, then choosing the best solution for each of us really works."

- "Sometimes I have to stop and look at what's really happening *behind* the anger."

- "I never thought I could do much about violence in the world; now I know it begins with each one of us working together. Anger and conflict will be around as long as we all live, so I aim for each of us to come out of the conflict feeling that nobody is a loser."

7-1. DIRECTIONS FOR THE CONFLICT-SOLVING QUIZ

This quiz may be used as a pre-test before Conflict Solving is introduced in your classroom. After you feel your students have completed a sufficient number of conflict-resolution activities, the quiz may again be given and the results compared with the pre-test. Below are the conflict-solving components you are assessing. If a student answer differs from the answer key below, it may be an indicator of weakness in that component and you will know specifically what his or her needs are.

Conflict Solving skills to be developed in students:

- **Control of Anger:** Able to stop and cool down
- **Collaborative Conflict Solving:** Both win; nobody is a *loser*
- **Problem Solving:** Able to identify the problem, to brainstorm several solutions, and to choose one that meets needs of both
- **Active Listening:** Able to listen to the feelings and needs of the other person involved in the conflict and to repeat back his/her words to him/her
- **Peace Contribution:** Feels he or she makes a difference to peace in own school and community

Answer Key:

1. NO; Control of Anger
2. NO; Collaborative Conflict Solving
3. NO; All areas
4. YES; All areas
5. YES; Collaborative Conflict Solving
6. NO; All areas
7. YES; Peace Contribution
8. YES; Control of Anger
9. YES; All areas
10. NO; Control of Anger

Teacher Evaluation—Notes on Weak Areas

Student: _____ Date: _____

Observed behavior in the area of: _____

My plan to help strengthen that area: _____

_____

_____

Name _____ Date _____

STUDENT CONFLICT-SOLVING QUIZ

Directions: Circle YES or NO depending how you *usually* feel about the statement. Your answers will not be shared with the rest of the class.

YES	**NO**	**1.**	When I am angry, the *anger controls* me.
YES	**NO**	**2.**	I have to win when I have a conflict with someone.
YES	**NO**	**3.**	I use physical force to get my way.
YES	**NO**	**4.**	It is important to me how the other person sees the problem in a conflict with me.
YES	**NO**	**5.**	I think *both* of us should feel like winners after we have solved a conflict together.
YES	**NO**	**6.**	Shouting when I'm angry is the best way to get what I want.
YES	**NO**	**7.**	I can make a difference to world peace even if I'm only one person.
YES	**NO**	**8.**	If I stop to calm down when I'm angry, I can plan what to do next.
YES	**NO**	**9.**	Conflict is a part of my life, so it's helpful to know how to solve our problems so that *nobody feels like a loser.*
YES	**NO**	**10.**	When I'm angry, I tell the person off right away.

Why I answered YES or NO on number(s):

_____

_____

_____

_____

_____

Here are my ideas for solving conflicts so nobody ends up feeling like a loser.

_____

_____

_____

_____

_____

193

Dear Parents and Guardians,

We feel that if we link together—home and school—we can make a difference to the growing trend of violence in our society. Here are some of the ways in which you can help at home. Your efforts will support our program by following the same approach to problems at home as we are using here at school.

We are studying Conflict Solving at school. We are learning how to handle our anger, how to cool down, and then plan a solution so that nobody feels like a *loser*. We are learning the value of listening to one another's feelings and needs (not just our own!) and repeating the words back to the other person so that he or she knows he or she is understood. The goal is for both persons involved in the conflict to end up feeling like winners. Please practice these approaches at home with your child so that there will be consistency as we change old patterns of verbal shouting and physical discipline into a more *tender loving care* approach from both sides. This conflict-solving approach promotes *power with* rather than *power over* your child. You are asked to remember this **BBQ Technique** and **TLC Recipe** when you and your child disagree.

First, **BBQ— Better Be Quiet**. *Cool down* and plan to listen to your child's point of view without judging. This does not mean you have to agree; just let your child know you understand his or her point of view. Then . . .

    T—TUNE IN to both of your feelings by taking turns saying, "When you . . . I feel . . . because . . . "

    L—LISTEN to how your child sees the problem, then take turns repeating back the other's words.

    C—CHOOSE a solution to meet both of your needs.

We are learning that nonviolence and peace begin right here—in our little corners of the world. How? Part of our approach to solving conflicts is for each one of us to do our part to solve conflicts peacefully. Then when we reach out to help others in need in our school, our neighborhoods and community, the first step toward global peace will have been taken! If kids take this approach in all our schools all over our country, what a difference it will make to end the growing trend of violence. What better place to start managing conflict peacefully than right here in our own school and playground and in our homes?

Please support our efforts at home with your child! We would like to see school, home, and community united in our efforts to promote *empathy*, thoughtfulness for others. Kids need to feel they belong somewhere. Let's enable our kids to fulfill their *need for belonging* with friends and educators here at school as well as from you at home. That way, they will not have the need to affiliate with gangs or individuals who may promote undesirable forms of belonging.

Thank you.

7-2. IT IS! IT ISN'T!

Because we are always faced with anger and conflict in our lives, it is an important life skill to learn to resolve them effectively so that everyone involved is satisfied with the outcome. An intended outcome of conflict resolution is that nobody emerges as the loser.

Arriving at this harmonious point involves some learned strategies. First, we are better able to plan our resolutions when we stop, cool off, and collect our thoughts. After cooling off, the next step is to take turns expressing our feelings and needs with the other person involved in the conflict, to brainstorm ideas, and then to choose a collaborative solution that will make both feel like winners.

Materials Needed:

- Yardsticks or masking tape
- Sheet with list of topics for discussion (several topics are listed below)
- Two large signs—one that reads IT ISN'T! and one that reads IT IS!

Room Preparation:

After clearing desks and chairs to the sides of the classroom to create an open space, divide the space as equally as possible into two parts by placing masking tape or several yardsticks as dividers. Put an IT ISN'T! sign in one section of the open space and an IT IS! sign in the other section of the open space.

Directions:

1. Announce to students you are going to play a game called, "It Is! It Isn't!" Explain that after the game begins, when you call out a statement, they are to *walk* (without running or shoving) to their choices of marked spaces: if they agree, they move to the It Is! space or if they disagree, they move to the It Isn't! space. Here are a few statements to help you get started:
   - The BEST spectator sport is college football!
   - The MOST DELICIOUS Italian food is spaghetti and meatballs.
   - Rap music is the BEST!
   - The MOST RELAXING way to "veg out" is to watch TV.
   - A mystery is the MOST INTERESTING type of book to read.
2. After you have done several different topics and students have moved to their chosen spaces, move the chairs and desks back to their original positions. Hold a class discus-

7–2. IT IS! IT ISN'T! (cont'd)

sion to introduce conflict resolution. Ask the students the following questions for a whole-class oral discussion.

- Did everyone think the same way about the same issues? *Response:* "We had a lot of differences during the game. We have different opinions in real life all the time."
- What is *conflict*? *Responses:* "Disagreement; opposing ideas or interests; clash; fight or struggle."
- Do you have to have another person(s) involved to experience a conflict? *Responses:* "No. A conflict can happen inside a person. For example, whenever I have to make a decision when I'm pulled in different ways, such as whether to study for my exam or watch my favorite TV show."
- When conflict involves a person other than yourself, how do people usually act? *Responses:* "They swear." "They are so mad they start hitting." "They start to give put-downs to the other person." "Their faces get red. Fights start happening."
- Does shouting, swearing, giving put-downs, and hitting or fighting usually work well for everyone involved in a conflict? *Responses:* "The person who did the swearing didn't really win because the other person is hurt and comes out the loser. The one who verbally attacked the other person might act like a winner but inside he or she usually does not feel that good about himself or herself. And the loser feels awful."
- How do you think we could solve conflicts with others and end up both feeling good about the results? *Responses:* "If you talked things out without shouting, swearing or hitting and tried to listen to the other person instead of only thinking about what *you* want."
- Is a conflict solved by using force or physical violence? *Response:* "It may put a quick end to the conflict but nobody is a winner in a physical abuse conflict solution. The person who was the victim of the abuse loses as well as the abuser."
- How should people feel when a conflict is over? *Response:* "They should come to some agreement and feel better than when they started. They should feel like they are winners. Nobody should go away feeling like a loser."

Evaluation:

After the discussion has ended, have your students list three effective ways to resolve a conflict in their lives.

7-3. A PEACEFUL JOURNEY

This imagination activity not only enables students to quietly relax but also to have a period for exploring inner strengths. The intended outcome, after they have mentally taken the journey in which you guide them, will be greater awareness of their abilities to create *inner peace* within themselves. Inner peace begins with *individuals* realizing the positive qualities they have within themselves, helping to create a feeling of inner peace. If there is conflict within themselves, they will be more likely to have conflicts with others. Conflicts with other races, religions, or cultures often stem from individuals or groups trying to overcome their own inner feelings of discord.

Atmosphere Needed:

A quiet, comfortable room with soft music playing, dimmed lights, covered windows and, if possible, carpet for the students to lie down if they choose. Otherwise, they may remain at their desks. A calm atmosphere is created by a relaxing musical selection.

Materials Needed:

- "A Peaceful Journey" activity sheet (for the follow-up)

Directions:

1. Create an atmosphere in which you guide your students during a relaxing period to soft music, picturing or imagining a scene in which they will discover or acknowledge an inner strength.

2. To introduce students to a guided imagination exercise, ask them to close their eyes (only if desired, as some children visualize with their eyes open and some feel more comfortable with their eyes open). Tell them to picture in their minds a favorite animal (a pet or an admired animal seen in books, movies, on TV, or at the zoo). Ask when they have chosen their animals to silently nod their heads. After they acknowledge that they have the images of the animals in their minds, tell them to imagine them moving in any way the students choose. Allow a short period of time for this visualization, then ask students to open their eyes if they closed them. Ask volunteers to share what they imagined. *Responses:* "I pictured a deer. Then it ran gracefully through the woods." "First, I pictured my pet kitten, Ziggy. Then I pictured her in a tree and my dad climbing a ladder. Then she jumped into his arms because she was too scared to climb down." Sharing these images will make students feel comfortable with guided imagining which is to follow. You may choose to substitute a topic other than "animals" that you feel would interest students as an introduction to this imagination activity.

3. Prepare students for the guided imagination exercise by comparing the experience to the one they have just had. Suggest to them to get comfortable for a relaxing time by putting their heads down on their desks or, if yours is a carpeted classroom and some

7–3. A PEACEFUL JOURNEY (cont'd)

would prefer to lie down, by choosing a spot on the floor. (*Note:* Some students may not be able to participate in this exercise for religious reasons. Although this imagination exercise is *not* a religious activity, some religions choose not to participate in visualization exercises. Or some younger students may hold a fear of imagining which is associated with bad dreams, etc. Although these cases may be isolated, it is important to respect those students who are not able to participate, while alleviating any embarrassment they may feel as a result of not joining the rest of the class. Perhaps they may be given a quiet activity to be completed in another section of the room as opposed to sending them out of the classroom, which may cause some students possible embarrassment. Ask them to respect the quiet atmosphere by not making any noise while the other students relax.)

4. After students are comfortable, begin playing your musical selection as relaxing background music. Speaking in a soft voice, you may then begin the following narrative.

This is going to be a private time for you to relax and to reflect. As you listen to me, you will begin to imagine pictures of the things I am saying to you. Enjoy this time just for YOU! Pretend you have a day ahead of yourself and you have NOTHING YOU HAVE TO DO TODAY!! You have a free day! Imagine yourself in a beautiful park with small blue and yellow wildflowers and long green grass. It is warm enough that you do not even need a sweater or jacket. The sun is shining and the sky is blue. You can even take off your shoes and socks! You hear water falling in the distance coming from a gently sloping mountain beyond the park. Since you have the entire day free, you decide to climb the mountain! It's an easy mountain to climb as you pass an awesome waterfall and feel the cool spray as the water swishes over the rocks. You want to get high enough to reach up to touch the soft cotton puffs which, as you get closer, look like white smoke or fog swirling gently all around you. Yes, you are now high enough to touch the clouds! You are greeted by a wizened mountain person who is quite happy to see you, as if expecting you. The wizened person asks you an important question, which is: *"What one strength or positive quality do you have within yourself that you can always count on?"* You have to stop and think about this question. The answer you discover is to be kept private between the two of you. You take your time thinking about a few of the good points you have noticed about yourself or perhaps someone else has pointed these strengths out to you. You are enjoying this time just for yourself! While trying to think of your very best strength, some negative self-talk may come into your mind, reminding you of times you did not feel good about yourself. Let that negative self-talk go! Replace it now with good things about yourself. (Pause.) Now the time has come for you to give your answer, only ONE strength to the wizened person. (Pause.)

After you give your answer, you feel awesome! A *peaceful* feeling floats all over you because you know that you can return to this place anytime you want to. Why? *That place is within yourself.* Slowly you descend the mountain, returning to the park and feeling an inner peace within yourself. Now you decide how you are going to spend the rest of your free day!" (Pause.)

Ask students to slowly focus on leaving their imaginary journeys and returning to the classroom. Lights, if dimmed, should not be turned on abruptly. Let the soft music continue a few more moments after you finish speaking. Allow for a moment or two of silence.

Follow-Up Activity:

The follow-up questions on the activity sheet may be completed orally or written either as a whole-class or as a small cooperative-group activity. Students may also enjoy drawing the scenes they have just imagined. Inner strengths that children uncovered in their visualization may be kept private for this activity and are thus not included in the questions. It is important to be sensitive to any child you suspect may have had difficulty finding an inner strength. Perhaps you could privately point out some qualities you know he or she possesses. It is not intended that the questions be judged "right" or "wrong." For example, the "wizened person" may have been pictured by some children as being female and others as being male. A "wizened person" usually connotes an *aged* person; however, some students may argue that a *young* person who has experienced and learned worthwhile lessons from challenging life issues emerges as a wise person! Item five on the activity sheet is intended to be a creative opportunity for students to make up their own visualizations. If you would like to enact these relaxation exercises as a special part of your class routine, perhaps some of their stories could be used and read orally by the author.

A PEACEFUL JOURNEY

After your imaginative mountain-climbing adventure, answer the questions below. The answers are what *you* want them to be. The last question gives you the chance to *create your own* imagination adventure!

1. Describe or draw the wizened person you saw as *you* imagined him or her.

   _____

   _____

2. Was this a journey you feel was best traveled *alone*? Why? Why not?

   _____

   _____

3. What feelings did you have as you were coming down the mountain ? Explain.

   _____

   _____

4. What does the feeling of peace inside one person have to do with world peace?

   _____

   _____

5. Make up an imagination story in which you lead your listeners on a peaceful journey. Where will you take them? What will you ask them to search for? (Use the back of this sheet for your story.)

7-4. PEACE BEGINS IN YOUR LITTLE CORNER OF THE WORLD

The relationship between inner peace and the desire to create peace outside ourselves is explored in this activity. If we begin to improve ourselves and to establish inner peace, we can then go forward outside our own little corners of the world to bring that same feeling of peace to our homes, neighborhoods, and communities.

Materials Needed:

- "Peace Begins in Your Little Corner of the World" activity sheet
- Scissors, paste

Directions:

1. After passing out the activity sheets, discuss the quotation by the English novelist and essayist Aldous Huxley, "There is only one corner of the universe you can be certain of improving and that is your own self." Discuss the meaning of the verb *improve*. *Response:* "To raise to a better quality by additions or changes."

2. Ask students what the quotation means to them. *Responses:* "We alone are responsible for how we feel about ourselves and how we can improve ourselves." "We can make improvements to areas of our lives, our little corners of the world, by additions or changes we plan." (Activities to develop these concepts may be found in the "Positive Identity" and "Goal Setting" chapters of this book). "If we first find peace within ourselves, we can then spread peace to others."

3. Hold a class discussion in which students discuss improvement in the following areas:

   HOME—Get along with others at home; contribute to family duties and household tasks; help out family members emotionally when needed. Other?

   NEIGHBORHOOD—Get along with other kids in the area; help the elderly to carry heavy bags; rake leaves and shovel snow. Other?

   COMMUNITY—Organize drives to collect used items for needy children, such as skates, books, coats, mittens, boots and Scout uniforms, that they may not be able to afford to purchase brand new; provide pleasure for the elderly by reading stories or poetry, or performing a class play or song at a local nursing home; donate some time organizing food donations at a local food bank. Other?

4. Direct the students' attention to putting their ideas for improvement inside each small globe on their activity sheets next to each of the three above-discussed areas.

Bulletin Board Link:

The students could then be asked to cut out each of their small numbered globes and paste them inside three large class globes. Each large globe can be labeled for classroom display with: 1. HOME; 2. NEIGHBORHOOD; 3. COMMUNITY.

PEACE BEGINS IN YOUR LITTLE CORNER OF THE WORLD

"There is only one corner of the universe
you can be certain of improving and that is your own self."

—*Aldous Huxley*

If we begin to work to establish inner peace within ourselves, then to our small corners of the world—in our homes, neighborhoods and communities—we can then go outside our own corners to spread that feeling of peace to others.

Think how you can plan to improve the following areas of your life: Home, Neighborhood, and Community. Write your answers in the globe beside each of the three areas.

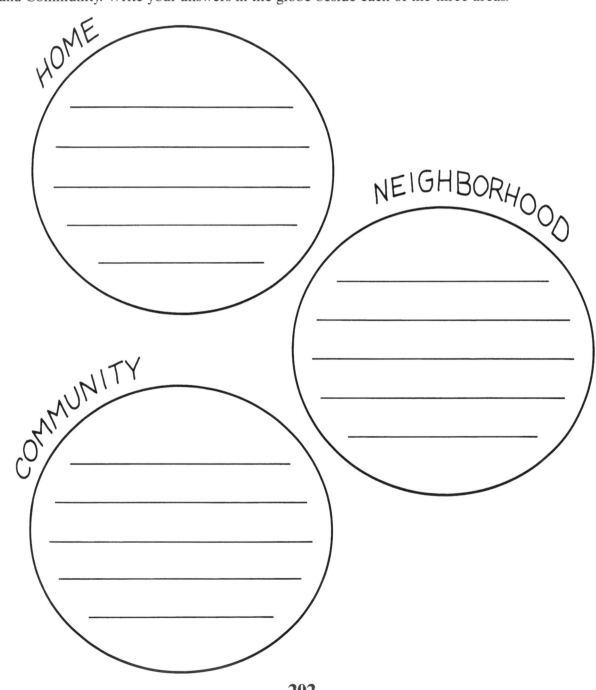

7-5. SOLE TALK

What if you were in the other person's shoes? Students have the opportunity to put themselves in the other person's shoes in this activity by seeing the problem from the other's point of view during a conflict situation.

Materials (Advance Preparation Needed):

- Ask students to bring pictures of three items from magazines or newspapers that they would like to receive as gifts. These pictures are due on the day you choose "Sole Talk" to be a class activity.
- "Sole Talk" activity sheet

Directions:

1. Announce to your class that they are going to play a game in which they are going to experience what it is like to be in someone else's shoes, to have a sole talk together ("sole" meaning the bottom part of a shoe). Tell the class they will be playing the game *"I Want What You Have."* Ask the class to take out the pictures they brought in of three items they would like to receive as gifts. The pictures should be kept "secret" by having students turn them face down until the game begins. (It would be helpful to certain students who may not have magazines or newspapers at home, if you asked for the class to bring in an extra picture for the "picture pool" from which students without pictures of their own could draw three pictures.)

2. Pass out the activity sheets to your class. Read the directions for the game "I Want What You Have." Make the point that they are to pretend they are in the other person's shoes when their partners are trying to convince them to give up their gifts, to look at the problem from the other's point of view! Stress again, after the directions have been read, that the pictures are *gifts* to you; that you have paid no money for the items and that no offer of money to convince the other to give up the gift will be accepted. Also, make it clear that no physical contact may be made between partners to convince them to give up the gift, such as physical force, hugs, pats, etc.

3. Before students divide into partner groups, tell them that the first thing they will do will be to try to see the problem of wanting the gift from the other person's point of view. The next thing they will do together will be to decide who is A and who is B.

4. Divide students into groups of two facing one another with their pictures/gifts face down. Remind them to decide on A and B. (Pause.) Instruct B to go first! This will cause some laughter as students usually expect A to be chosen to begin. B then picks *one* gift from A's collection. B has to then convince A why A should give up the gift to her or him. Remind students of the no-force or offer-of-money rule; you are interested in their *creative approaches to the problem* of getting the other's gift.

5. Each partner should have the same length of time to try to convince the other to give up the gift, about two minutes. After the time is up, the partners switch roles, carrying

7-5. SOLE TALK (cont'd)

out the same approach. After both partners have had their turns, ask students to return to their seats.

6. Ask students, "How did it go?" *Responses:* "It felt really weird to think about what it was like for my partner trying to convince me to give the gift to him or her. I usually only think about it from my own point of view." "I got to think about where somebody else was coming from—for a change."

7. Ask students to answer the follow-up questions at the bottom of the activity sheet. Discuss the answers together as a whole-class activity.

SOLE TALK

Have you ever stopped during a conflict to look at the problem from the other's viewpoint? What if you were in the other person's shoes? Try it! Play **Sole Talk** while you listen to your partner trying to convince you to give up your "gift" during the game of "I Want What You Have."

1. While you play "I Want What You Have," imagine what the problem (he or she is trying to get you to give up your "gift") looks like from his or her point of view.

2. Think about how things look from someone else's shoes.

3. When it's the other partner's turn to try to get the "gift," think about what it is like from his or her shoes!

How Did It Go?

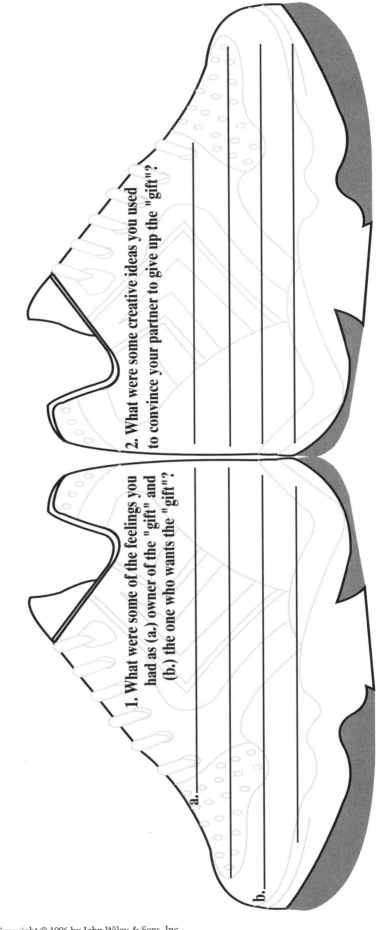

1. What were some of the feelings you had as (a.) owner of the "gift" and (b.) the one who wants the "gift"?

   a.

   b.

2. What were some creative ideas you used to convince your partner to give up the "gift"?

7–6. LINK TOGETHER FOR A PEACEFUL WORLD

This activity links students together as they discuss, first in small groups, then as a whole class, why they agree or disagree with controversial issues and how the issues are linked to a peaceful world.

Materials Needed:

- "Link Together for a Peaceful World" activity sheet
- Paper and pen for recorder of each team

Directions:

1. Pass out activity sheets to your class. Explain that this will first be an oral activity in which they will form small groups to discuss *controversial* issues. Write the term "controversial" on a chart or the board. Ask students for its meaning. *Responses:* "A statement that is intended to have several different responses." "Argumentative." "There will be as many different answers as there are different opinions."

2. Students may form their regular cooperative groups if you have already formed them or you may choose to make up new groups for this activity. A recorder will be needed for each group, appointed by yourself or by the group. The recorders will need paper and pen when they go into their small groups. The job of the recorder will be to write down, in summary form, the following points from group members:

   a. Why they agree or disagree with each issue

   b. How they see the issue linked to a peaceful world

   c. The *final total number of agrees and disagrees* in the spaces next to the numbers of their teams

   It should be stressed to students that the recorder will also be responsible for monitoring the group, ensuring that there are no judgments or put-downs of one another's opinions and that each group member has the same amount of time to express his or her views. The names of the group members should not be included in the recording next to their individual opinions. The names should be kept anonymous and not discussed outside the group unless permission is given by the one who issued the opinion statement. He or she will also orally report the recording to the class when students have completed their small-group discussions.

3. After students have formed their small groups, give each group a number that will correspond to the controversial statement they will discuss. Depending upon your number of students and the number of members to a group, you will have several statements you will not choose to give to the small groups. Perhaps these issues could be used for language arts activities later. The final results of the total numbers of agrees and disagrees from each group may be written by the recorders in the spaces next to the numbers of the teams on the activity sheets.

Language Arts Link:

The controversial statements on the activity sheets provide students with eight choices of topics for written essays or poems. The essays should include the above three questions used for the small groups.

LINK TOGETHER FOR A PEACEFUL WORLD

After forming teams, each team receives a number (from a box) that corresponds to the controversial statements below. This is the number for the issue they will discuss. A recorder should be appointed for each group. Team members are to include in their discussions:
1. Why they *agree or disagree* with the controversial issues
2. How the issue is *linked to a peaceful world*

Discuss first as a small group, followed by sharing as a whole class. It is not intended for team members to share the same opinions within their groups. Recorders write their teams' total number of "agrees" and "disagrees" in the spaces under their teams' numbers below.

Controversial Statements:

1. "Children *learn* to be violent."
2. "If everyone would just *stay within their own racial and ethnic groups*, we would not have any conflicts."
3. "One country *should not get involved* in another country's war."
4. "Everybody *should be allowed* to buy a gun."
5. "A country with an abundance of food, clothing, and medical supplies *should help* countries that suffer from a shortage of them."
6. "If people feel positive about themselves, they *will not have a need to "put down" or hold power over* other racial groups or other countries."
7. "People *should volunteer* to help the homeless in their communities."
8. "Natural disasters such as earthquakes, floods, droughts, and fires are *not really our problems* if they happen far away from our community."

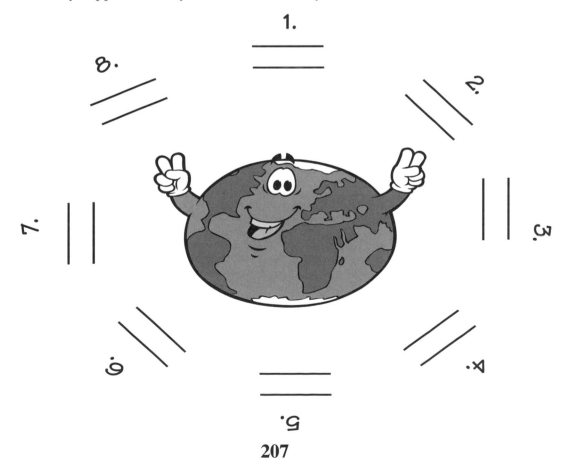

207

7-7. PEACE ACTIVITIES CELEBRATION

Why not enhance your unit of study of conflict solving with a day or a part of a day dedicated to celebrating peace and nonviolent ways of conflict solving? Suggestions are given below for planning a Peace Activities Celebration. You may want to culminate the day with an all-school assembly in which classes perform skits and lead the assembly in selected peace songs. Peace and nonviolence begin with you, your students and their families, and your school—in your little corner of the world.

1. After receiving agreement to hold a schoolwide Peace Activities Celebration from your school administrators and faculty, enlist a planning committee of supportive teachers, principal or vice principal, along with students. Your committee may want to select a creative title for the day such as *We Are Links in the Peace Chain*; *Peace Begins in Our Little Corner of the World*; or *Doves of Peace*.

2. Each participating classroom teacher chooses a conflict-solving activity to do with his or her groups and indicates it on the included sign-up sheet. A list of classroom activity suggestions is provided or teachers may prefer to choose activities of their own. (The activities listed are found in the conflict-solving section unless otherwise indicated.) You may decide to rotate your students within grade-level divisions if your school has a large number of students.

3. Each class meets for 20 minutes, then rotates. If the entire school is participating, the bell could ring every 20 minutes so that everyone is on schedule to rotate. If only a certain number of classes is participating, a timer or the student aide could remind each class to rotate. Students are then to be instructed as to the location of their next classroom activities. There are five-minute intervals for rotating. Student aides guide younger students to their next activities as well as assist with the preparation for the activities.

4. The faculty or the Peace Activities Celebration committee decides whether or not to hold an all-school assembly, either as a way of starting off the day or as a culmination activity at the close. If there is to be an assembly, decide which classes will be participating and what each will contribute.

5. Nametags for each student are provided in the form of the peace symbol—a dove. (Doves and ready-to-send Dove Invitations are provided in the Handouts section of this book.) The dove nametags will also enable teachers to learn names of students in the school other than those in his or her own classroom. The dove forms could alternatively be used for students to write peace poems. The peace doves may be hung in the front hall, welcoming all to the Peace Activities Celebration!

IDEAS FOR PEACE ACTIVITIES

1. **I'm a Hit.** Activity for primary students. Paper baseballs and bats are available in bright colors. Children fill in with drawings, dictation or writing how they handle their anger by completing the sentence stem, "I'm a HIT when I handle my anger this way . . . " (Not found in this book.)

2. **It Is! It Isn't! Game.** Section the room into two areas. Controversial statements are read and kids go to one of the above areas to show if they agree or disagree.

3. **It's Your Move!** Activity sheets. Plan your moves in a conflict situation so everybody is a winner.

4. **We're AMAZING!** Role plays. Groups perform their own renditions of "Steamed in Line" or "Give Me a Little Credit!" (role plays found in "Amazing Ways to Make Your Point"). Or situations may be made up in which the undesirable aggressive style is performed first, followed by the desirable way of assertively approaching the problem.

5. **Cool Sounds.** Activity sheets, "Cool Sounds," or musical notes cut out of colorful paper are available for each child to fill in a present conflict in their lives. Use "When you . . . I feel . . . because . . ." statements inside the musical notes.

6. **Don't Get Ticked!** Games of tic-tac-toe found on the "Don't Get Ticked!" activity sheets are played individually while children look at how they handle their angry feelings.

7. **Sole Talk.** The game of "I Want What You Have" is played with each partner trying to convince the other to give up the "gift" (a picture of the gift) without offer of money or force. Students see what a problem is like from another's viewpoint when they reverse the roles.

8. **Soda Shop.** Milkshakes from "Look for a Smooth Solution" are given to students (or make your own sundaes or sodas out of white paper so kids can color in their favorite flavors) to plan how they will handle their anger to get a smooth solution next time they're *all shook up*!

9. **A Peaceful Journey.** Relaxation time. Soft music is played while children are taken through an imagination journey in which they picture a peaceful situation. You may use "A Peaceful Journey" from the book or make up your own journey for the children.

10. **Smart Signals.** Activity sheets. After deciding which stoplight should be used for the situations on the sheet, kids may form groups to role play the situations on the activity sheet.

11. **Brush Up on TLC.** Students use the TLC Recipe to solve the "toothpaste problem" in the "Brush It Off? No Way!" activity sheet. Some humorous solutions can be role played.

12. **Sticky Situations.** Kids form pairs and share "sticky situations" as explained on the activity sheet "Oops! Wilbert Put His Foot in His Mouth." They then role play their humorous acts.

13. **Jumpin' Jellybeans!** Colorful paper is cut into jellybean shapes and, from everyday conflict situations (provided by the students and written on a chart or the board), one is chosen to be worked out by students individually on their jellybeans using the TLC

Recipe so that nobody feels like a *loser*. Primary students may dictate or draw pictures on their jellybeans.

14. **We Paint a TLC Approach to Conflict Solving.** Bright paper is cut into shapes of paint blobs for students to write about how they would solve a conflict using the TLC Recipe. *Conflict situation:* Two friends go to a movie together and leave a third friend behind. Display with the caption "Color Us Unique at Solving Conflicts" on a large easel, with palette and brush. (Not found in this book)

15. **What's Wrong with This Picture?** Review listening skills on this activity sheet. Divide kids into pairs. One is A (whose last name is closer to the beginning of the alphabet) and the other is B. Tell them when you call out a particular listening skill for B's, for example, "B's, let me see you using *open body language!*" B's are to *do the opposite* to their partners! B's would *cross their arms and legs and avoid eye contact*. The partners then tell them how that makes them feel ("Not listened to.") A's are to then do the skill the *right way*! They *use direct eye contact, bodies open to their partners*.

16. **Three's Company!** "Plug in to Mediation" activity sheets. The ten points on the sheet are visible on a chart or the board along with three real-life conflict situations from which each group will choose to mediate. Divide students into groups of three and designate who's A, B, and C. Students take turns as to who will mediate the conflict.

17. **Line Up Against V-I-O-L-E-N-C-E.** Each student receives one letter of the word "violence." They write a word that begins with that letter and a short paragraph about how they feel the word they chose contributes to violence. *Example:* **V**engeance. How does vengeance contribute to violence? Choose the most expressive words and articles for each letter. They are then recited by their authors at your Peace Day assembly. Each child holds up a large poster with his or her letter, forming a line to spell the word "violence." (Not found in this book)

18. **Showcase of MAD Events.** Cut out hats with the five conflict styles and pass one to each student. (See "Stylish Lifesavers.") Given a real-life conflict, the students act out the style on his or her hat in a role play with a partner. Then host a "Mad Hatters' Tea Party" and serve a snack. *Conflict situation:* A child loans a video to a friend and the friend loses it. (Not found in this book)

19. **We're Hot Stuff! (at Cooling Down!)** Hot chili peppers are cut out of bright red paper. Students write their best ways to "cool down" when they're angry. All are displayed together hanging from twine "branches." (Not found in this book)

20. **We're Out of This World (Handling Our Anger)** Activity for primary students. Cut out colorful spaceships for each child to write or dictate how he or she should first "cool off" when angry as an alternative to "taking off" when angry by hitting or shouting. (Not found in this book)

MUSIC FOR PEACE ACTIVITIES CELEBRATION:

Enable students to enjoy music while learning peace and conflict solving from the lyrics of one of the songs suggested below or of your own or the students' choices. If you aren't musically gifted, borrow a recording of the song, play it a couple of times for the group—and soon the whole group will be singing along! Words to the song should be visually available on paper and/or a chart or the board. (Your student aides could help to prepare a copy of the words to the song ahead of time.) If an assembly is planned, you may choose to teach each of your classes one of the songs that will be performed by a class at the assembly so that all classes can join in singing together. Sign up your chosen song on the Peace Activities Celebration Sign-Up List or join together with another class (or more) to perform a song at the assembly.

* "Celebration" by Kool and the Gang (as a "kick-off" entrance song)
* "Circle of Life" by Elton John
* "Hero" by Mariah Carey
* "Lean on Me" by Bill Withers
* "One Moment in Time" by Whitney Houston
* "The Rose" by Bette Midler
* "The Living Years" by Mike and the Mechanics
* "The Dance" by Garth Brooks
* "Yes, I Can" by Baldy

  "Forever Yesterday, for the Children" by Gladys Knight

  "From a Distance" by Bette Midler

  "He Ain't Heavy; He's My Brother" by the Hollies

  "I Know" by Beautiful World

  "Put a Little Love in Your Heart" by Jackie DeShannon

  "Shower the People" by James Taylor

  "Stand by Me" by Ben E. King

  "The Heart of the Matter" by Don Henley

  "The Greatest Love of All" by Whitney Houston

  "What the World Needs Now Is Love" by Dionne Warwick

  "You've Got a Friend" by Carole King or James Taylor

* "Between Friends" by Richard Samuels

  "New Attitude" by Patti Labelle

* "What a Wonderful World" by Louis Armstrong

  "Rise Up" by Parachute Club

  "Angels Among Us" by Alabama

  "Can You Feel the Love Tonight?" by Elton John

*Indicates meaningful songs to be performed by classes at graduation as well as peace ceremonies.

PEACE ACTIVITIES CELEBRATION SIGN-UP SHEET

Sign up below for one of our Peace Activities Celebration activities! If you have an activity of your own, feel free to use it. If you're looking for an idea, check the attached list.

Name   **Activity**

1. _____   _____

2. _____   _____

3. _____   _____

4. _____   _____

5. _____   _____

6. _____   _____

7. _____   _____

8. _____   _____

9. _____   _____

10. _____   _____

11. _____   _____

12. _____   _____

13. _____   _____

14. _____   _____

15. _____   _____

16. _____   _____

17. _____   _____

18. _____   _____

19. _____   _____

20. _____   _____

7–8. HOT BBQ SIZZLER—TLC RECIPE

This activity sheet is intended to give students an easy way to remember some guidelines for handling a conflict in a way that nobody ends up feeling like a *loser*. The **BBQ Technique** and the **TLC Recipe** give children the ingredients needed to emerge from the conflict feeling as if the needs of both have been met so that everyone feels happy with the outcome.

Materials Needed:

- "Hot BBQ Sizzler—TLC Recipe" activity sheet
- Scissors
- Props for role plays (optional): chef's hat, apron, cooking utensils, portable chalkboard for use as menu

Directions:

1. Announce to your class that you have a great recipe for them to try, one easy enough for all to have great success. The "fixings" are readily available to each one of them: they all have the ingredients within themselves. They don't even have to go out and buy anything for this recipe! Pass out the activity sheets and choose a student to read aloud the TLC introductory recipe at the top of the sheet.

2. Introduce the **BBQ Technique** and the **TLC Recipe** by writing both on a "menu" chart or board. Explain as you write out the BBQ Technique that these initials (BBQ) serve as a sizzling way to remember **Better Be Quiet** when first facing a conflict situation in which one feels very angry. This technique gives those involved in the conflict time to cool down and to plan how best to proceed. Taking a deep breath and counting to at least ten enables them to control their anger before it controls them. Hold a class discussion about conflicts they have had (volunteers only in order to avoid any embarrassing displays of anger a student would prefer not to disclose in front of classmates) in which they felt their anger controlled them. Ask, "If you had stopped quietly to cool down first, might you have handled your anger more effectively?" *Response:* "I was so mad, I didn't stop to think ahead. I just blurted out some angry shouting and started punching!" Ask if they feel the BBQ Technique would have changed the way the conflict was handled. *Response:* "If I had cooled off, I would not have said and done the things I did that hurt the other person."

3. Give students the ingredients that come after the BBQ Technique, the **TLC Recipe**. Write on your "menu" as you explain each letter of the recipe.

    T: Tune in to *both* of your feelings by taking turns saying, "When you . . . I feel . . . because . . ."

    L: Listen to how the other person sees the problem, then take turns repeating back the other's words.

    C: Choose a solution to meet *both* persons' needs so nobody feels like a *loser*.

7–8. HOT BBQ SIZZLER—TLC RECIPE (cont'd)

Discuss each of the above points by doing some examples of conflict situations given to you by students (real or imagined) and go through the conflict using each of the steps above.

4. After passing out the activity sheets, ask students to think of a real or made-up conflict situation they would like to role play with a partner. Their lines for the role play are to be written after each of the TLC letters, following the guidelines for each letter as given in the TLC Recipe.

5. Students may cut out their TLC Recipes to tape to their notebooks for easy reference. You may want to leave your "menu" on display during your Conflict Resolution unit until the students have internalized the desired behavior during conflicts.

HOT SIZZLER!!

Here's a SIZZLER: When a conflict gets "too hot to handle," first remember the **BBQ** technique: Better Be Quiet! Count at least to ten! Then follow this recipe: Don't try to be a hot dog when you find yourself in a pickle. Relish the care you give, turn over gently so nobody gets burned, hold the HOT stuff, and top with TLC (Tender Loving Care)! Grate! Remember to use a little "tenderizer" to soften your conflict by following the **TLC RECIPE** below. Then you can say to yourself, "Well done!"

Role play a conflict situation (real or made-up) with a partner. First, act out how you will use the **BBQ Technique** to cool off. Then role play using the **TLC RECIPE** to solve your conflict.

TLC RECIPE

*<u>TUNE IN</u> to *both* of your feelings by taking turns saying, "When you . . . I feel . . . because . . ."

*<u>LISTEN</u> to how the other sees the problem, then take turns repeating back the other's words.

*<u>CHOOSE A SOLUTION</u> to meet *both* persons' needs so nobody feels like a *loser*.

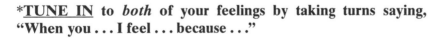

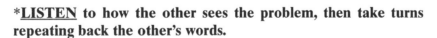

7-9. BRUSH UP ON TLC
AND 7-10. BRUSH IT OFF? NO WAY!

This activity provides students the opportunity to *brush up* on the **TLC Recipe**. They are encouraged to describe how they will approach a conflict using the **BBQ (Better Be Quiet) Technique** to calm down, then the **TLC Recipe** to solve the conflict.

Materials Needed:

- "Brush Up on TLC" and "Brush It Off? No Way!" activity sheets*
- Colored pencils, markers

Directions:

1. Announce to your class that they are going to receive a tube of Truthpaste (on paper!) for this activity so that they can brush up on their BBQ Technique and TLC Recipe for handling their conflicts. Explain that the Truthpaste is to remind them to *stick to an honest approach* when telling the other person their feelings and their needs.

2. Pass out both activity sheets. Ask for a student volunteer to orally read the activity directions at the top of the activity sheet, "Brush Up on TLC." Students refer to their "Brush It Off? No Way!" activity sheets and read together the story about Perly White's dilemma. Ask students to fill in on their "Brush Up on TLC" activity sheets the solution they would use to solve Perly White's toothpaste problem. They place their solutions in each of the T–L–C letters on the sheet.

3. Students will enjoy using this story as a humorous role-play to act out. Or students could use the idea of this story for their own stories they write about a humorous problem situation they create or one they have experienced. Students then write out the stories and, if desired, role play for the class.

* See reproducible handout on page 288.

BRUSH UP ON TLC

Remember to first cool off with the **BBQ Technique** (Better Be Quiet) and then use the **TLC Recipe: T**une in to both of your feelings by taking turns saying, "When you . . . I feel . . . because . . ." **L**isten to how the other sees the problem, then take turns repeating back the other's words. **C**hoose a solution to meet both person's needs so nobody feels like a *loser*. Don't give the other person the *brush-off*!

Think of a conflict you are now having in your life—or use the story of Perly White. Write beside each TLC letter written with Truthpaste (be honest!) how you will approach your conflict. Then give yourself some "Way to go, (your name)!" positive strokes!

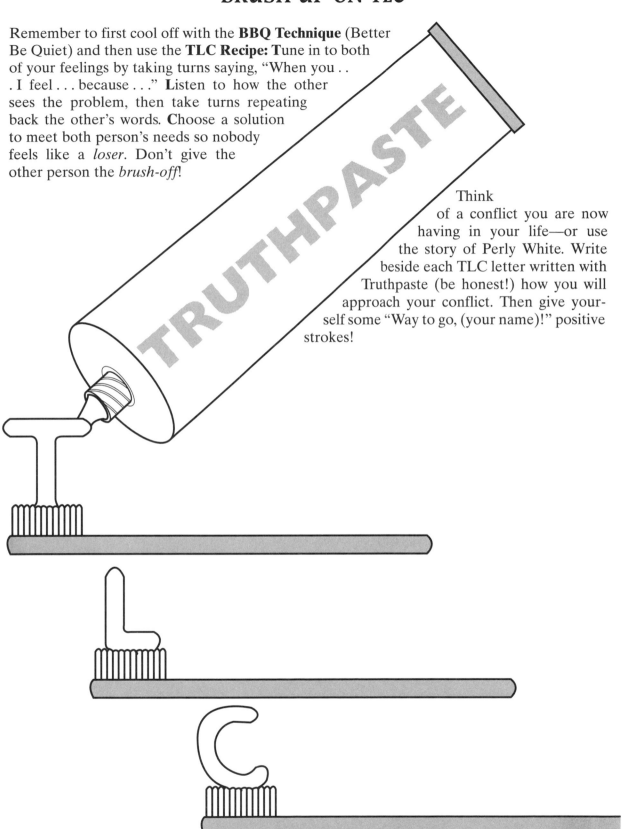

217

BRUSH IT OFF? NO WAY!

Hi, my name's Perly White and here's the situation: My family has different opinions on how to squeeze our toothpaste, which six people share, supposedly, two or three times a day. We're just about split on how to squeeze the tube. Half of our family members squeeze the tube from the middle or even from the top so they can quickly get the toothpaste out, put it onto the toothbrush, and then hurry off. The other family members take the time to squeeze the tube from the bottom, like civilized people, rolling the bottom up as the tube is gradually emptied, which seems to me to be the practical thing to do, even though it may take an extra nine seconds or so. The same people who squeeze from the bottom also take the time to clean the toothpaste off the top of the tube so it doesn't get goopy! Guess which ones don't put the cap on when they're finished? You guessed it, the middle-of-the-tube squeezers! I usually try to *cap* my annoyance at what to me is an extremely lazy approach by those who don't care when the tube starts to look like a twisty toy. Do you have an issue like this in your family? Maybe you can brush it off better than I can. How would *you* solve this, although small, conflict which is still *really annoying* to a neat person?

Directions:

Use the above story to fill out your "Brush Up on TLC" activity sheet. Go through the problems this family has with their toothpaste using the TLC Recipe. This story may give you a "stroke of genius" for a fun story you could write about a similar ordinary problem you have. *Brush up* on your dramatic role-playing skills using your own similar humorous problem situations and stories (real or made-up) describing how to come up with solutions.

7-11. DON'T GET CARRIED AWAY!

How do you usually let off "hot air"? Do you get *carried away* by your anger? These questions are explored in this activity. Analyzing their usual reactions when angry, who they are often angry with, and what they are often angry about enables students to take a look at patterns that emerge each time they feel anger. They can then think about some different ways they could begin to handle their anger in the future and how they will feel about the changes.

Materials Needed:

- "Don't Get Carried Away!" activity sheet
- Pencils, pens

Directions:

1. Pass out activity sheets as you ask students to be on the lookout for poor Wilbert, who has gotten himself into trouble again. This time he is being carried away in a hot air balloon when he couldn't let out his own "hot air" very well and shouted before he stopped to cool down.

2. Ask for a volunteer to read the top of the activity sheet, which asks that students try to help Wilbert handle his anger differently next time.

3. Go through the questions once together with volunteers who are willing to share their experiences involving anger.

4. When you prepare students to answer the questions individually, point out to them that they will see emerging patterns as to what often **triggers** or sets off their anger. They will also become aware of **traps** they often fall into each time they get angry. Give your class an example of a trigger that always makes Wilbert fly into a shouting tirade. Every time he is called "geeky," Wilbert gets *triggered* because he gets embarrassed that kids think he is a geek. His checkered shirt, which he thinks looks cool, is often laughed at! Wilbert gets *trapped* because he has some doubts about himself, feeling maybe he really is a geek. When someone triggers him, he gets stuck in the same old trap of shouting and flailing his arms about wildly. Of course, this makes kids laugh harder at Wilbert, so he shouts louder. Ask students, "How would you suggest Wilbert treat his triggers and traps next time?" *Responses:* "Wilbert should stop to cool down next time kids make fun of him." "Kids know how to trigger him *to get carried away* by his own anger and they think it's funny. If he would remain calm, ignore them or plan to say something clever back to them, they would get bored and stop making fun of him."

5. Instruct students to answer the questions on the numbered lines that correspond to the questions. Assure the class that these answers will not be shared with the rest of the class. Advise them to start the new way of handling their anger the next time they feel

7–11. DON'T GET CARRIED AWAY! (cont'd)

they are getting *carried away*. Tell them to notice how reactions from others change when they control their anger instead of letting anger control them.

Bulletin Board Link:

Students will enjoy making their own hot air balloons, drawing Wilbert being carried away, if desired, or themselves inside the balloons. They have two choices for writing inside the balloon: (a) Advice for Wilbert so that he doesn't get carried away or (b) different ways they will handle their own anger next time they feel they are getting carried away!

Language Arts Link:

Students write *MAD Metaphors!* expressing how they feel when they are angry. For example, "I'm mad as a raging fire." "Anger is a tornado twisting your temper with rage." "Anger is a hurricane whirling you into a spin of violence."

DON'T GET CARRIED AWAY!

Do you get carried away by your anger? Remember, *you* control your anger; it doesn't control you! Think about how you usually "let off hot air." Tell how you would like to change this method (if you feel you could do better) by answering the questions below on the corresponding numbered lines beside the hot air balloon. Poor Wilbert got carried away by a hot air balloon because he didn't know what to do with his anger! Your answers will help bring him back down, showing him a more peaceful way of dealing with his anger next time.

1. Describe how you usually react when you're angry. Are you *trapped* or stuck in the same pattern of handling your anger?
2. Who or what often *triggers* or sets off your anger?
3. What are you often angry about?
4. What are some different ways you could handle your anger?
5. How do you think you will feel when you handle your anger in a different way?

1. _____

_____

2. _____

_____

3. _____

_____

4. _____

_____

5. _____

_____

7–12. DON'T BLOW IT BY EXPLODING!
AND 7–13. OSY

The different stages of anger are compared to various stages of volcanic action in this activity. Students realize they have choices as to how they handle their anger. The graphic comparison to a volcano creates a visual to which they can relate their own styles of releasing angry emotions. Repression of angry feelings, avoidance, and denying anger are undesirable ways of handling anger, which may result in emotional harm to the student.

Materials Needed:

- "Don't Blow It by Exploding!" and "Osy" activity sheets
- Pens, pencils, paper

Directions:

1. Ask your students if they have ever stopped to think about the way they *let off steam* when they are angry. Are they able to find a pattern that is usually the same? *Responses:* "I start shouting loudly when I get mad." "I really blow up, my face gets red, and I start punching!"

2. Ask the class to think how they feel about the way they usually handle their anger. Have they ever made others angry with them by exploding? *Responses:* "I had a friend who said she got fed up with my temper blow-ups. She said she didn't want to hang out with me until I could control them better." "I used to get in trouble at school for starting fights every time I got mad. Now I try to cool down and not get physical when I'm mad."

3. Pass out the activity sheets. Assure your class that *anger is a natural emotion* and that as long as we are alive, we will all get angry sometimes! Because it will always be part of our lives, we need to learn to handle our anger the best way we can so that we do not harm ourselves or others, physically or emotionally, by our "losing it" when we get mad.

4. Call upon a volunteer to read the activity introduction at the top of the "Don't Bow It by Exploding" activity page. Tell students to look at the stages of volcanic eruptions on the page and decide which one best describes themselves most of the time. (You may decide to have your class answer these questions privately, not sharing orally with the rest of the class; or you may want to ask for volunteers to share their answers orally.) Then inquire if they are usually satisfied after the conflict is over with the way they handled their anger.

5. Instruct your class to fill out the questions at the bottom of the activity page, which ask for three examples of their own angry incidents and a comparison of their angry behavior at the time of each incident to the volcano descriptions listed on the page. Because of embarrassment some children may feel about their past behavior when angry, assure the class that their answers need not be shared with the rest of the class.

6. While discussing the fact that anger is a natural emotion, it is how we handle anger that can be harmful. It should also be stressed to students that bottling up anger within ourselves and *not* letting it out is also undesirable. This bottled-up, repressed anger can be unhealthy. Also, we tend to let the anger out on people other than the ones to whom our bottled-up anger is really directed. An example to the students of repressed anger is the story of Osy.

7-13. OSY

1. Pass out the "Osy" activity sheets to your students. Read Osy's story together as a class.

2. Ask students to answer the questions at the bottom of the sheet. The questions should be answered individually and then discussed together.

3. The purpose of the activity sheet is twofold: Students should realize that *repressed anger*, or anger that is held inside, *is not desirable*. Osy should have expressed his quiet, hidden anger for having to support his family, moving away from everything he had loved, being laughed at, and punished for falling asleep in class. He could have talked his problems over with a teacher, a counselor, or a classmate instead of keeping his emotions inside himself. The other intended objective is *empathy* created for Osy. Students need to learn to place themselves in others' situations and try to share their emotions and feelings.

4. Role play Osy's story: first the way it is told in this book, then followed by another where the students share Osy's feelings and emotions. In the second role play students will create ways to boost Osy when he is feeling down; Osy will express rather than repress his frustration and anger.

DON'T BLOW IT BY EXPLODING!

There are different ways of expressing anger we should be aware of so that we won't blow it by exploding! Take a look at the stages shown in the volcanoes and see which one best describes your behavior most times when you're angry. Remember, anger is a natural feeling everyone has and is not bad in itself. It is *how you handle the anger that can be bad*— if it hurts someone else or yourself.

Imagine your anger as *stages of volcanic action:*

1. **Inactive volcano**—"I can't make it to rent a video with you as we planned." *(hidden anger)*

2. **Smoldering volcano**—"You'll be sorry for this one of these days!" *(revenge, get even)*

3. **Erupting volcano**—"You lost the tape I loaned you? You loser!! I've had it with you!" *(exploding anger)*

4. **Active volcano**—"I got a D in Math. It's my Mom's fault! She makes me do so many jobs that I don't have time to study!" *(misplaced anger)*

5. **Expressive volcano**—"When you always choose which video we are going to watch, I feel left out." *(active, honest expression of why you feel anger)*

1. Think of three times you got angry. Tell about how you expressed your anger and which one of the above volcanoes could best describe your angry behavior.

   a. _____

   My volcanic action was: _____

   b. _____

   My volcanic action was: _____

   c. _____

   My volcanic action was: _____

2. Which volcanic action would you use *now* to express your anger for the three incidents? Why?

   a: _____

   b: _____

   c: _____

OSY

Osy's Mom, a single parent, just got laid off from work. She has health problems so she cannot find another job. To help with the bills, Osy has to work at a pizzeria in the kitchen washing dishes and cleaning up. His job ends late on week nights. Osy, his Mom, and his little sister have to move to another housing project. Osy feels angry he has to leave all his good friends behind in his old school, where he loved to play soccer after school. At his new school, Osy does not know anyone and has a new teacher. One day while the class was watching a video, Osy, who was exhausted from working late nights, fell asleep. When the lights were turned back on and students noticed him sleeping, they began to laugh. The laughter awakened Osy and he turned red from inner anger and embarrassment. His teacher was annoyed when he could not answer any of the video quiz questions. She told him he would have to stay after school to view the video and answer the questions. He knew he could not miss his job at the pizzeria. He was lucky to have the job because he was only 14 years old. Osy *appears* not to react to the students laughing at him. He nods quietly to his teacher's demands. Osy does not try to explain, shout, talk back, swear, or lash out at anyone. He only looks down at his rough, dishwasher's hands, crying silent tears deep inside where nobody can see.

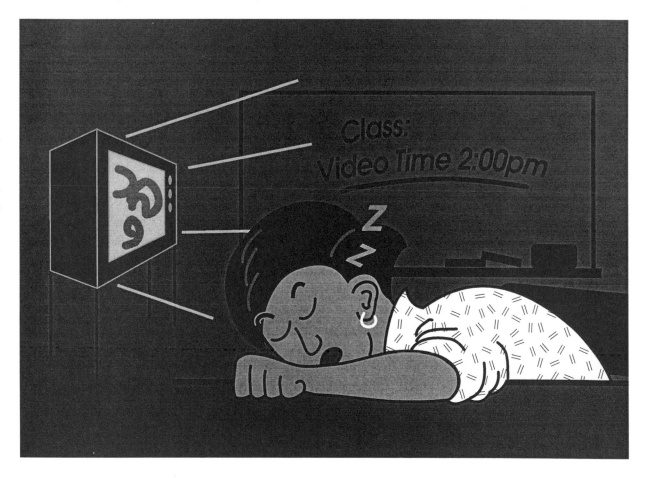

OSY

Answer the following questions, sharing the feelings you have about Osy.

1. Describe Osy's feelings throughout the story.

   _____

   _____

2. What would you do if Osy fell asleep in your class?

   _____

   _____

3. How would you feel if kids laughed at you for falling asleep in class after working late?

   _____

   _____

4. Describe how you would feel if your single parent was out of work and you had little money.

   _____

   _____

5. How can people help kids like Osy?

   _____

   _____

6. What would you advise Osy to do when the kids laughed at him and the teacher was angry with him for falling asleep in class?

   _____

   _____

7. Would you like to have Osy as a friend? Why or why not?

   _____

   _____

7-14. SMART SIGNALS

A plan that younger students can easily remember when they are *so angry that they see RED* is the **Traffic Signal Strategy**. This method enables them to remember steps to take to cool down when their behavior is a *signal* to them that their anger is getting out of hand!

Materials Needed:

- "Smart Signals" activity sheet
- Colored pencils, markers or crayons
- Large traffic light drawn on a chart or the board with strategies for cooling down

Directions:

1. Pass out the activity sheets. Tell students that if they sometimes get so angry that their faces turn red, we use the phrase, "He (or she) sees red!" Ask for a show of hands as to who has ever felt that they were seeing red. *Responses:* Most hands will probably go up. Remind them that anger is a natural emotion everyone feels at times; it is only when anger controls us rather than our controlling the anger that it is a *signal* we need to cool down.

2. Announce to your class that, speaking of signals, there is an easy method they can use the next time their anger makes them feel like they are "seeing red." It is called the **Traffic Signal Strategy**. Ask for volunteers to read the points written beside the traffic light on the activity sheet.

3. Direct students' attention to the conflict quotations at the bottom of the activity sheet. They are to decide which color of the stoplight should be used for each problem and to then write the stoplight color on the lines before each number. On the line under each conflict quotation, they are to decide what the kids in conflict should say *after* they have used the traffic signal strategies. They may create their own conflict situations for #5 and then write which traffic light is needed to help resolve the conflict.

4. Proceed as an individual or as an oral whole-class activity. If done individually, discussion should be held after students have completed the five questions. Students may then share the next step—what the kids in the conflict situations should say next to resolve the conflict. Tell students there are no single responses to each situation; if their responses "work"—that is, if they accomplish cooling down so that they can then plan to solve the conflict so that nobody feels like a loser—then they have used the Traffic Signal Strategy well!

SMART SIGNALS

When you find yourself so angry that you "see red"—STOP! Use The **Traffic Signal Strategy**. Follow these signals:

Red Light—STOP! Remember the BBQ Technique—Better Be Quiet—and count at least to ten!

Yellow Light—PROCEED WITH CAUTION! Plan to solve the conflict with *Tender Loving Care* using the TLC Recipe you have learned.

Green Light—GO! Move ahead when you feel calmer, **T**une in to both your feelings, **L**isten to how the other sees the problem, and **C**hoose a solution so nobody is a *loser*.

Which traffic light do the kids below need to use? Write in the traffic light color before each statement to help them out with their conflict situations. On the line under each, fill in what they should say next. Create your own conflict situation for number 5 and tell what you would say next.

1. _____ "I wish I had a different sister! You ate the last mini pizza! You also ate the other three!"

   _____

2. _____ "I was really ticked off at you until you explained what happened to the baseball mitt I let you borrow."

   _____

3. _____ "Now I'm planning what to do. I almost just quit this team because the coach is always on my case."

   _____

4. _____ "I'll make you sorry you ever said that about my skin color!"

   _____

5. _____   _____

   _____

7-15. LOOK FOR A SMOOTH SOLUTION

The following activity gives students the opportunity to take a look at how they behave when they are angry and then to analyze if that behavior is desirable or undesirable. Looking for a smooth solution the next time they feel "shook up" is the intended outcome.

Materials Needed:

- "Smooth Solutions" activity sheet
- Colored pencils or crayons

Directions:

1. Review with your class the fact that anger is a natural feeling we all experience. It is the way we handle our anger that results in appropriate or inappropriate behavior. Introduce the activity sheet by telling students they will be looking for smooth solutions when they feel shook up!

2. After students have received their "milkshakes," ask for volunteers who would like to share any experiences in which they felt shook up. Ask volunteers, "What was your behavior at the time?" and "How did you feel about your behavior afterward?" Provide students with an example of a situation in which a big sister gets "all shook up." The "Losin' It" scenario may be read to the class and then role played in two ways:

   a. The big sister loses her temper and speaks in an angry voice to her little brother.

   b. The big sister calmly explains to her little brother the way she feels when he breaks her things.

Losin' It!

BIG SISTER: "I really lost it with my little seven-year-old brother when he unraveled my tape. I yelled at him and he cried, then when I cooled off later, I felt guilty."

Ask the students, "How could the anger have been handled differently? Should she repeat the same behavior? If not, how should she change it next time?" *Responses:* "Next time she will remember how guilty she felt before when the yelling made her little brother cry. She will try not to get so shook up and instead explain to him how she feels when he breaks her things." "Maybe she could also remember to put her tapes away so her little brother can't reach them."

3. Direct the students' attention to their milkshake activity sheets. Ask them to recall a time when they felt all shook up and how they handled their anger at the time. Ask what were their feelings about their behavior and its effect on the person with whom they were angry. Finally, tell the class to write about what aspect of their behavior they will change in future situations. Assure them that this is going to be a learning process for the whole class. Nobody should feel embarrassed by the way they handled their anger as long as they realize *now* that there are alternative ways of handling their behavior when they are angry.

LOOK FOR A SMOOTH SOLUTION

If you find yourself in a conflict with someone, don't get all shook up! Choose a solution so that both of you feel like winners. Practice being able to look at your feelings when you are frustrated or angry by filling in the milkshake below with a SMOOTH SOLUTION.

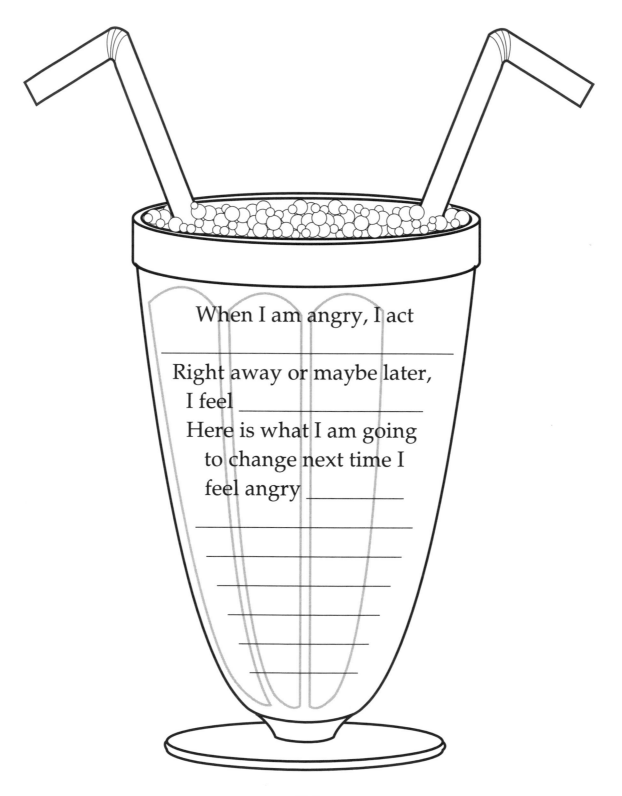

When I am angry, I act

_____

Right away or maybe later,
I feel _____

Here is what I am going
    to change next time I
    feel angry _____

_____

_____

_____

_____

_____

7–16. COOL SOUNDS

"When you . . . I feel . . . because . . ." expressions are the focus of this activity sheet. Students can relate to resolving conflicts using *cool sounds*. These statements make up the first step of the **TLC Recipe**, which is to: **Tune In** to both of your feelings by taking turns saying, "When you . . . I feel . . . because . . ." The steps to follow will make for a *soundsational* conflict resolution!

Materials Needed:

- "Cool Sounds" activity sheet
- TLC Recipe visually displayed
- Colored pencils or markers

Directions:

1. Before you pass out activity sheets, as a warm-up activity, ask students to think about some of the things said to them that are "music to their ears," that make them feel happy. Then ask for volunteers to share their favorites. *Example responses:* "When my Mom tells me I don't have to do a job for the second time because the first time it was good enough." "When I hear I can go out with my friends!" After you have heard a few pleasant oral experiences volunteered, tell students you are going to discuss some *cool sounds* we can make to others during conflicts.

2. Display visually the TLC Recipe and review the **Tune In to both of your feelings by taking turns saying, "When you . . . I feel . . . because . . ."** These statements of honest expression can also be *cool sounds* to your ears because they tell you specifically *why* the other person feels angry or frustrated and how he or she *feels*. They enable you to look at the conflict from the other's point of view.

3. After passing out the activity sheets, direct the students' attention to the three points that will help them in tuning in to the other person involved in the conflict. Ask them to read first silently, then ask a volunteer to orally read the three points that explain in detail how to use these expressions:

   - Be specific about the behavior you want to point out. Begin with "When you . . ."
   - Be honest about your own feelings concerning the situation. Say, "I feel . . ." then explain your feelings.
   - Explain how the situation bothers you. Say, "because . . ." and give the specific problem as you see it.

4. You may want to give your class an example of a conflict between two friends using this method of resolution. "*When you* always decide which movie we are going to watch, *I feel* angry (frustrated or resentful) *because* I would like us to take turns choosing our movies."

5. Instruct the class to write inside the musical notes on their activity sheets the cool sounds of "When you . . . I feel . . . because . . ." to strike some notes of accord in solv-

7-16. COOL SOUNDS (cont'd)

ing their conflicts. They may choose to make the notes more colorful by using colored pencils or markers. The conflicts they choose to express may be real or imaginary. (Some students may not want to reveal private conflicts in their lives.) A different conflict should be chosen for each musical note.

Bulletin Board Link:

A caption for a bulletin board display could read, "Music to Our Ears," "Class Notes of Accord," or "Soundsational Notes" with larger musical notes made of bristol board or art paper filled with "When you . . . I feel . . . because . . ." statements by students.

COOL SOUNDS

When you are in a conflict with someone about an issue, here are some *cool sounds* that may help resolve your conflict so that nobody feels like a loser. Take turns using "When you . . . I feel . . . because . . ." statements when you **Tune In** (the first step in the TLC Recipe) to both of your feelings. Remember the following three points that will help you be *soundsational*!

1. Be specific about the behavior you want to point out. Begin with "When you . . ."
2. Be honest about your own feelings about the situation. Say, "I feel . . ." then explain your feelings.
3. Explain how the situation bothers you. Say "because . . ." For example, "When you always decide which movie we are going to watch, I feel angry and frustrated because I would like us to take turns choosing our movies."

Fill in the musical notes below with "When you . . . I feel . . . because . . ." *cool sounds* while thinking about a conflict situation in your life now or in the past.

7-17. IT'S YOUR MOVE!

Comparing conflict resolution to a chess game in this activity emphasizes to students the value of careful planning of their "moves" in a conflict situation and the consequences that will follow. Students are encouraged to choose the best move so that nobody feels like a loser.

Materials Needed:

- "It's Your Move" activity sheet
- Large chessboard made of art paper or bristol board showing large chess player with questions from activity sheet printed inside *(optional)*

Directions:

1. After passing out the activity sheets, ask your class, "Who knows how to play the game of chess?" Choose one of the volunteers to explain what must be done before each chess piece is moved. *Response:* "Each move has to be planned ahead of time while stopping to give some thought to the strategy you want to use." Ask your students, "How is this planning similar to solving conflicts?" *Response:* "You need to stop when you're angry and plan your next move in the conflict."

2. Ask, "What is the difference in a game of chess that we do not look for in the way we have learned to solve conflicts?" *Response:* "In chess, there is a winner and a loser. We've learned in conflict our goal is to work out a solution so there is no loser—everyone wins."

3. Direct students to their activity sheets to fill in the answers while thinking of a conflict going on in their lives now or in the past. Remind them to choose "moves" they would take so that everyone involved in the conflict will come out feeling like a winner!

Bulletin Board Link:

A group of students could make a chessboard as background for a large chess player containing the conflict resolution questions from the activity sheet, "It's Your Move." Students could cut out chess figures they have drawn as people in their own conflicts, showing the words they have used to resolve their conflicts and attach them to the large chessboard entitled "It's Your Move," "Cool Moves," or "Smart Players." Any game could be substituted for the chess game, e.g., checkers with large black and red circles used on a checkerboard background.

IT'S YOUR MOVE!

A. When you are involved in a conflict, after you have stopped to "cool off," it is time to plan or set up your next move or goal. Remember, your goal should be: "Nobody is the loser—everyone involved in the conflict comes out feeling like a winner." A difference in comparing conflict solving to a game of chess is that in chess there is a winner and a loser. The value in comparing conflict resolution to a chess game is that you choose your moves after considering several possibilities. Try to choose the best move so that nobody feels like a loser. Think about a conflict you would like to solve so that "everybody comes out a winner."

Set up your next move in a conflict you would like to solve by answering the following questions:

1. With whom am I angry? _____

2. What am I angry about? _____

3. What are both our needs? _____

4. What are some possible ways to solve our conflict so nobody loses? _____

_____

_____

_____

5. What does A and B's body language say about their conflict solving?

_____

_____

_____

B.

6. How will you both feel as a result of your solution?

_____

_____

_____

235

7–18. OOPS! WILBERT PUT HIS FOOT IN HIS MOUTH

Students can relate to the "sticky situations" humorous Wilbert experiences. Learning how to speak calmly and assertively in tense situations is a life skill students will use frequently. *Empathy* for the feelings of others is also an intended outcome of this activity.

Materials Needed:

- "Oops! Wilbert Put His Foot In His Mouth" activity sheet
- Props for role plays *(optional)*

Directions:

1. As you distribute the activity sheets, students will be amused to see their old friend, Wilbert, with his foot stuck in his mouth! Ask if they are familiar with the meaning of the phrase, "I've put my foot in my mouth!" *Responses:* "I've said the wrong thing!" "I've said something to embarrass someone else—or myself!"

2. Choose a student to read the activity introduction at the top of the sheet, explaining how Wilbert always seems to say the wrong thing during "sticky situations" or times of conflict. Ask, "How many of you can relate to Wilbert by sometimes saying the wrong thing in a 'sticky situation'?" Responses: Most hands will probably go up! Assure students that it is natural to make some mistakes at times, especially when we are faced with a conflict in which we feel emotionally upset.

3. You may choose to use the activity sheet as a whole-class activity, having each of the four "sticky situations" read aloud as students choose the better responses for each, followed by the role plays. Or you may prefer to assign students the roles and play them out after the class finishes individually filling in the better responses. Students will enjoy the humorous names and the way Wilbert gets himself into trouble in the "sticky situations."

4. Introduce the term *empathy*. After writing the term on a chart or the board, explain that empathy is "the ability to share in another's emotions or feelings."

Language Arts Link:

Students may enjoy an extension of this activity by making "Sticky Situations" journals in which they record personal incidents they have had similar to Wilbert's, accompanied by drawings of the incidents, if desired. Students should include how they responded *before* this activity to the situations and how they would *now* respond with empathy for the feelings of others while expressing themselves calmly. Students' creative titles are encouraged. *Examples:* "Journal of My Stickiest Situations" or "Unmentionables Now Told" or "No-Fail Ways to Turn Your Face Red!"

Sticky Situations Answers: 1.B 2. C 3. D 4. A

OOPS! WILBERT PUT HIS FOOT IN HIS MOUTH

Wilbert can't seem to say the right thing in "sticky situations" or times of conflict. When he's upset, he doesn't stop to think before he speaks. He blurts out angry words, putting his "foot in his mouth," or saying the wrong thing. Of course, then the conflict only gets worse! Help Wilbert find the right way to approach a disagreement. Put the right words *right* into Wilbert's mouth by putting the letter of the answer you choose for Wilbert under the STICKY SITUATION. Your goal is for both persons involved in the conflict to feel happy with Wilbert's new knack of saying the *right* thing! Role-play the sticky situations first using the wrong methods, then role-play the same situations using the conflict-solving skills you have learned.

1. **STICKY SITUATION:**
   Wilbert dropped his pencil during an English test and his teacher, Mrs. Sharpeyes, asked him suspiciously what he was doing. "It's not fair! You thought I was cheating, didn't you, Mrs. Sharpeyes?" Wilbert then received a lecture.
   A BETTER RESPONSE: _____

2. **STICKY SITUATION:**
   Wilbert's mom came home to find him watching TV. What she didn't know was he had completed his homework after school and had just sat down to watch TV. "Wilbert, turn off that TV and study!" his Mom said. "I can't even relax around here! You're so mean to me!" Wilbert shouted and ran to his bedroom.
   A BETTER RESPONSE: _____

3. **STICKY SITUATION:**
   Wilbert asked Sandy Beach when her birthday was because he was nosy about whether she was 12 yet. She thought it meant he wanted to buy her a gift! When Wilbert found out, he blurted out, "Sandy, I just wanted to know hold old you are because you look a lot younger than 12 and not so I could buy you something. I don't even like you, really!" Sandy's face turned red from embarrassment.
   A BETTER RESPONSE: _____

4. **STICKY SITUATION:**
   Injured with a sprained ankle after he slipped on a banana peel at recess, Wilbert shouted loudly at Ian Ocent, who happened to be carrying a lunchbox, "Hey! Haven't you heard of throwing your leftovers into the trash bin? You'll be sorry for this accident!" Ian Ocent had not dropped the peel. He then got angry with Wilbert, followed by a fight which left Wilbert with a swollen eye.
   A BETTER RESPONSE: _____

Help Wilbert with Better Responses He Could Have Chosen:

A. "Next time I'll watch where I'm heading! Could someone help? 'I've fallen and I can't get up' as the saying goes!"

B. "I was picking up my pencil which I dropped."

C. "I changed my routine and did my studying right after school today, before the TV time we agreed I could watch every day. You had no way of knowing because you were at work."

D. "Hey, it's cool you have a birthday in May. I just wondered if you'd turned 12 yet."

7–19. DON'T' GET TICKED!

This activity provides a **review** of handling anger in the form of a tic-tac-toe game. Students will enjoy trying to obtain a win with three X's or O's in a row while answering review questions about the emotions involved when angry and cooling off before using the TLC Recipe.

Materials Needed:

- "Don't Get Ticked!" activity sheet
- Pencils, pens
- Large tic-tac-toe grid numbered one to nine inside each square on a chart or the board

Directions:

1. Ask your class to raise their hands if they have played the game of tic-tac-toe. After seeing the show of hands, ask for a volunteer to explain the object of this game. *Response:* "To win the game, you must complete a straight or diagonal row of three X's or three O's." Demonstrate the various possibilities of the X's or O's in winning rows on your large tic-tac-toe grid or chart.

2. Pass out activity sheets to students as you announce that they will now be playing a game of tic-tac-toe as they answer questions reviewing what they have learned about handling their anger.

3. Call on a student to read the activity instructions at the top of the page. As an additional reminder to them as they fill in their tic-tac-toe grids, write X = YES and O = NO on a chart or the board.

4. Instruct students to answer the questions on their worksheets by filling in an " X" or an "O" in the corresponding number inside the tic-tac-toe grids on their activity sheets. Tell students that although tic-tac-toe is usually played between two people, they are going to play it individually for this activity. Ask them not to share with others the numbers of the squares in which they had their winning rows before, as a class, you have discussed each question and answer. Write, or have student volunteers write as students give you the correct answers, onto your large tic-tac-toe grid on your chart or board. The answers are as follows:

1. NO—O; 2. YES—X; 3. YES—X; 4. YES—X; 5. NO—O; 6. YES—X; 7. NO—O; 8. YES—X; 9. NO—O.

DON'T GET TICKED!

How do you handle your angry feelings? Answer the following questions in the numbered squares in the "Don't Get Ticked!" tic-tac-toe game. Answer with an "X" for YES and "O" for NO. If you complete a straight or diagonal row of three X's or three O's, you win at "Don't Get Ticked!"

1.	2.	3.
4.	5.	6.
7.	8.	9.

1. Shouting is the first step to take when you find yourself in a conflict because it lets the other person know he or she is in for it.

2. Anger is not bad in itself; it's how you react to another person when you are angry or what you do with your anger that can be bad.

3. Anger is an emotion everybody feels.

4. Sometimes a conflict isn't about what just happened; it's about built-up anger from what's been happening with the other person at other times.

5. When you're angry with someone, plunge right in to tell him or her off.

6. It's a good idea in a conflict to repeat back the other's words to him or her so they know that you understand how they see the problem.

7. You need to look out *only for yourself* in a conflict—your concerns are all that really matter.

8. Both persons involved in a conflict should feel like winners; nobody should feel like a loser.

9. The best way to get what you want is to use physical force.

7–20. STYLISH LIFESAVERS

We have choices of conflict styles to use when we are angry. This activity explains these conflict-style choices to children. It points out the need to "cool off" before planning how to "dive in," using the conflict style that has the highest regard for all involved in the conflict.

Materials Needed:

- "Stylish Lifesavers" activity sheet
- Five large lifesavers drawn on the board or a chart OR large lifesavers made from colorful art paper, a different color for each style. These could be strung in a corner of the classroom along with a colorful, real inflatable lifesaver.

Directions:

1. After reviewing the fact that anger is an emotion everyone feels, explain that we all have choices as to how we are going to handle our anger after using the **BBQ Technique** (Better Be Quiet and count at least to ten, while cooling off).

2. As you explain the conflict styles, you may want to provide visual display written on a chart or board or to provide colorful lifesavers containing the different styles.

3. Introduce the different ways of handling conflicts by asking students, "What are all the various possibilities that both people involved will feel when a conflict ends?" Write the answers as they are volunteered on the chart, board or paper lifesavers so that the responses are visible to all. *Responses:* "There is a winner and there is a loser." "One gives in and the other wins." "One avoids the conflict and loses." "Both people give and take, a 50/50 situation." "Both work together toward a solution and both feel they have a 100/100 win."

4. As students volunteer responses, fill in each lifesaver, helping with the wording when needed so that the answers read as follows, while you introduce each conflict-style term:

   ACCOMMODATOR: I give in—You win.

   AVOIDER: I leave—I (sometimes) lose.

   COMPETITOR: I win—You lose.

   COMPROMISER: You and I give and take, a 50/50 win.

   COLLABORATOR: We work together. We both win, 100/100.

5. Ask students which of the above styles they have chosen when involved in a past conflict and how that style worked out for both involved. Ask them to include how they would handle the conflict now that they are aware of different approaches. *Response:* "Usually, when we choose which TV program to watch, one of us wins and one of us loses. I'd feel better, and I think the other person would also feel better, if we tried the COLLABORATOR style because both of us would totally win! We will both agree on only watching both our favorite shows."

6. Ask the class to discuss each of the five conflict styles, giving an example of each. The examples may be real or made-up situations. Point out that the AVOIDER, the person who "walks away" or puts an imaginary paper bag over his or her head, *sometimes* loses an opportunity to win by avoiding. However, there are some conflicts that *benefit by this avoidance*, at least for the time being if, for example, more time is needed to cool off and plan. Thus, these styles are subject to the components of individual conflict situations.

7. As you pass out activity sheets, tell the class that they are each going to get their own lifesavers from which to choose how to cool off, then to plunge in for the best resolution to their own personal experiences with conflicts.

STYLISH LIFESAVERS

When you feel a wave of anger in a conflict, don't let the anger overcome you! Handle your anger by first cooling off, then by planning how you are going to approach the conflict. The life-savers below offer you different *conflict styles* for solving your problems. Read the approaches for each style of conflict solving. Ask yourself, "How do I want everyone involved in the conflict to feel with the solution?" Then reach out for the best approach before you plunge in to solve your conflict.

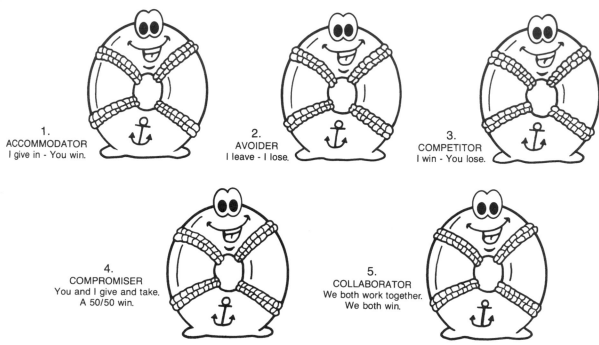

1. ACCOMMODATOR
I give in - You win.

2. AVOIDER
I leave - I lose.

3. COMPETITOR
I win - You lose.

4. COMPROMISER
You and I give and take.
A 50/50 win.

5. COLLABORATOR
We both work together.
We both win.

1. Think of a conflict you are now having. Choose which conflict style number above you would reach out for as a "lifesaver". Write the number and why you have chosen this style for your conflict._____

_____

_____

2. Recall a past conflict you have had and write the number of the conflict style you used to solve it. _____ How did it work out?

_____

_____

3. Would you repeat the same conflict style for the past conflict in #2 now that you are aware of other ways of solving conflicts?_____ Why? Why not?

_____

_____

_____

7–21. HAUNTED!

What's *really* happening here? What is the real issue, communication, or personal feeling going on with this conflict? Is it the present situation or a "ghost of the past"? This activity deals with exploring what is behind the behavior displayed. At times, the issue is not about the present but about an unresolved past issue.

Materials Needed:

- "Haunted!" activity sheet
- Pencils, pens

Directions:

1. Pass out the activity sheets to students, explaining that sometimes we confuse unsolved issues or problems in our pasts with present problems. Introduce the term "ghosts of past conflicts" as you prepare to write the elements usually involved in conflicts on a chart or the board.

2. Write the following terms and discuss each point, all of which answer the question, "What's *really* happening here?" Begin by asking for the meaning of the term "resolve." *Response:* "To find the solution or answer to a problem."

   - **ISSUES**—What are the problems that need to be **resolved** about the issue at hand or the issue now? Is there underlying anger about an issue that happened before, a ghost of a past conflict?

   - **COMMUNICATION**—Are you giving each other enough information about your feelings and needs with respect to the conflict now? Are you sure you are not dealing with a past conflict? What kind of body language are you giving? Closed body language—crossed arms, legs or your eyes or body positioned away from your partner, along with frowns or scowls, can "haunt" your best oral conflict-resolving efforts!

   - **PERSONAL FEELINGS**—Are you dealing with angry or hurt feelings about this present conflict or are your feelings really about a past conflict? Are you expressing your feelings openly and honestly?

3. Hold a class discussion asking for volunteers to recount a conflict they experienced and, looking back, reacted not to the issue at hand or the present issue, but to something that took place in the past. As an example for the students, you may want to give them the scenario of a past conflict showing up to ruin Saturday afternoon plans for two friends:

Bowled-Over Gerry

Gerry arrived to meet Henry and happily announced he had reserved a bowling lane for them. Henry said he couldn't go bowling, even though he had promised to get together with Gerry that Saturday afternoon. Gerry angrily said, "We planned to do something together and now you're backing out. That leaves me

7–21. HAUNTED! (cont'd)

with nothing to do." Henry lost his cool and shouted, "Why does everything have to be what *you* want to do? Chill out!" Henry then looked as if he was going to hit Gerry, but instead angrily took off down the street. Gerry scratched his head, stunned, saying to himself, "What's with him? I only arranged a game of bowling." Problem was, the last four times the two boys had gotten together, Gerry had suggested, then pushed for his choice of activity with no thought of what Henry wanted to do. The past caught up with Gerry because he never listened to what Henry's interests were, which had included some outdoor sports, soccer, and basketball.

Ask students to look at the conflict from each boy's point of view and discuss the following:

a. What was the real issue? Gerry's? Henry's? *Responses:* "Gerry did not consider what Henry had, at other times, said he wanted to do—soccer and basketball." "Henry was angry at never having his needs met. He wasn't angry just about the bowling game, but the other times his activity requests were ignored."

b. How would you have suggested the communication be changed? *Responses:* "Gerry needs to listen to the needs of Henry also and take turns choosing their mutual activities." "Henry needs to make his needs known each time they make plans and not to let his anger pile up from past disappointments and finally explode as it did about the Saturday bowling game."

c. Was Henry's anger only about the bowling game that Saturday? If not, what was the issue? *Response:* "The truth was that Henry enjoyed bowling. The issue he was angry about was that he had not been included in the decision to make the activity plans when they arranged to meet that day. He remembered how many times before plans had been made with no consideration of his requests."

4. Students may now be directed to think of their own personal experiences and fill their answers inside the ghost with past conflicts that came back to *haunt* their present conflicts.

HAUNTED!

When you find yourself in a conflict situation with another person, there are usually three elements involved: **issues**, **communication**, and **personal feelings**. Consider the following points that all answer the real question, *"Hey what's <u>really</u> happening here?"*

- **ISSUES**—What are the problems that need to be **resolved** or worked out about the issue at hand now? Is there underlying anger about an issue that happened before, a ghost of a past conflict?
- **COMMUNICATION**—Are you giving each other enough information about your feelings and needs with respect to the conflict now? Are you sure you are not dealing with a past conflict? What kind of body language are you giving? Closed body language—crossed arms, legs or your body positioned away from your partner, along with frowns or scowls, can haunt your best oral conflict-resolving efforts!
- **PERSONAL FEELINGS**—Are you dealing with angry or hurt feelings about this present conflict or are your feelings really about a past conflict? Are you expressing your feelings openly and honestly?

Think of a past conflict in which the real problem was not what was going on about the issue at hand, but about something that happened before, a ghost of a past conflict. Fill in your answers in the numbered spaces in the ghost, now that you are aware of what's really happening.

1. The issue seemed to be about . . .

2. The thing I was really angry about was . . .

3. The way I communicated was . . .

4. My personal feelings I showed were . . .

5. Now I would handle the issue like this . . .

PAST
CONFLICTS

RIP

7-22. WHAT'S WRONG WITH THIS PICTURE?

Learning how to listen in everyday conversations is a life skill emphasized in this activity. The ability to listen nonjudgmentally without interrupting, in an interested manner while using open body language and direct eye contact is an activity we all would like to recommend to others at times!

Materials Needed:

- "What's Wrong with This Picture?" activity sheet
- Pencils, pens

Directions:

1. Announce to your class that they are about to receive a valuable life skill they will use often in their futures. Tell them the skill they are about to study is **listening**. Ask if any of them can think of someone (no names are to be mentioned!) they have spoken with whom they would like to recommend for a listening course! *Responses:* Most hands will probably go up! Follow these responses with asking for specific annoying habits others show when listening—or appearing to listen. *Responses:* "They don't really pay attention to what I'm saying. If I asked them to repeat back what I'd just said they wouldn't be able to." "They start to talk about their own things, as if I hadn't even been talking first." "I receive offers of advice when all I want to do is have someone listen to me without judging or offering what I *should* do."

2. Introduce the listening skills after passing out activity sheets. Discuss each skill as it is read aloud. Have a student demonstrate Open Body Language while sitting or standing next to another student to whom he or she is listening. Point body toward the person, arms and legs uncrossed, and make direct eye contact. The face and body should appear to offer the unspoken words, "I'm eager to listen to what you have to say."

3. Direct the students' attention to the illustrations at the bottom of the activity sheet. Ask them to fill in the number on the line under the illustration of the listening skill the person is ignoring.

4. Remind your class that by developing their listening skills, the more others will enjoy speaking with them and they will seek their company more often.

5. Now divide students into groups of three. One student tells a partner the highlights of what he or she did from the end of school until bed time the previous day of school. The partner listens according to the listening skills described. The role of the third person is to observe how the listener follows the skills, making notes of observation. The notes should also record how the listener remembered and repeated back what was said. The person being listened to tells how well received he or she felt as the story unfolded. Were there interruptions? Was there open body language and eye contact? Were there judgments or put-downs? Did the other person seem interested? Each person in the group of three should have a turn at each role.

Answers:

2, 3, 4; 2; 3, 4, 5

WHAT'S WRONG WITH THIS PICTURE?

When you are talking to others, do you like them to *listen* to what you are saying? If you could list some picture-perfect rules for how you would like others to listen to you, would there be any from the list below?

Listening Skills:

1. **Be interested in learning what others have to say to you.**
2. **Think about what they are saying; not what <u>you</u> are going to say next!**
3. **Make direct eye contact while you are listening, showing that you care about what they are saying.**
4. **Use open body language—avoid crossed arms and legs.**
5. **Listen to others as you enjoy others listening to you—without interruption and judgment.**

Look at the illustrations below. What's wrong with these pictures? Which of the listening skills have been forgotten? Put the numbers of the above listening skill(s) needed under each of the illustrations that need a retake. Next, form groups of three and take turns being: (a) the speaker; (b) the listener; (c) the observor who evaluates how well the listener follows the above listening skills. Choose your own topics or highlight everything you did after school until bed time the previous day of school. Each student plays each of the three roles.

7–23. IT'S A BRAINSTORM!

A valuable part of the problem-solving process is brainstorming. This activity likens brainstorming to a thunderstorm in which Wilbert has "lightning bolts of brainwaves" with the steps involved in brainstorming.

Materials Needed

- "It's a Brainstorm!" activity sheet
- Props for role play *(optional)*

Directions:

1. Intoduce the term "brainstorming," which is written on a chart or the board. Ask students to give you their definitions of this term. Tell them you would like to hear the first ideas that come to mind, that there will be no judgment or put-downs among classmates and, lastly, every idea will be written on a chart or the board. After you have heard all volunteers, decide which definitions to eliminate and which are the most accurate descriptions. *Responses:* "Getting lots of ideas from lots of different people to find a solution to a problem." "Choosing the best problem solution from a lot of possibilities given without putting down others for their ideas." When responses are completed, congratulate students on having just completed a brainstorming session themselves!

2. Pass out activity sheets showing familiar Wilbert with lightning bolts of brainwaves emitting from his head, pointing out the steps involved in brainstorming. In order to both enjoy and to remember these points more easily, the activity is compared to a thunderstorm. Students may think of their own scenarios to brainstorm and write on bottom of activity sheet.

3. As a whole-class or small-group activity:

   a. Brainstorm to get the best solution for each scenario.

   b. Role play the problem.

   c. Role play the solution decided upon after brainstorming.

Bulletin Board Link:

Title for the heading is taken from the activity, "It's a Brainstorm" or "Our Class Brainwaves." Show Wilbert with his brainwaves along with the brainstorming points. Staple an upside-down paper umbrella to the bulletin board so that there is a pouch for students to place real or made-up problems (with no names required) for the class to brainstorm at a future brainstorming session. As an alternative to the umbrella, hang large paper raindrops with problems to brainstorm written inside the raindrops.

Name _____ Date _____

IT'S A BRAINSTORM!

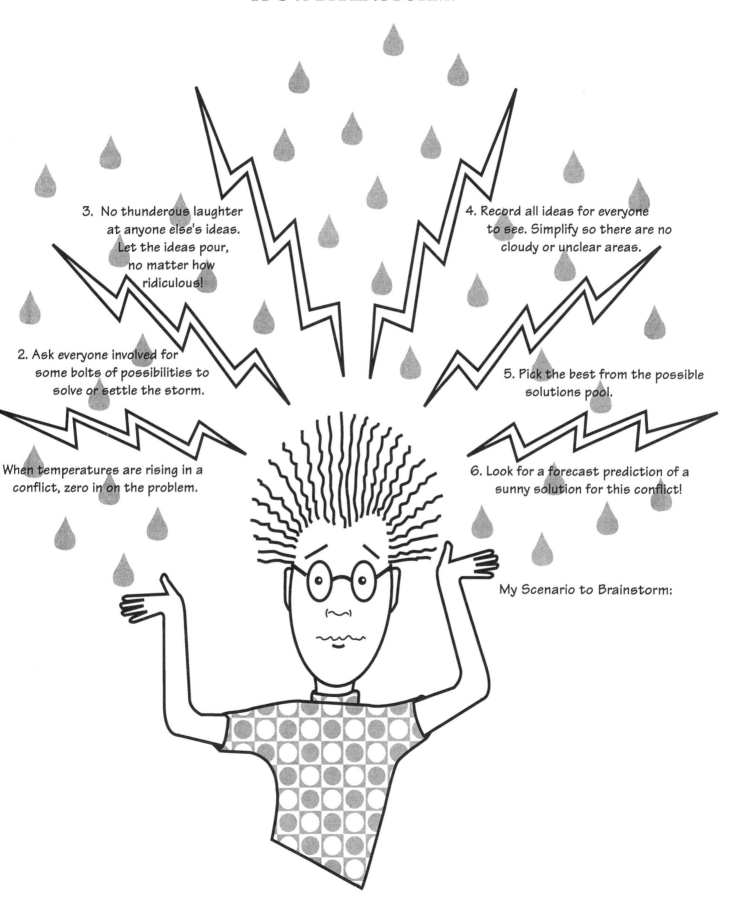

3. No thunderous laughter at anyone else's ideas. Let the ideas pour, no matter how ridiculous!

4. Record all ideas for everyone to see. Simplify so there are no cloudy or unclear areas.

2. Ask everyone involved for some bolts of possibilities to solve or settle the storm.

5. Pick the best from the possible solutions pool.

When temperatures are rising in a conflict, zero in on the problem.

6. Look for a forecast prediction of a sunny solution for this conflict!

My Scenario to Brainstorm:

7–24. AMAZING WAYS TO MAKE YOUR POINT

The ability to handle conflicts assertively is the intended outcome of this activity. This approach enables students to have their needs met without making the other person feel put down. The result is that both feel pleased with the outcome. The difference between an *assertive* versus an *aggressive* approach is pointed out through role playing depicting the loud, pushy actions of an aggressor and the calm, direct manner of the assertive person.

Materials Needed:

- "Amazing Ways to Make Your Point" activity sheet
- Role-play props *(optional)*
- Pencils, pens

Directions:

1. Write the terms "aggressive" and "assertive" on a chart or the board. Introduce the terms by asking the class how many have had an experience with a loudly demanding, pushy person who ended up getting his or her way at the expense of others' feelings. *Responses:* Most hands will go up. Ask for a few volunteers to relate some of these experiences, describing the way people involved in the conflict reacted to the demanding person. Summarize the stories by explaining that the term we use for this behavior is an "aggressive" approach to a conflict. Fill in the definition using students' definitions so that the definition reads something like, **"An approach in which people get their ways by loudly demanding, pushy means."**

2. Ask students for examples of **"An approach in which people obtain what they want in a direct, calm manner."** Write this definition of "assertive" on a chart or the board. Ask students to include descriptions of the ways people involved in the conflict reacted to the assertive approach.

3. Pass out the activity sheets. Ask a student to read aloud the opening paragraph. Direct their attention to the activity and have them circle what they feel is the best way to handle the conflict *assertively* in each of the two scenarios.

4. After the activity sheets have been completed, go over the correct answers. Discuss the approaches not chosen as the best approaches and talk about how the aggressive approach antagonizes or "turns off" others.

5. After both assertive and aggressive approaches are discussed, each scenario may be role played first with the pushy, aggressive approach, followed by the calm, assertive approach. You may choose the same students to perform both approaches or change the students for each approach.

6. Students may enjoy making up some of their own assertive versus aggressive role plays.

Answers:

1. B; 2. B

WAYS TO MAKE YOUR POINT

When you are involved in a conflict, express your feelings openly and honestly in an **assertive** approach, which enables you to have your needs met without making the other person feel put down. The result of this approach is *both* of you feeling pleased with the outcome. Some people confuse "assertive" with an "aggressive" approach. There is a big difference! Do you like others who get their way by being loud and pushy or **aggressive**? Even if the aggressive person does get what he or she wants, it often comes at the expense of the other's hurt and angry feelings.

Read the following conflict-situation scenarios and circle the better way to handle the conflict *assertively*. Then role play the scenes with a partner in the following order:

1. First, role play the (wrong) pushy, **aggressive** approach you *did not circle*.
2. Role play the (correct) **assertive** approach you *did circle* to make your needs known, while respecting the other's needs.

Scenario 1: "Steamed in Line"

You have been waiting in line at the checkout counter at the drugstore when a pushy lady cuts in front of you in line, saying, "I just have to pay for one item, this newspaper, and I have my change ready." You are steamed as the clerk takes her money ahead of you! You . . .

A. Look angrily at the sales clerk and shout, "Hey, man, this woman shoved her way into line in front of me and I've been waiting! I'm next!"

B. Look directly at the sales clerk while saying firmly, "Excuse me, sir, I have been waiting in line for my turn and this lady got in front of me. I need to to pay for my item *now* and not wait any longer."

Scenario 2: "Give Me a Little Credit!"

You thought of a great title for your annual conflict-resolution class play. Tom, a member of your planning committee for the play, tells the teacher *he* thought of the title. You . . .

A. Flip out and loudly say to the teacher, "*I'm* the one who should get the credit for thinking of that title! Tom wouldn't even be able to come up with a clever title!"

B. Look calmly at Tom, saying, "Tom, do you remember when our committee met and we discussed a title for our play? Do you recall <u>my</u> suggestion of the title *Class Acts of Accord*? Tom, you've done a great job planning the props. *When you* take credit for the title, *I feel* hurt because it was my idea just as which props to use were yours. I need you to acknowledge me for thinking of the title of the play and I will continue to give you credit for the props."

251

7–25. PLUG IN TO MEDIATION

Mediation is a method of conflict solving in which one person listens without assessment while helping to resolve a problem for others. The role of the mediator is to enable both involved in the conflict to plug into one another's needs and feelings in order to come to an agreement in which both involved in the conflict are happy with the outcome. Guidelines for mediation are presented in this activity.

Materials Needed:

- "Plug In to Mediation" activity sheet
- Mediation Guidelines displayed on a chart or the board

Directions:

1. Pass out the activity sheets. Ask for a volunteer to read aloud the explanation of the role of a mediator in a conflict-solving situation. Before reading the guidelines together orally, announce that all points are based on the goal of each person involved in the conflict "plugging in" to one another's needs and feelings. As an outcome, an agreement in which everyone feels good about the resolution is intended.

2. Students can read along on their activity sheets with the visual display of the Mediation Guidelines as each point is orally read and discussed.

3. After completing the oral reading and discussion of the guidelines, ask students to form groups of three for the purpose of implementing the mediation techniques. You may want to caution students that mediation for conflicts in which physical contact is involved should be left up to adults to intervene. However well intended their mediation attempts, student mediation must be reserved for certain types of conflicts and monitored by adults. Ethnic and racial conflict mediation also require training and expertise. Student mediators who do receive mediation training should be monitored by educators during any conflict the educator feels may escalate into a potential physically violent or racially explosive disagreement. (References are given in the Bibliography for student-mediation training programs.)

4. After students are sitting in groups of three, explain that each person in the group will have a turn as mediator. Each student may choose a conflict (one they have experienced or an imaginary conflict) to mediate when it is his or her turn to be mediator. Conflict scenes should not be limited to the school. Scenes from conflicts in the home, extracurricular activities or in sports as well as other situations the students think of should be included. The idea is that real-life scenarios are mediated because these are the events kids relate to. Each group will go through the same conflict three times. In this way, they will view different ways of approaching the conflict as each student plays a different role.

5. After each group member has taken a turn as mediator, evaluate their roles as mediators by asking students the following questions:

   - How well did you enable the two who were in conflict to "plug in" to the feelings and needs of one another?
   - Did you have difficulty finding a common point that both shared?
   - Did you have to help them brainstorm solutions?
   - Was agreement easy or difficult to reach in choosing a solution so that nobody felt like a loser?
   - Did you validate both persons involved in the conflict for reaching a fair solution that made both feel like winners?
   - Did you validate yourself for helping others come to a peaceful agreement?

Peace Link:

Select volunteers who would like to be part of a PEACE group. The purpose of the group will be to:

Plug into
Every
Action of
Conflict
Eruption

After receiving training in mediation skills, members are available when a minor conflict arises in the halls, the classroom, or on the school grounds. They mediate the dispute between the two who are in conflict. A room in the school should be made available for the three to sit down, cool off, and then begin the mediation process. A teacher should first be asked for permission to use the room and made aware of what the conflict is about. It should be noted that a serious conflict or any conflict involving weapons or physical violence of any kind must have the intervention of an adult and no attempt should be made by a student mediator to settle the conflict. It is then the PEACE member's job to immediately look for an adult to intervene or to call for assistance. The point of having an appointed PEACE group is that sometimes students can relate more openly to kids their own age.

PLUG IN TO MEDIATION

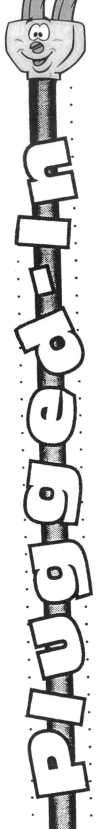

MEDIATION is a method of conflict solving in which one person listens without judgment while helping to resolve a conflict for others. The role of the mediator is to enable everyone involved in the conflict **to plug in** to one another's needs and feelings in order to come to an agreement. A mediator should follow the guidelines below:

1. Choose one person involved in the conflict to state the problem as he or she sees it while the other listens.

2. Ask the person who listened to the stated problem to repeat back his or her words to him or her.

3. The person who was the listener repeats the same process while the other person listens.

4. Summarize what each person has said and make sure each person is "plugged in" to what the other's needs and feelings are regarding the problem.

5. Ask each person to take turns describing how he or she is feeling. Ask each person to repeat how the other feels.

6. State a common point they share, such as both feeling frustrated, hurt or angry, or their mutual desire to come to a fair agreement.

7. Brainstorm ideas for solutions from each person, followed by your own suggestions if you have any possibilities that were not mentioned.

8. Ask each person which solution will work so that nobody will come out as a *loser*.

9. Validate or affirm each person for being fair with one another in choosing a solution. Let each one know you are available for any future get-togethers to reinforce what they have just agreed upon.

10. Validate yourself for helping others come to a peaceful agreement.

Group Activity:

Form groups of three. Take turns so that each member of your group has a turn being the *mediator* in a conflict between the other two people in your group. Follow the above guidelines as you plug in to the feelings and needs of others. When it is your turn to be mediator, you may be the one to choose a real conflict in your own life or you may make up a conflict for the role-playing mediation.

7-26. CONNECTIONS

How well students have learned to *connect* with one another is reviewed in this activity. Making a good connection with another person in a conflict determines the final outcome of both feeling their needs have been met.

Materials Needed

- "Connections" activity sheet
- Pencils, pens

Directions:

1. Pass out the activity sheets. Ask for a volunteer to read the "connections" opening and the instructions for the questions below. Tell students this will be an opportunity for them *to repeat back* what they have learned in this conflict-solving section.

2. Remind students to put the letter of the best connection on the line next to each conflict-solving statement.

3. When completed, you may choose to collect the activity sheets so that you may correct the reviews yourself in order to determine if any students need further skill development in certain areas of conflict solving. If a weakness is indicated, you may wish to look also at results from the Conflict-Solving Quiz. Repeating some conflict-solving activities may be needed to reinforce those concepts in the weak areas.

Answers:

1. L	6. I
2. B	7. J
3. G	8. C
4. H	9. E
5. F	10. M

Connections

The way we "connect" to one another when solving conflicts can make the difference between a solution in which both people involved feel their needs have been met and a solution in which one person comes out of the conflict feeling like a *loser*. Make a *good connection* with the other person by addressing both your needs. Put the letter of the best connection on the line next to each conflict-solving statement below.

_____ 1. When you feel very angry at the start of a conflict

_____ 2. A method of thinking of several possible solutions to the problem

_____ 3. These qualities are important when making your needs known

_____ 4. The first step in the TLC Recipe

_____ 5. In Active Listening, it's important to

_____ 6. World peace begins here

_____ 7. Using a calm, firm approach to have your needs met

_____ 8. It may not be the issue now that is bothering you; it may be

_____ 9. This is what you like to say and to hear from the other person involved in a conflict

_____ 10. You should control this emotion; it shouldn't control you

A. Dominate by force if you don't get your own way
B. Brainstorming
C. Things that bothered you other times before
D. Look at the needs both persons in the conflict have
E. Hey! Nobody's a loser
F. Repeat back the other's words to him or her
G. Honesty and openness
H. Tune in to both persons' feelings
I. Inner peace within yourself
J. Assertiveness
K. Plunge right in to tell off the person you're angry with
L. Better Be Quiet! Cool down and plan your TLC Approach
M. Anger
N. Ask, "What's in it only for me?"

7–27. I'M ALL GREEN THUMBS!

A great way to develop "down to earth" kids is to do just that—take them right down to the earth! A natural way to accomplish this task is **school ground naturalization**. Instead of waiting for a field trip to develop environmental appreciation, why not turn a section of your school's carpet of asphalt into a living, growing outdoor classroom?

What is naturalization? Plants are arranged to simulate a native plant community in which natural processes create a web of relationships. The goal is to create a natural ecosystem so that students can study the natural associations of plants and the animals, insects and birds they attract.

Why is planning for a school ground naturalization project found in a conflict-solving unit? A less hostile, not-so-sterile space will be developed with assistance from the children, and consequently, will be respected by them upon completion. If given responsibility for planning, planting and maintaining a special area, children will find ways to **peacefully solve the conflicts** that will naturally arise as they work together. Children learn that when working with others, conflicts are inevitable and they will achieve desired results if they manage their anger and use a collaborative approach so that nobody feels like a loser. They learn to listen to one another in an active way and discover the conflict style and assertive approach that works best to accomplish their tasks. A **sense of community** will be a natural outgrowth of this naturalization plan.

This project is a microcosm of environmental problems we face globally. Problem-solving skills will be called upon often when starting a brand new project such as this. Participation in planning, planting and maintaining a naturalized area provides many opportunities for children of varying levels of ability. The child who has never experienced academic success and feels socially inept *can succeed* in planning and watching something he or she has planted grow! The sense of stewardship in planning and producing a naturalized area calls upon a child to use all the components of **skills for self-esteem**: *security* (this is *my* safe space *I* helped to create), *affiliation* (being part of a planning group), *goal setting* (planning what and where to plant), *problem solving* (fundraising, enlisting people to help with landscaping, what plants grow best, etc.), *creative problem solving* (when asked, "How are we going to get needed items when we have a small budget?") In addition, *competence* is developed as *responsibility* for the role each child is to play is accepted (a feeling of *capability* and positive identity as children reap the benefits of their living, growing finished products).

Conflict-solving skills development is an integral part of this naturalization process as children learn to work cooperatively toward a common goal—their naturalized areas—just as global cooperation is needed for a peaceful world. Children learn that when working with others, conflicts are inevitable and they will benefit from the results if they manage their anger and use a collaborative approach so that nobody feels like a loser.

Materials Needed

- "I'm All Green Thumbs" activity sheet
- "Green Thumbs Certificate of Participation" activity sheet
- Magazines and catalogs of seeds and plants

Directions:

1. Creating a sense of community within your children must first come from community assistance as you begin to plan your school ground naturalization project. You will

need the support of your principal or vice principal and a *steering committee* set up. Enlist parents who can provide support for your project. Ask for volunteers who have some knowledge of landscaping and gardening to help plan your area. Seek horticultural societies, garden and naturalist clubs, and community agencies or corporations for assistance. Local nurseries might offer your school topsoil, plants, and seeds at a discount price. Local farmers may provide peat moss and manure. Your PTA may also lend assistance. Caretakers should be included in the project. They will play a crucial role to assist with maintenance of your project. Once your committee is set up, set your schedule for meetings and your *target date for planting*. A schedule that includes when to order seeds and plants and when to prepare your ground plot should be set with the planting date in mind.

2. When beginning to plan your naturalization, ask, "What would we like to see happen in this space?" With the goal of starting out with a simple plan (unless you have a wealth of volunteers with gardening expertise and generous funding assistance), decide on what to plant and a site. Ideally, use solely native plants that are indigenous to your locality. You can always add non-native or carefully chosen exotic plants later on. Start simply and your naturalized space can mature as your experience grows! If a courtyard is feasible (or perhaps the only alternative in an urban school setting), decide on your vision for this space.

3. Decide on the location of your naturalization space when planning which flowers or plants you will be using and determine the sunlight and soil conditions they will need. Are you going to have a vegetable patch? Your committee will need to find out which vegetables grow best in your climate and soil. How about wildflowers? Enlist a volunteer with a love of gardening (this doesn't have to be a professional landscape architect) to plan a design of the area on graph paper. An overhead map of the planting area should be drawn to a common working scale. North should be indicated in the plan. A water supply source, pathways, seating areas (such as logs or benches), bed edging, and, if lighting is to be included, a source of electricity. Plan to take before and after photos.

4. Each child and every class should be involved in this project in some way. A theme could be assigned or chosen by each grade division or each grade level. In addition to essential class contributions, some "extras" to enhance the naturalized area could include:
   - habitat boxes
   - bird feeder
   - compost container(s)
   - hibernation boxes for butterflies

   Because one of the main aims of this project is to instill a feeling of community cooperation, the opportunity for every child to participate and experience success and to practice his or her conflict-solving skills, it is *crucial to encourage your low self-esteem students to participate in some way.* If they resist or say they *can't*, tell them they *can*; then find a position for them in which they can succeed! For example, he or she could be one of the following "key" plotters:
   - **Chief engineer**—in charge of working with the landscape architect and planning what and where to plant
   - **Chief gardener**—in charge of who in the class is assigned to: help prepare the soil with peat moss and manure, plant the seeds, help with the maintenance, help with the watering, and assist with pruning

- **Chief artist**—designs and paints wooden signs for the various plants or flowers in the naturalized area
- **Member of an environmental appreciation group**, named **Green Thumbs Plotters** or **Down to Earth Kidz**—decides on fundraising projects such as making gift tags or cards from recycled paper, having an all-natural bake sale, or selling some of the wooden signs they paint to raise money for the naturalization project
- **Chief contractor**—keeps track of contracts each child who is willing to accept responsibility signs detailing the job he or she promises to do to contribute to the new naturalized ground; after the project is established, the chief contractor passes out certificates of appreciation signed by the chief contractor and the project coordinator to students for performing their tasks
- **Botanical buddies**—committee that researches the botanical names for the plants that will be included
- **We're Naturally Grateful**—committee that thanks all in the school and community who volunteered and contributed to the project

5. Some examples of plots to plant are:
   - **Vegetable**—herbs, pumpkins, tomatoes, cucumbers, beans, carrots, green peppers, etc.
   - **Woodland**—cedar, birch, berry bushes, shrubs, trees
   - **Butterfly garden**—plants to use to attract the butterflies are researched by the students; seed heads can be collected for planting the next year
   - **Flowers**—perennials are preferable so you don't have to plant each year; add a few annuals the first year so you'll see some color right away
   - **Wildflowers**—start seeds of wildflowers indoors and plant outdoors in the spring
   - **Compost area**—outdoor compost area should be included in your plans so that children can deposit eggshells, fruit skins, coffee grounds, tea bags, etc.
   - **Trees**—native trees are best to plant

   Try to get donated or discounted topsoil, peat moss, manure, mulch, and protective snow fencing for your naturalization space while it is being established. You will also need mulch to protect seedlings and to conserve moisture after planting.

6. Celebrate your beautiful new naturalized space with an art mural of a naturalized school ground or courtyard to adorn your halls. Come up with a creative design for your naturalized space. For example, Beethoven School, a Chicago public school with over 800 students, created a "geography garden" in the shape of the seven continents and forty oceans! This may be ambitious for most first naturalization projects, so whatever comes up naturally, plot, plant and enjoy!

Naturalization Project References:

American Horticultural Society
7931 E. Boulevard Drive
Alexandria, VA 22308-1300
703-768-5700

In Canada:
Evergreen Foundation
24 Mercer
Toronto, Ontario, M5R 3B9
416-596-1495

I'M ALL GREEN THUMBS!

Write inside the thumbs the numbers, from the choices below, of the five best ways you can help with naturalization. Then color those thumbs *green*!

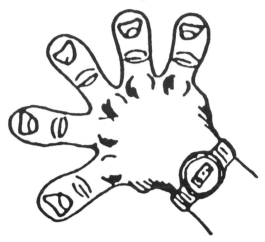

On the back of this sheet, write about and draw a picture of how you picture your project to look when it's finished.

Plotters, Sign Up for How You'll Contribute to Our Naturalization Project!

Here's how I will accept responsibility to help with our naturalization project. I'll check off *one* area in which I think I can best contribute:

_____ **1. Engineer**—I'll plot what we will plant, where vegetables, flowers, and other plants will grow best. I'll work with the landscape architect.

_____ **2. Tiller**—I'll prepare the soil for planting, peat moss, fertilizing, tilling, etc.

_____ **3. Planter**—I'll plant the seeds and plants.

_____ **4. Research Scientist**—I'll research the botanical names for the plants and link with artists to put them on signs.

_____ **5. Artist**—I'll paint names for the plants on small wooden signs, etc., in the naturalized area. I'll help plan and draw with the hall garden mural.

_____ **6. Fundraising**—I'll plot ideas to raise money for the seeds, signs, plants, etc.

_____ **7. Maintenance Crew**—I'll take care of watering and do supervised pruning to take care of and to establish the seeds and plants after planting. I'll also help weed and put mulch over them to help them grow.

_____ **8. Green Thumbs Club**—I'll help establish a Green Thumbs Club to help fundraise for our project and help to get it going.

_____ **9. Grateful Gardeners**—I'll help write thank-you letters to everyone in the school and community who helps us with our project.

_____ **10. Other**—Here's an area that will need attention. I'll _____

GREEN THUMBs

CERTIFICATE OF
APPRECIATION

THIS CERTIFICATE IS
PRESENTED TO :

FOR

FOR OUR SCHOOL GROUND
NATURALIZATION PROJECT

THIS KID'S A
NATURAL!

7–28. JUMPIN' JELLYBEANS!

Wilbert will jump for joy if you help him put together the letters in the jellybean jar so he can discover the message they spell. Can you help him? Don't forget to add the jumpin' jellybeans that have escaped from the jar! The message answer is found at the bottom of the page. **Hint:** The message is important in solving conflicts!

Message: _____

Message: NOBODY FEELS LIKE A LOSER

8

Behavior That's Driving You Up the Wall

WHAT TO DO ABOUT BEHAVIOR THAT'S DRIVING YOU UP THE WALL!

When a student is disruptive, the student is telling us something. Listen! It's a silent plea in the guise of an anything-but-silent exterior. A misbehaving child is usually a *discouraged* child. If you are patient enough to look beneath the misbehavior, you will slowly uncover the layers beneath it. What you will often expose is a discouraged child filled with underlying *anger*; and hidden beneath that layer, *fear*. Often, after many failed attempts to discipline or to reason with this child, and finally because of the disruption to your class and your own sanity, you send the child out of the classroom and off to the principal to "deal with."

Included here are several suggestions that have been successful with other educators who have felt driven "up the wall" with misbehaving kids. Perhaps a combination of each or one idea in particular will help to build the self-esteem of your discouraged child.

Validate children's feelings. When they are angry, don't tell children they shouldn't feel angry. If they feel sad, don't tell them they shouldn't be feeling sad. Instead, assure them that you understand they are angry or sad, that anger and sadness are both natural feelings which are okay to have. As your validations begin to calm them down, explain to them that what they do with their anger or sadness, if it harms themselves or another person, is *not* okay. For example, explain that losing their tempers and hitting another child as a result of their anger is *not* okay. Once their anger is validated, they will then be more open to appropriate alternatives to hitting. Let them know you are there *with them* if they want to talk about their feelings with you. If they need more time to cool off or if they are being verbally abusive to you, let them know you will be *with* them when they are ready to talk with you respectfully, just as you will respect them. After they have had time to calm down, the next step will be to discuss conflict-solving alternatives to physical and verbal aggression. The important thing here is to let children know you understand their feelings, that you are going to give them quiet time to calm down, and that you will then be there *with* them for a "chill-out chat" together. Following are feelings we hope to instill in children after validating their feelings: "I feel like there is somebody who listens to me. My feelings aren't the problem; it's when I don't control my behavior that's the problem. I know my feelings are separate from my actions."

Try to find something to **sincerely encourage** in this child. You can best find out where his or her interests lie if you take a few minutes at the start of recess or during the lunch period for several sessions of "chill-out" time together. (A "chill-out" chart is available in this section.) This is intended to be a private time between just the two of you to talk about anything other than academics. School grades and behavior may emerge as your chats increase, but the purpose of the talks, until you get to know the child, is to listen nonjudgmentally to any topic initiated by the child. If you share some of your own private hopes, fears, successes and failures, perhaps the child will feel like sharing, also. "You really should . . . better not again . . . if I catch you . . . next time I see you . . ." are phrases to avoid.

Implement Dr. Michele Borba's *Three Week Plan* from *Esteem Builders* with a child who is discouraged. She recommends finding one positive quality, talent or accomplishment you can point out to the student *daily* for a period of three weeks (the length of time it takes for the plan to be effective with the child to begin to believe this unaccustomed positivism). Encouragement of this positive quality must be made not only daily, but is also crucial it be made *privately* to the student. The reason for privacy is that this discouraged child is not used to hearing positive compliments about himself or herself and will, at first, probably resist your efforts. If done in front of others, the child will be embarrassed by the positive attention in front of peers. Misbehavior may temporarily escalate. The child will be struggling to get out of a negative comfort zone in which he or she has always heard negative comments and will not believe he or she is capable of anything positive. This disbelief will slowly turn into a flicker of pleasure and emerging belief — if you are patient enough to wait for the conviction from this child that perhaps there really is something good in him or her! It is imperative that the positive quality you choose is an honest appraisal of something positive the child possesses. If there is no apparent academic, artistic or musical talent, is there a hobby or interest you discovered during your private talks together? If there are no interests or talents, why not **create an opportunity for this child to succeed**? Make up a position in the classroom as the "designer" designated to display and decorate bulletin board and around-the-room work by the students. How about a class photographer? Show the child how to take a picture, supply a photo album, and he or she has the job! Or you may need a library liaison to take care of books, tapes and videos related to topics being studied. If you make music a daily part of your routine, this child could be the "Much Music DJ" in charge of lining up tapes, getting them ready, playing, and rewinding. If there is a "Superbuddy" program in your school pairing older and younger students together, choosing this child to "help" a younger child is an effective self-esteem booster.

Any job, however menial, may be the first time someone gave this child the opportunity to be responsible. If it does not proceed smoothly at first, it's crucial not to give up. The child will test you. Everyone else has always given up on him or her before; isn't this "big chance" going to prove to be the same failure? Your confidence and attitude say to the child, *"It is different this time because I believe in you."* Studies have proven students will live up — or down — to the expectations you have of them. They will watch for your anticipations, which you cannot fake with kids! So it's important to first convince yourself that this time he or she *will succeed*!

Articles debunking building self-esteem in children claim they cannot understand the approach of pointing out their positive qualities to children. (Please request information about the backgrounds of those who oppose self-esteem and other life skills programs, to see if they have a background in elementary education, having been trained and experienced in educating elementary children. Also, ask which specific self-esteem programs they oppose, which activities they object to, and their reasons for opposition. Many opponents, upon being questioned as to specifics, cannot give any and have no training in the area; they say they are simply against the idea of self-esteem building!) The self-esteem opponents advise, "Self-esteem is false praise, touchy, feel-good nonsense. Just make kids work hard and succeed. That's all they really need to feel good about themselves." But what about the students we have discussed above who are "stuck" in one of these negative behavior patterns, those who never succeed? It is imperative that they be given an *opportunity to succeed* and *to see how good it feels*. That must be the first step. Without it, they will always be "stuck" because, sadly, they will never know the difference.

Give misbehaving children some power of their own rather than feeling you have to be the power over them. Enable students to take responsibility for their own behavior rather than looming over them as the authoritarian figure. Ask children when they misbehave, *"What is the cost and what is the benefit?"* For example, if a child pushes to get in front of the bus line, ask the child if the benefit is worth the cost. Explain that the kids in the line resent the shoving and then they don't want to sit by the pushy child on the bus. Ask the child if getting on the bus ahead of everyone else (the benefit) is worth not having kids wanting to sit by him or her once he or she is on the bus (the cost). Most will reply that they really would like other kids to want to sit by them and that they are not really getting ahead by their pushy behavior. Or you may ask the child to think about the cost–benefit privately and ask that they give a silent response. Some children may not want to admit aloud that they would be *thrilled* if other kids—or even one kid—wanted to sit next to them! However, they will think it over themselves. Eva Fugitt in *Skills of Peacemaking* recommends asking a misbehaving student privately, *"How is this (behavior) helping you, (name of student)? You don't need to answer me out loud, just quietly go inside yourself and think about it."* This helps a student to take responsibility for his or her behavior, taking the authority away from the teacher. Eva Fugitt says, "I am constantly amazed at the strength of this question. It has never failed to evoke some form of self-correction. I call it the magic question."

As difficult as it may be, ignore the misbehaving child's bids for negative attention as much as possible except, of course, in the case of physical safety concerning other students. Concentrate on quietly rewarding the child's attempts to avoid physical aggression in the form of bullying or disrupting the class by negative attention-seeking, which may be a real stretch for a student who has never before attempted to follow a rule. We need to be hesitant to say, "Catch the student doing something *right*." *Right* has a different meaning to many discouraged children than our definition of the term. For example, if our misbehaving, discouraged children succeed in controlling themselves from beating up another child and instead yell and swear, they have, in their minds, done the "right" thing by not resorting to violence. Although we certainly don't condone swearing, that student is making headway in avoiding previous violent behavior! Swearing isn't "right." But in this case, the child should be **acknowledged for curbing the urge to be violent**. The next step will be to curb the swearing. If he or she is punished for swearing with no encouragement of the huge step (for this child) of holding back physical violence, in the next argument he or she may resort again to violence. Why not? The punishment, the child figures, is the same anyway.

Enlist the parent(s) or guardian(s) of your misbehaving child as your partner(s). Find out by talking with them about what is taking place in the home that may be contributing to the misbehavior. Stress to them the importance that they find something positive in the child to point out to him or her. Ask them to assist if you have decided to use the Three Week Plan to overlook negative feedback for three weeks (unless it involves physical harm to another, which cannot be ignored). Ask them to instead focus on positive feedback for efforts that may have gone previously unnoticed. Explain to the parents that they will be put to the test, so ingrained is the negative pattern the child is probably used to. Assure them you are making the same efforts at school and—with their patience—within a few weeks you will begin to see improved behavior. Tell them to *believe themselves that the child will succeed* and *to show those expectations to the child*.

Below are a few of the many studies done linking positive self-image to success in all areas.

- A four-year study by Gail Dusa at Silver Creek High School in San Jose, CA (from a Report to the National Council on Self-Esteem, 1989) showed great gains by the group that had self-esteem training at least one 45-minute period per week. The teacher had three criteria for herself while teaching these students:

  1. No put-downs
  2. Dare to dream
  3. Unconditional positive regard

As a result, a list of some of the comparisons between the **Control Group** and the **Self-Esteem Group** are as follows:

	Control Group	Self-Esteem Group
Days absent per semester	16	1
Completing 90% or more of homework	26%	75%
Parental involvement per year	1.9	9.5
Graduates from high school	50%	82%
Honor roll	5%	25%

- After a five-year study by the teacher T. Hall, who formed the Harlem Chess Players in order to involve students in a non-academic activity, it was found that the *60%* dropout rate before the students became positively motivated through chess changed to a *15%* dropout rate.

- Prescott Lecky, pioneer in self-image psychology, found as a result of his studies that if the student would change his or her self-definition, the student could also change his or her learning ability. Suffering from poor self-images, they identified with their failures and consistently expected to fail. An example is a student who changed her negative self-image into a positive self-image. She had been told she had no aptitude for English; she received and previously made grades that lived up to that expectation. "Honorable Mention" in a literary contest was awarded to her the following year after she changed her expectation of herself.

- Psychologist Emmy Werner conducted a 30-year study following the development of one thousand children from abusive homes. The students among this high-risk group who did not become high school dropout statistics all had one thing in common— someone who cared enough to nurture them in some area of their lives. In most cases, it was a *teacher*.

- This self-image concept is further substantiated by William Purkey. In *Self Concept and School Achievement*, he points out that a major determining factor in how a student sees himself or herself is how others see him or her. Students' failures in basic subjects, school dropouts, drug abusers, teen pregnancies, and suicides are due in large measure to the consequence of faulty perceptions children have of themselves. Many students have difficulty in school, not participating in school activities—not because of low intelligence or lack of ability—but because *they have learned to see themselves as incapable.*

The National Education Association held a 1995 Safety Summit and gave some statistics regarding our youth and violence. Especially disturbing is the fact that more youth were killed by guns between 1970 and 1990 than the soldiers who died in Vietnam. Statistics from the 1994 Children's Defense Fund show that every two hours a child dies of a gunshot wound in our country. One out of nine youths carries a handgun. Many of our children live in fear and carry weapons to protect themselves. Before they graduate from elementary school, the average child will have witnessed 100,000 acts of violence and 8,000 murders in the media.

If a gun is kept in the home, there is a five-fold risk of suicide. In 1993, 8% of young people reported carrying a firearm, which was up from 5.5% in 1991. A comparison was made between youth deaths in the United States related to guns and youth deaths related to guns in Canada, Australia, and Japan. In these three countries, there is no right to own guns and the deaths of young people by guns is very low. The punishment received by our violent youth—jail terms—isn't really worse than many of their home lives and, in many cases, it's an improvement.

What can we, as educators, do about violence? We can do so much! We can offer *values education* in our schools, character education that teaches what's right and what's wrong to children who have never been exposed to values, lack of values being one of the factors contributing to crime. We can teach them to feel *empathy* for others, a feeling we see simply not present in most of the youth gang violence committed. The offenders don't feel empathy for their victims nor, in many cases, do they regret their actions. We can make them take *responsibility* for their actions by teaching them from an early age that their locus of control is within themselves. We can enable them to feel *capable*, if not in many areas, at least in one area in which they *succeed*!

At the Safety Summit, we heard from the kids themselves. They suggest that adults offer fewer lectures on violence and that they instead ask the youth, "What can we do about violence?" One successful program out of many started in schools across the country is the Red and Blue Ribbon Committee at Cleveland High School in Reseda, CA. It is an anti-violence group that offers peer counseling (with the assistance of adult mentors). Anyone is welcome to join. Open-arena meetings are held once a week, in which kids talk openly about stereotypes, racism, and religion. These are elements that often contribute to violence. Their goal is to understand one another so that youth will get along together better. These youth find that often it's a misunderstanding about one of these elements that starts a gang or an individual fight. Teachers who are involved in this program help break down the teacher-student barrier that often inhibits communication. In this open forum, they are all friends. Elementary school is not too soon to begin one of these programs as a *prevention program* before the children reach high school!

Patience, effort, and time—all of the above suggestions require these but will enable you to make a lasting contribution to the misbehaving child. And neither of you will be climbing the walls any longer!

CHILL OUT!

Use the TLC approach to conflicts

T — TUNE IN to <u>both</u> of your feelings by taking turns saying, "When you… I feel… because…"

L — LISTEN to how the other sees the problem, then take turns repeating back the other's words.

C — CHOOSE A SOLUTION to meet <u>both</u> persons' needs so nobody feels like a loser.

9

Ready-to-Use Handouts

READY-TO-USE HANDOUTS

Light Up a Student's Day with a "Gram"

"Children value themselves to the degree that they have been valued."

Although we encourage students to praise their own efforts intrinsically, it is very uplifting to a student to receive a "gram" from a teacher to take home for progress in academic or life skills areas.

A good deed, an act of kindness or help to another classmate or teacher, or simply an effort made should be acknowledged. Too often a parent hears from a teacher only when a student has misbehaved in school or from the periodic report cards sent home.

Grams for students to fill in for others should be encouraged. Have several grams run off and readily available; it will only take a moment of your time to fill in and will make such a difference to a child!

♥ ♥

HEART GRAM

♥ ♥

The kindness _____ showed to another student was exemplary. A lot of "heart" was shown!

Signed: _____

Date: _____

♥ ♥

♥ ♥

---

news FLASH GRAM

_____ *made news in our classroom.*

Here's how:

_____

_____

Signed: _____

Date: _____

☺ ☺

PROBLEM SOLVING GRAM

Finding a solution is no problem for _____

who used the problem-solving steps and came up with a solution for

_____

Signed: _____

Date: _____

☺ ☺

GRAM-FROM-A-STUDENT

You're a winner in my eyes!

for _____

You are a great _____

Signed: _____

Date: _____

PEACEMAKING GRAM

During a conflict, _____ showed responsible conflict resolution skills.

It is realized that WORLD peace begins in our little corner of the world.

Signed: _____

Date: _____

BIRTHDAY GRAM

HAPPY BIRTHDAY   **TO:** _____

YOU ARE SPECIAL TO ME

You are special to me because

_____

Signed: _____

Date: _____

Directions: Fill in the name or initials of your school. Write why you feel your school is a special place for you. Collect several classes' grams and form your school's name or initials in your front hall.

is a
special place
because...

_____
_____
_____
_____
_____
_____

is a
special place
because...

_____
_____
_____
_____
_____

PEACE DOVE

This peace dove may be used for a front hall or classroom display. Students may fill in doves with how they will contribute to peace in their own schools. In addition, doves may be used as name tags for your all-school Peace Activities Celebration. (See the Conflict Solving Section.)

PLEASE COME

TO OUR

PEACE

ACTIVITIES

CELEBRATION

DATE: _____

TIME: _____

SIGNED: _____

PLEASE COME

TO OUR

PEACE

ACTIVITIES

CELEBRATION

DATE: _____

TIME: _____

SIGNED: _____

DO YOU ENJOY...
SONGS? SKITS? ART
DISPLAYS?
DECORATED HALLS?
AND LOTS MORE!
THEN COME TO OUR
SKILLS FOR LIFE
ACTIVITIES DAY

DATE: _____

TIME: _____

SIGNED: _____

WE HOPE YOU CAN
COME!

ROLE-PLAYS

CHARACTER: _____

LINES: _____

_____

_____

_____

_____

_____

_____

COSTUME: _____

_____

- -

ROLE-PLAYS

CHARACTER: _____

LINES: _____

_____

_____

_____

_____

_____

_____

COSTUME: _____

_____

HALLOWEEN

NOTHING IS SCARY IF YOU BELIEVE IN YOURSELF

Here is a list of times I will be myself and not put on a "mask" to cover up my real feelings.

1. _____

_____

_____

2. _____

_____

_____

3. _____

_____

_____

If you were asked to write a song about yourself—a concert—what would you say?

A CONCERT FOR YOU

HAPPY VALENTINE'S DAY!

TO:

YOU ARE SPECIAL TO ME BECAUSE:

HAPPY ST. PATRICK'S DAY

St. Patrick was a missionary who converted Ireland to Christianity. He felt good about helping people. He is the Patron Saint of Ireland.

Directions: Think about someone you will help. Write the ways you will go about it.

Example:

A younger brother or sister who is having trouble in math; your Mom or Dad in need of some support from you; a discouraged classmate.

Help my younger brother or sister with his or her math problems.

Whom will I help?

_____

How I plan to help:

_____

_____

_____

_____

_____

Extra!

Research why the island is split into the independent Irish Free State and Northern Ireland.

Christmas is a time for giving and not just receiving gifts. This Christmas, give presents to your family and friends by giving them kind words and helpful actions as presents. Plan your Christmas List with these gifts below.

Here is my Christmas Gift List:

1. I will _____ for _____.

2. I will _____ for _____.

3. I will _____ for _____.

4. I will _____ for _____.

5. I will _____ for _____.

HAPPY HANUKKAH

During the celebration of Hanukkah, think of eight strengths for which you are thankful. Write one for each of the eight days of the "Feast of Lights."

1. _____

2. _____

3. _____

4. _____

5. _____

6. _____

7. _____

8. _____

HAPPY EASTER

Fill the basket with colored eggs with names of special people and why they are special.

Bibliography

BIBLIOGRAPHY

Skills-for-Life Resources for Educators

Albert, Linda. *A Teacher's Guide to Cooperative Discipline.* Circle Pines, MN: American Guidance Service, 1989.

Borba, Michele. *The Esteem Builders' Complete Program.* Rolling Hills Estates, CA: Jalmar Press, 1994.

Borba, Michele and Craig Borba. *Self-Esteem: A Classroom Affair, Volume 2 (More Ways to Help Children Like Themselves).* Minneapolis, MN: Winston Press, 1982.

_____. *Self-Esteem: A Classroom Affair, (101 Ways to Help Children Like Themselves).* Minneapolis, MN: Winston Press, 1978.

Bosch, Carl W. *Bully on the Bus.* Seattle: Parenting Press, 1988.

Branden, Nathaniel. *Honoring the Self.* New York: Bantam, 1983.

_____. *The Six Pillars of Self-Esteem.* New York: Bantam, 1994.

Canfield, Jack and Mark Hansen. *Chicken Soup for the Soul.* Deerfield Beach, FL: Health Communications, Inc., 1993.

_____. *A Second Helping of Chicken Soup for the Soul.* Deerfield Beach, FL: Health Communications, Inc., 1995.

Canfield, Jack. *100 Ways to Enhance Self-Esteem in the Classroom.* Boston: Allyn & Bacon, Division of Simon & Schuster, 1994.

Canter, Lee and Marlene Canter. *Assertive Discipline.* Santa Monica, CA: Lee Canter & Associates, 1976.

Chase, Larry. *The Other Side of the Report Card: How-to-Do-It Program for Affective Education.* Santa Monica, CA: Goodyear Publishing Co., 1994.

Coopersmith, Stanley. *The Antecedents of Self-Esteem.* San Francisco: W. H. Freeman, 1967.

_____. *Developing Motivation in Young Children.* San Francisco: Albion, 1975.

Crary, Elizabeth. *I Can't Wait.* Seattle: Parenting Press, 1982.

_____. *My Name Is Not Dummy.* Seattle: Parenting Press, 1982.

_____. *I Want It.* Seattle: Parenting Press, 1982.

_____. *Without Spanking or Spoiling.* Seattle: Parenting Press, 1982.

_____. *I Want to Play.* Seattle: Parenting Press, 1982.

_____. *Kids Can Cooperate.* Seattle: Parenting Press, 1984.

_____. *Mommy Don't Go.* Seattle: Parenting Press, 1982.

Elkind, David. *Miseducation: Preschoolers at Risk.* New York: Alfred A. Knopf, 1987.

Faber, Adele and Elaine Mazlish. *How to Talk So Kids Will Listen & Listen So Kids Will Talk.* New York: Avon Books, 1980.

Fugitt, Eva D. *He Hit Me Back First!* Rolling Hills Estates, CA: Jalmar Press, 1982.

Gibbs, Jeanne. *Tribes. A Process for Social Development and Cooperative Learning.* Santa Rosa, CA: Prima Publishing & Communications, 1987.

Girard, Kathryn, Janet Rifkin, and Annette Townley. *Peaceful Persuasion.* Amherst, MA: The Mediation Project at the University of Massachusetts, 1985.

Glenn, H. Stephen and Jane Nelsen. *Raising Self-Reliant Children in a Self-Indulgent World.* Rocklin, CA: Prima Publishing, 1988.

Glenn, H. Stephen, Jane Nelsen, and Lynn Lott. *Positive Discipline in the Classroom.* Rocklin, CA: Prima Publishing, 1993.

Grevious, Saundrah Clark. *Multicultural Activities for Primary Children.* West Nyack, NY: The Center for Applied Research in Education, 1993.

Huggins, Pat. *Helping Kids Handle Anger—Teaching Self Control.* Mercer Island, WA: ASSIST (A Validated Washington State Innovative Education Program), 1988.

Johnson, David W. and Roger T. Johnson. *Creative Conflict.* Minneapolis: Cooperative Learning Center, 1987.

Johnson, D.W., R.T. Johnson, E. Johnson Holubec, and Patricia Roy. *Circles of Learning.* Association for Supervision and Curriculum Development, 1984.

Kerr, Robert. *Positively!* Portland, ME: J. Weston Walch, 1987.

Kreidler, William J. *Creative Conflict Resolution.* Glenview, IL: Goodyear Books, 1984.

Lawyer, John W. and Neil H. Katz. *Communication and Conflict Management Skills.* Dubuque, IA: Kendall/Hunt Publishing Co., 1985.

Martin, Robert. *Teaching Through Encouragement.* Englewood Cliffs, NJ: Prentice-Hall, 1970.

Maslow, Abraham. *Toward a Psychology of Being.* New York: Van Nostrand Reinhold, 1968.

Moorman, Chick and Dishon Moorman. *Our Classroom: We Can Learn Together.* Englewood Cliffs, NJ: Prentice-Hall, 1977.

Nelsen, Jane. *Positive Discipline.* New York: Ballantine Books, 1987.

Nelsen, Jane and Lynn Lott. *Positive Discipline for Teenagers.* Rocklin, CA: Prima Publishing, 1994.

Palmer, Pat. *The Mouse, The Monster and Me.* San Luis Obispo, CA: Impact Publishers, 1977.

_____. *Liking Myself.* San Luis Obispo, CA: Impact Publishers, 1977.

Reasoner, Robert. *Building Self-Esteem: A Comprehensive Program.* Palo Alto, CA: Consulting Psychologists Press, 1982.

Rubenstein, Judith and Catherine Woolner. *Discovery Sessions.* Greenfield, MA: Franklin Mediation Service, 1989.

Sadalla, Gail, Meg Holmberg, and Jim Halligan. *Conflict Resolution: An Elementary School Curriculum.* San Francisco: The Community Board Program, Inc., 1990.

Sadalla, Gail, Manti Henriquez, and Meg Holmberg. *Conflict Resolution: A Secondary School Curriculum.* San Francisco: The Community Board Program, Inc., 1987.

Schmidt, Fran and Alice Friedman. *Creative Conflict Solving for Kids.* Miami Beach: The Grace Contrino Abrams Peace Education Foundation, 1985.

School Initiatives Program. *Classroom Conflict Resolution Training for Elementary Schools.* San Francisco: The Community Board Program, Inc., 1987.

Sloane, Paul. *Lateral Thinking Puzzles.* New York: Sterling Publishing Co., 1992.

Sloane, Paul and Des McHale. *Challenging Lateral Thinking Puzzles.* New York: Sterling Publishing Co., 1993.

Skills for Life Resources for Parents

Bean, Reynold and Harris Clemes. *Self-Esteem: The Key to Your Child's Well Being.* New York: Kensington Publishing, 1981.

Bloom, Benjamin. *Developing Talent in Young People.* New York: Simon and Schuster, 1987.

Bloomfield, Harold H. *Making Peace with Your Parents.* New York: Random Houe, 1983.

Bolton, Robert. *People Skills.* New York: Simon and Schuster, 1979.

Borba, Michele. *Home Esteem Builders.* Rolling Hills Estates, CA: Jalmar Press, 1989.

Borenstein, Sasha and Zo A. Rudman. *Learning to Lean: An Approach to Study Skills.* Dubuque, IA: Kendall/Hunt Publishing Co., 1985.

Branden, Nathaniel. *The Psychology of Self-Esteem.* New York: Bantam, 1982.

———. *The Six Pillars of Self-Esteem.* New York: Bantam, 1994.

———. *The Power of Self-Esteem.* Deerfield Beach, FL: Health Communications, Inc., 1992.

Briggs, Dorothy Corkille. *Celebrate Yourself.* Garden City, NY: Doubleday, 1977.

———. *Your Child's Self-Esteem.* Garden City, NY: Doubleday, 1975.

Canfield, Jack and Mark Hansen. *Chicken Soup for the Soul.* Deerfield Beach, FL: Health Communications, Inc., 1993.

———. *A Second Helping of Chicken Soup for the Soul.* Deerfield Beach, FL: Health Communications, Inc., 1995.

Clark, Aminah, Reynold Bean, and Harris Clemes. *Raising Teenagers' Self-Esteem.* Capitola, CA: APOD Publishers, 1992.

Clarke, Jean Ilsley. *Self-Esteem: A Family Affair.* New York: Harper Collins, 1978.

Coloroso, Barbara. *Kids Are Worth It! Giving Your Child the Gift of Inner Discipline.* Toronto, Ontario: Sommerville House, 1994.

Coopersmith, Stanley. *The Antecedents of Self-Esteem.* San Franciso: W. H. Freeman, 1967.

de Bono, Edward. *Six Thinking Hats.* New York: Penguin Books, 1985.

———. *Serious Creativity.* Toronto, Ontario: Harper Collins, 1992.

———. *de Bono's Thinking Course.* New York: Facts on File, 1985.

———. *The Happiness Purpose.* New York: Penguin Books, 1990.

Dobson, James. *Hide or Seek.* Old Tappan, NJ: Revell, 1974.

Dreikurs, Rudolf and Pearl Cassel. *Children, the Challenge.* New York: Elsevier-Dutton, 1974.

———. *Discipline Without Tears.* New York: Hawthorn Books, 1974.

Dyer, Wayne. *What Do You Really Want for Your Children?* New York: Avon Books, 1985.

Elkind, David. *The Hurried Child.* New York: Addison-Wesley, 1988.

———. *Miseducation: Preschoolers at Risk.* New York: Alfred A. Knopf, 1987.

———. *All Grown Up & No Place to Go.* Reading, MA: Addison-Wesley, 1988.

Eyre, Linda and Richard. *Teaching Your Children Values.* New York: Simon & Schuster, 1993.

Felker, Donald W. *Helping Children to Like Themselves.* Minneapolis: Burgess Publishing Co., 1973.

Fugitt, Eva D. *He Hit Me Back First!* Rolling Hills Estates, CA: Jalmar Press, 1983.

Gardner, James E. *Turbulent Teens.* Rolling Hills Estates, CA: Jalmar Press, 1983.

Garfield, Charles A. *Peak Performance.* Los Angeles: Houghton Mifflin, 1984.

Glenn, H. Stephen and Jane Nelsen. *Raising Self-Reliant Children in a Self-Indulgent World.* Rocklin, CA: Prima, 1988.

Harrill, Suzanne. *You Could Feel Good.* Houston, TX: Innerworks, 1987.

Helmstetter, Shad. *The Self-Talk Solution.* New York: Pocket Books, 1987.

Hillman, Carolyn. *Recovery of Your Self-Esteem: A Guide for Women.* New York: Simon and Schuster, 1992.

Holt, John. *How Children Fail.* New York: Delta Books, 1982.

_____. *How Children Learn.* New York: Delta Books, 1967.

LaBenne, Wallace and Bert Greene. *Educational Implication of Self-Concept Theory.* Pacific Palisades, CA: Goodyear Publishing Co., 1969.

Leman, Dr. Kevin. *Parenthood Without Hassles* Well Almost.* Eugene, OR: Harvest House, 1979.

Lorrayne, Harry. *Good Memory, Good Student!* New York: Stein and Day, 1976.

Maslow, Abraham. *Toward a Psychology of Being.* New York: Van Nostrand Reinhold, 1968.

Nelsen, Jane. *Positive Discipline.* New York: Ballantine Books, 1987.

Nelsen, Jane and Lynn Lott. *Positive Discipline for Teenagers.* Rocklin, CA: Prima Publishing, 1994.

Newman, James W. *Release Your Brakes.* Costa Mesa, CA: H.D.L. Publishing Co., 1977.

Peale, Norman Vincent. *You Can if You Think You Can.* Pauling, NY: Foundation for Christian Living, 1974.

_____. *The Power of Positive Thinking.* New York: Fawcett Crest, 1956.

Pearce, Joseph Chilton. *The Magical Child Matures.* New York: E. P. Dutton, 1985.

Purkey, William. *Self Concept and School Achievement.* Englewood Cliffs, NJ: Prentice-Hall, 1970.

Purkey, William and John Novak. *Inviting School Success (2nd edition).* Belmont, CA: Wadsworth Publishing Co., 1984.

Sanford, Linda and Mary Ellen Donovan. *Women and Self-Esteem.* New York: Penguin Books, 1984.

Satir, Virginia. *Self-Esteem.* Millbrae, CA: Celestial Arts, 1975.

Sloane, Paul. *Lateral Thinking Puzzles.* New York: Sterling Publishing Co., 1992.

Sloane, Paul and Des McHale. *Challenging Lateral Thinking Puzzles.* New York: Sterling Publishing Co., 1993.

Stewart, Emery. *Actualizations: You Don't Have to Rehearse to Be Yourself.* New York: Doubleday/Dolphin, 1978.

Vitale, Barbara Meister. *Unicorns Are Real: A Right-Brained Approach to Learning.* Rolling Hills Estates, CA: Jalmar Press, 1982.

Waitley, Denis. *Being the Best.* New York: Pocket Books, 1987.

_____. *Seeds of Greatness.* Old Tappan, NJ: Revell, 1983.

_____. *The Winner's Edge.* New York: Times Books, 1980.

Resources on Eating Disorders

American Anorexia/Bulimia Association (AABA)
c/o Regent Hospital
25 E. 61st Street, 6th Floor
New York, NY 10021
(212) 891-8686

For eating disorder referrals other than East Coast, contact:
National Eating Disorders Organization (NEDO)
Laureate Psychiatric Clinic and Hospital
P.O. Box 470207
Tulsa, Oklahoma 74147-2027
(918) 481-4092

Blinder, B.J., B.F. Chaitin, and R.S. Goldstein, *The Eating Disorders.* New York: PMA Publishing Corporation, 1988.

Bruch, H. *Eating Disorders.* New York: Basic Books, 1973.

_____. *The Golden Cage. The Enigma of Anorexia Nervosa.* New York: Vintage Books, 1978.

_____. "Four Decades of Eating Disorders." In D.M. Garner and P.E. Gardinkel, (eds.): *Handbook of Psychotherapy for Anorexia Nervosa and Bulimia.* New York: The Guilford Press,

_____. *Conversations with Anorexics.* New York: Basic Books, 1988.

Byrnie, K. *A Parent's Guide to Anorexia and Bulimia.* New York: Schocken Books, 1987.

Cauwels, J.M. *Bulimia: The Binge-Purge Compulsion.* Garden City, NY: Doubleday, 1983.

Chernin, K. *The Obsession Reflections on the Tyranny of Slenderness.* New York: Harper Colophon Books, 1982.

Crisp, A.H. *Anorexia Nervosa: Let Me Be.* Orlando, FL: Grune and Stratton, 1980.

_____. "The Psychopathology of Anorexia Nervosa: Getting the Heat Out of the System." In A.J. Stunkard and E. Stellar, (eds.): *Eating and Its Disorders.* New York: Raven Press, 1984.

Giesey, G. and F. H. Trieder. "Attending to Family Issues in Anorexia Nervosa." In M. Gross, (ed.): *Anorexia Nervosa: A Comprehensive Approach.* Lexington, MA: The Collamore Press, 1982.

Marx, Russell. *It's Not Your Fault: Overcoming Anorexia and Bulimia Through Biopsychiatry.* Villard Books, 1991.

Orbach, Susie. *Fat Is a Feminist Issue:* New York: Berkley Books, 1978.

_____. *Hunger Strike: The Anorectic Struggle as a Metaphor for Our Age.* New York: Norton, 1986.

Sacker, I.M. and M. A. Zimmer. *Dying to Be Thin: Understanding and Defeating Anorexia Nervosa and Bulimia—A Practical Lifesaving Guide.* New York: Warner Books, 1987.

Siegal, M. J. and M. Weinshel Brusman. *Surviving an Eating Disorder.* New York: Harper & Row, 1988.

Sours, J. A. *Starving to Death in a Sea of Objects.* New York: Jason Aranson, 1980.

Weiss, L, M. A. Katzman, and S. A. Wolchik. *Treating Bulimia: A Psychoeducational Approach.* New York: Pergamon International Library, 1985.

_____. *You Can't Have Your Cake and Eat It Too: A Program for Controlling Bulimia.* Saratoga, CA: R & E Publishers, 1985.